SALSA RISING

SALSA RISING

*New York Latin Music
of the Sixties Generation*

Juan Flores

OXFORD
UNIVERSITY PRESS

Oxford University Press is a department of the University of Oxford. It furthers the University's objective of excellence in research, scholarship, and education by publishing worldwide. Oxford is a registered trade mark of Oxford University Press in the UK and certain other countries.

Published in the United States of America by Oxford University Press
198 Madison Avenue, New York, NY 10016, United States of America.

Library of Congress Cataloging-in-Publication Data
Flores, Juan, 1943–2014
Salsa rising : New York Latin music of the sixties generation / Juan Flores.
pages cm
Includes bibliographical references and index.
ISBN 978-0-19-976489-1 (hbk. : alk. paper) — ISBN 978-0-19-976490-7 (pbk. : alk. paper)   1. Salsa (Music)—New York (State)—New York—1961-1970—History and criticism.   2. Salsa (Music)—New York (State)—New York—1971-1980—History and criticism.   I. Title.
ML3535.5.F66 2014
781.64089'680747—dc23
2014022910

In memory of Tato Laviera (1950–2013)

a blackness in spanish
a blackness in English
mixture-met on jam sessions in central park,
there were no differences in
the sounds emerging from inside
        —*the salsa at bethesda fountain*

Contents

List of Illustrations

Preface

New York City has been home to Latin music for the better part
of a century. Already in the 1920s and 30s, as the city's Latino
population began its steady growth, musicians from Latin
America and the Caribbean were flocking to NewYork, lured by
the burgeoning recording studios and lucrative entertainment
venues. In the late 1940s and 50s, the big-band mambo dance
scene at the famed Palladium Ballroom was the stuff of legend,
while modern-day music history was made when the masters of
Afro-Cuban and jazz idioms conspired to create Cubop, the first
incarnation of Latin jazz. Then, in the 1960s, as the Latino
population swelled to exceed a million strong, a new generation of New York Latinos, mostly Puerto Ricans born and
raised in the city, went on to create the music that came to be
called salsa, which continues to enjoy avid popularity around
the world. And finally, in our own times, the children of the
mambo and salsa generations contributed to the making of hip
hop, while also finding inspiration by reviving ancestral Afro-
Caribbean forms like Cuban rumba, Puerto Rican bomba, and
Dominican palo.

It is a rich and exciting story, a tale of remarkable resilience and creativity in the face of widespread indifference

and sometimes crushing adversity. The relentless sequence of stylistic innovations and bold fusions, buttressed by a steadfast allegiance to native traditions and cultural practices, serves as a convenient and revealing trustworthy window on the social circumstances of massive Latino migration and community settlement. Indeed, the history of Latin music in New York is of such telling significance as to impel a new understanding of both Caribbean and U.S. cultural experience and social identities, and of the aesthetic expression of diaspora populations on a global scale.

As gripping and significant as it may be, it is a story that remains to be told in a single volume. Significant portions and aspects have been narrated and analyzed in publications through the years, starting with John Storm Roberts' classic overview of "the impact of Latin American music on the United States" in his 1979 book *The Latin Tinge*, and the more recent and updated coverage of similar terrain by Ed Morales in *The Latin Beat* (2003). These geographically and historically wide-ranging syntheses are complemented by the invaluable, New York-focused study of the early decades by Ruth Glasser in *My Music Is My Flag: Puerto Rican Musicians and Their New York Communities* (1993), and by Latin music historian Max Salazar in his many journal articles over the decades, finally compiled in *Mambo Kingdom: Latin Music in New York, 1926–1990*.

As for historical focus, while a preponderance of journalistic and scholarly writing has been dedicated to the ever-exciting and transformative mambo period and the "Afro-Cuban revolution" of jazz history, ample attention has also gone to the "salsa phenomenon," often characterized as a stylistic expression of the 1970s but with a staying power as a kind of Latin "world music" persisting through the subsequent decades and down to the present generation. It is this elusive, highly contested term "salsa", its historical context, and its multiple cultural referents, that I have taken as the central concern of the present book. In large measure because of this very controversial, multifaceted and emotionally charged quality of "salsa" and all that bears on it that I must begin with some caveats and delimitations by setting forth what my study is not, and the many aspects and dimensions of the theme that I do not treat or elucidate in any consistent way. I will then articulate what *Salsa Rising* does seek to contribute and what angles and aspects I hope to illuminate on the basis of my research and critical analysis.

First of all, though it had been my original intention, this book does not tell that rich and dynamic story of Latin music in New York that I appeared to be promising. It quickly became obvious to me that the full historical trajectory was far too huge a field for me to take on in one volume, and that my main interest was actually riveted on the salsa conundrum and that pivotal chapter in the longer historical narrative. However, still intent on an historical approach to the subject, I set as a goal placing the salsa period—which I define as 1960–75—in a more carefully calibrated temporal and cultural context than has generally been the case. My more modest aim is thus to retain a sense of the full historical arc by leading up to the circumscribed period with an overview of the antecedent musical generations, and then at the end fading off from that period with some suggestions as to the new tendencies evident as the most intense salsa years showed their earliest signs of waning. Thus in my introduction I discuss the main tendencies and musical exponents between 1930 (and earlier) and 1960 in terms of two prior generations cusping around 1945, while my final chapter seeks to identify some of the sprouts of musical innovation surfacing in the early to mid-1970s just as the name "salsa" comes into broad currency and the music by that name reaches the apex of its popular success. Those incipient countercurrents to what had become a mainstream salsa agenda—namely hip hop, Afro-Caribbean roots music, and Latin jazz—have come to define the contours of Latin music history in more recent times. The book has therefore taken on a bell-curve shape, stretching way back and arriving fairly close to the contemporary soundscape, but with the bulging mid-section training a close focus on that one complex and still resonant generational stage in the process.

Salsa Rising is also circumscribed geographically, my view being limited to the primary locus and birthplace of salsa by any account, New York City. Both the roots and the diffusion of the styles are of course strongly transnational in scope, since salsa is clearly grounded in Cuban and other Caribbean musical structures, and most of its ongoing afterlife has played out on the world stage. Its creative sources and ultimate creative base and audience are thus located outside of New York City, such that for both reasons the centrality of that founding, originating location is sometimes minimized or denied. Further, some important developments of the music even during those formative years of the 1960s and 70s transpire in other places, notably California, Puerto Rico, Venezuela, and Cuba. Yet while the salsa spills in many directions, and comes in many flavors, I nevertheless feel justified in limiting myself to the New York setting because it is in that city that the musical sensibility incubates and takes hold among a local cultural community, and in it's barrios that the musical emergence most directly correlates with demographically and historically based generational change. I readily admit to privileging such socially grounded creative innovation, or instances where such a correlation is definitive of cultural emergence.

Emergence here is the key word, and is the rationale for my title in its use of the term "rising." For I am also not trying to track the full life-span of salsa as it reaches back prior to the 1960 start-off point and extends on through the 1980s and beyond, most prominently in its guise as "salsa romántica."

Rather, in line with others who have thought about how to define the term, I treat "salsa" not as musical style, nor even a particular music-making practice (as Willie Colón would have it) or guiding cultural concept (according to Rubén Blades and others), but as a generation, the cultural voice and spirit of a historical span of time marked off by an initial collective inspiration and shared socio-historical experience, and lasting until the next set of redefining conditions and expressive languages begin to show up on the horizon. Therefore, as the title indicates, this book is about salsa as a musical generation among Latinos in New York City, one which transpires for as long as a full decade before even being named such, and which already ceases to be the musical dominant while it still seems in full swing. Both in my introduction spanning thirty years and in my central narrative of the 1960–75 period, I have found that the 15-year arc identified in much of the theoretical literature on "the problem of generations" corresponded best to my own sense of the chronological proportions at play in marking off the stylistic stages of New York's Latin music history.[1]

The origin, and "originator," of the term salsa is a point of avid and boundless contention, and is sure to forever remain so; I mention and assess many of these claims during the course of my narrative without taking a definitive stance on any of them in particular. There is even a reasonable claim that "salsa" in its widest and eventually established usage first emerged not in New York but in Venezuela, long before it took hold in its heralded baptism by Fania Records and *Latin New York* magazine around 1975. (I return to this fascinating back story to the coining of the term at the end of chapter 4, as part of the crucial late 1960s period.) It is journalist Ed Morales who has come up with perhaps the most circumspect grasp of the term's dynamic, multiply determined meaning when he refers to it as "Nuyorican salsa," and states that it is "at once a modern marketing concept and the cultural voice of a new generation."[2] While avoiding simplistic dualisms, the naming process has been primarily conditioned by two primary and often contrary sources of meaning and value, the music and broader cultural industry on one end and the socially based cultural community on the other. Consumption and production, commercial interests and creative needs—with a highly porous line between them. The two previous books on salsa that I have found most useful, Vernon Boggs' compilation of interviews and articles *Salsiology: Afro-Cuban Music and the Evolution of Salsa in New York City* (1992) and especially César Miguel Rondón's *El libro de la salsa: Crónica de la música del Caribe urbano* (1979, English translation, *The Book of Salsa: A Chronicle of Urban Music from the Caribbean to New York City*, 2008), are both significantly if implicitly framed by this dialectical concept. Rondón's remarkable book in particular has been guiding me through this subject for many years, and served as a constant object of reference, and some lively contention, as I was writing.

Beyond those broader delimitations of my effort there are of course sundry other important omissions and caveats. Most obviously, I have not sought to consider all of the many major musicians, groups, venues or recordings that stand out and characterize in a more expansive way the expression and enjoyment of the music of the salsa era. Many will be the questions and objections as to "what about" this or that important singer or drummer or album or concert or dance hall? I further only sparingly address the obviously key place of dance in the story of what is preeminently dance music, nor the important but elusive role of women, or the many crucial musicological dimensions of the analysis that might help bring my account to life, or lend it greater technical precision. Many will be the collector, aficionado, musician, journalist, or avid, well-informed fan likely to fault this study on many counts, and for leaving out those many areas of knowledge that are central to the full version of events.

While well aware of and sensitive to those many drawbacks and shortcomings, I am still hopeful that a carefully plotted and historically rigorous charting of the step-by-step emergence of salsa and its naming will nevertheless contribute to our understanding of this complex and (for many) emotionally charged field of expressive innovation and cultural creativity. For my sharpest attention remains riveted throughout on the signs and wellsprings of stylistic inventiveness, harbingers of the new, those forms and practices of aesthetic expressiveness that each new generation, especially the youth of any given cultural community, introduce to give appropriate articulation to its reality. With that aspect of music history as my lodestar I seek to identify among the wealth of musicians, bands, stylistic possibilities those which surface as pioneers, groundbreakers, rebels if you will, respectful of powerful traditions yet never deferential to the point of restraining the force of originality and that inner urge to strike out in new directions no matter the consequences. Rather than amassing a compendium of all that has happened and all who have participated in the music of the period, my view is fixed on the moments of shift, of transition, quick or gradual, from one stylistic temper to another. I have thus considered it necessary to be highly selective and as a result found my attention turning back again and again to the same individual bandleaders and other practitioners by way of instrumentalists, vocalists, arrangers, producers or other catalysts, and tracking their changing roles within the historical narrative. Thus the Palmieri brothers Charlie and Eddie, Johnny Pacheco, Al Santiago, Mongo Santamaría, Ray Barretto, Willie Colón, Joe Bataan, Joe Cuba, and a few other key figures are ubiquitous in these pages, the interactions and contrasts among them the building blocks of the salsa story. Thematically, the dialectics between tradition and experimentation, roots and ruptures, community and commerce, entertainment and politics, musical eras as defined by short lived dance crazes or by deeper demographic and historical shifts, "Latin" as an enclosed, internally structured ethnicity or as a locus of dynamic cross-cultural intersections and crossings—these and other conceptual tensions should provide a running analytical coherence to my account and, hopefully, lead to new understandings of this rich and widely shared cultural domain.

The books and articles mentioned, and many others, have proved indispensable sources for me in my research, as have some key journal publications such as *Latin New York, Latin Beat, Descarga Newsletter,* and the on-line service "Herencia Latina." I have also greatly enjoyed the many hours spent listening avidly and extensively to slews of great (and not-so-great) popular music, both Latin and African American, to keep my bearings and to track musical developments with the necessary historical precision. The endless listening sessions, combined with teaching the music in various educational contexts, have also been a central part of my life while writing the book, even more intensively so than they have been for many years prior. But far more than any of these sources, and an integral presence in every day of my life in recent years, have been the people in the music world, those infinitely generous and amazingly knowledgeable cognoscenti who eat, drink, and sleep the music every day and have done so all their lives. My list, even if limited to those I have had recourse to in the past three years while this book has incubated, seems endless, and I will present it in mortal fear that it won't be complete, and that I am very likely to leave someone out. If I do, may their consolation be that they are that much less responsible for the objectionable and erroneous things I might come up with in the course of my analysis. Not that any of them are to be blamed anyway, for I am painfully aware that whatever bullshit remains is my doing, and due to my relatively limited insider knowledge of the subject.

I would start with those who have seen me through the whole project, and been accompanying me in the music field for some years by now, my utterly indispensable sources. They are my main "bullshit blockers," and those who have helped me align my own sometimes irreverent judgments with something of a knowing consensus, a process that has allowed me to articulate views rarely if ever stated in print but nonetheless consensual among some of those most internal to and knowledgeable about the material and its complex dynamics. The following have been my closest confidants and have given of themselves to read the manuscript at various stages of its evolution: René López, David Carp, Andy González, Marty Sheller, and Pablo Yglesias. Then there are those friends and contacts to whom I have turned repeatedly for conversations and consultation on specific issues, and who have often generously shared with me valued materials to illuminate my work: Benny Bonilla, Nelson González, Joe Bataan, Jaime Flores, Louis Lafitte, Mike Amadeo, Richie Bonilla, Aurora Flores, Elena Martínez, Harry Sepúlveda, Pepe Flores, Juan Gutiérrez, Andy Kaufman, Willie Torres, Jorge Pérez, Roberta Singer, Chris Washburne. Finally, there are the dozens of musicians and others in the Latin music world who have shared their experience and knowledge with me in the course of wide-ranging conversations and interviews, sometimes under less than convenient circumstances: Johnny "Dandy" Rodriguez, Orlando Marín, David Pérez, Pete Rodríguez, Cheo Feliciano, Jairo Moreno, Héctor Maysonave, Johnny Palomo, Art Sato, Joe Quijano, Pablo Guzmán, Robin Moore, Mickie Meléndez, Roberto Berson, Leonardo Acosta, Richie Ray, Jesús Blanco, John Santos, Jimmy Sabater, Eddie

Zervigón, Alfredo Alvarado, Juan Otero, Larry Harlow, Sonny Bravo, Nicky Marrero, Jorge Pérez, and José Malavé. While working on chapter 1, I was delighted to talk at length with some of the community people with vivid recollections of the Tritons Club and those early 1960s years at the onset of the "salsa generation." Thank you Pee Wee López, Carmen Costas Vázquez, Julito Vázquez, Iris Meléndez, and Yogi .In my search for photos and other unpublished materials I was kindly assisted by Mary Yearwoood of the Photos and Prints Division at the Schomburg Center for Research in Black Culture, Pedro Juan Hernández of the Archives of the Centro de Estudios Puertorriqueños, and Laura and Elizabeth Nico of the Bronx County Historical Society.

Last but not least, two people have, for very diverse reasons, been of central importance to my work on this book. I must thank Eddie Palmieri for sharing many highly instructive and hilarious hours with me in recorded and unrecorded conversation, many of them accompanied by delicious food and drink; these formal and informal interviews provided me the privilege of a unique insider's view of my subject as recounted by an undisputed pioneer of the Latin music called salsa who, tellingly, has always hated the word salsa.

Finally, my beloved wife Miriam Jiménez Román, whose formative adolescent years span the period covered by the book and whose ear and feel for the great salsa and soul sounds never cease to amaze me. Whatever is worthwhile about *Salsa Rising* I owe to you more than anyone. *Te lo agradezco con todo el corazón!*

SALSA RISING

Introduction

Guaracha to Mambo, Soundscapes of the Early Decades (1930–1960)

Boleros, Guarachas, and the "Rhumba" Craze (1925–1945)

In the summer of 1930, at the onset of the Great Depression, New York's Latino neighborhoods were filled with the unforgettable sound of "Lamento Borincano," a new song by the famous Puerto Rican composer Rafael Hernández. From storefronts and tenement windows resounded the haunting melody and mournful lyrics of that historic recording. It is a "lament" over the fate of poor migrants in the face of economic crisis, and it immediately struck a chord not only with the "Borincanos" (Puerto Ricans) in El Barrio, but with Latino working people throughout the hemisphere. Indeed, "Lamento Borincano" has become the unofficial anthem not only of Puerto Ricans but of Latino migrants everywhere and has been called "the first Latin American protest song."[1] There are by now hundreds of versions of the song, in myriad musical styles and from many Latin American countries, sometimes with the title adjusted to "Lamento Argentino" or "Lamento Cubano." And that all-time standard, by a young Puerto Rican musician who went on to write over two thousand songs and become one of the preeminent Latin American composers of all time, was composed and recorded in New York city.

That same year, 1930, also saw the recording and immediate popularity of another classic song, the Latin and jazz classic "El Manisero" ("The Peanut Vendor"). That recording of the signature Moisés Simóns composition, not the first but by far the most influential, was played by the famed Don Azpiazú band, the Havana Casino Orchestra, with lead vocalist Antonio Machín (and, of some historical note, with the young Mario Bauzá playing saxophone). The contagious tune, with its seductive swaying rhythm, "tropical" maraca and muted trumpet, and playful double entendres, captured national and international audiences of the time, to the point that it actually initiated a decade-long craze, the so-called rhumba craze of the 1930s. Like "Lamento Borincano," "The Peanut Vendor" generated numerous versions in subsequent years, notably those by the Trio Matamoros, Louis Armstrong, Duke Ellington, and Stan Kenton. "El Manisero" was not actually a "rhumba-fox trot" as it was labeled (the widespread misspelling of "rumba" is indicative), but rather a *son pregón*, that is, a Cuban *son* based on the call of a street *pregón* (vendor)—in this case, a man in the street selling peanuts. Though the song was first popularized and recorded by the idolized Cuban vocalist Rita Montaner, the appeal of that historic RCA recording of the song is never in question: it is sheer entertainment in tune with the bustling popular culture of the time; indeed, it was first introduced to American audiences at its premiere on Broadway earlier that year. Along with its enticing vaudeville flavor and exotically tropical yet reasonably "authentic" Cuban sound, the smooth, magnificently modulated voice of lead singer Antonio Machín had much to do with its feverish reception. Machín, popularly known as "Cuba's Rudy Vallee," spent many years in New York with his influential group Cuarteto Machín, becoming the premier Latin vocalist of the 1930s period along with the beloved "Davilita." Interestingly, Pedro Ortíz Dávila, a young Afro-Puerto Rican singer who had just arrived to New York a few months earlier, began his prolific recording career singing the original version of "Lamento Borincano."

Despite their many historical coincidences, however, these two all-time favorites of the Latin American repertoire, both of them recorded in mid-1930 at New York's RCA Victor studio, bore quite different relations to the New York Latino community and its budding social and cultural presence. The popularity of the two compositions does, of course, attest to the growing size of that population, already exceeding 100,000 by that time, and also illustrates the powerful role of the nascent New York–based recording industry in shaping popular musical taste and public

FIGURE 1 Poster for Don Azpiazu and his Havana Casino Orchestra, 1930. John Storm Roberts Collection, Photos and Prints Division, Schomburg Center, New York Public Library. Photo by Raúl Azpiazu.

opinion among and about Latinos. It is interesting that appearing as they did at the onset of the financial crisis, both songs are about economic transactions, whether the *jíbaro* carting his produce to the desolate town market or the street vendor hawking his little paper cones of peanuts in the street.

But the difference in tone and intention is palpable: "Lamento Borincano" offers a narrative commentary on the crushing social conditions facing the Latino and Latin American masses in times of grave economic crisis and has remained popular mainly among Latinos; "El Manisero," however, was the first Latin crossover hit, providing Latinos and non-Latinos alike entertainment and diversion in the face of the decidedly grim Depression. Rafael Hernández's signature song evokes real-life suffering and struggle, disillusion, pride, and nostalgia for a distant homeland while the peanut vendor's cry is a playful, passing serenade, an invitation to sensual delights as a momentary respite from the misery of the everyday world. Though both have wide-ranging reach and appeal, one is firmly grounded in Puerto Rican historical experience and musical sensibilities while the other is unmistakably of Cuban vintage.

The two songs provide a striking contrast and point up a sharp duality of style and meaning which is at the same time expressive of the wide-ranging divergences in the musical, cultural, and social experiences of New York's Latino communities over the decades. The implicit class, ethnic, and ideological differences between these two early Latino megahits correspond to those evident in the earliest concentrations of Cubans and Puerto Ricans in New York in the later nineteenth century: it was a community which, though voicing and exhibiting strong solidarity in the face of lingering Spanish colonial rule, was composed of the professional and intellectual elite on the one hand and the far more numerous artisan workers on the other. Bernardo Vega, the foremost chronicler of nearly a century of Latino experience in New York from 1850 to 1950, offers a detailed account of these complex class interactions in his invaluable memoir and draws repeated reference to musical and other cultural events of those early years.[2] During the late nineteenth and early twentieth centuries, prior to the advent of commercial recording, established genres like the danzón, the danza, the *bolero*, and the *guaracha* enjoyed broad appeal across class and ethnic lines. But it was the Puerto Rican danza and the Cuban danzón, generally associated with the better-off elite sectors and popularized in periodic performances by touring operatic and orchestral troupes, that drew the most attention from the Spanish-language press of the time and were thus most generally identified with the tastes of the entire community. Vega makes no mention of more directly popular forms like *guajira* and *jíbaro* music (genres like *décima, punto, seis, aguinaldo* and *controversia* stemming from the Cuban and Puerto Rican peasant or country repertoires) or the Afro-Cuban and Afro-Puerto Rican forms of *rumba* and *son*, or *bomba* and *plena*, though there can be little doubt that those styles were favored and often played among the artisans and working people who made up the majority of the exile populations. Songs with social themes were of course very widespread among these highly politicized communities, with the many patriotic, anti-colonial compositions in a range of musical and poetic genres appealing to both professional and working-class sectors. But the abundant repertoire of proletarian hymns and calls to battle generally remained exclusive to the more impoverished and less formally educated among the militant activists of the period.

Even prior to the earliest studio recordings in the mid-1920s, the tango rage of the new century's opening decades introduced American audiences to exotic, commercially packaged Latin offerings and helped establish a gulf between presumptively "Latin" music and dance styles for the general public and the tastes of the Latino community itself. The tango did of course enjoy a long life of immense popularity among Latinos of all nationalities, especially as part of the repertoire, along with the bolero, of the traditional guitar and voice small groups, the trios and quartets. Rafael Hernández's Trio Borinquen was the earliest such ensemble to emerge in New York, but revered groups like the Trio Matamoros, Trio Mayarí, Cuarteto Marcano, and Cuarteto Flores held sway through the 1930s and beyond. The tango that landed in New York and the rest of the United States around 1914 was generally a watered-down version of the genre, rich in exotic and erotic allure but often thin in musical quality and of course far removed from its humble and African diasporic roots in the underworld of turn-of-the-century Buenos Aires. Instead, the tango came to New York by way of Paris and Broadway, with some of its earliest propagators describing it as a "descendant of the eighteenth-century minuet" and as "courtly and artistic." Its derivation from the prodigiously influential *habanera* of Afro-Cuban roots was effectively erased—and thus its relation to ragtime and the beginnings of jazz. Again, though representative of "Latino" musical style for the broad listening and dancing public, the tango of that first Latin dance fad bore scant if any relation to New York's Latino community. It was an early example of what music journalist and historian John Storm Roberts called "the Latin tinge," in his pathbreaking book of that title first published in 1979. Indeed, as Roberts was first to emphasize, the difference between the tango craze and the "rhumba" fever that followed in the 1930s was the very existence of a bustling Latin community with its own musical and cultural tastes and institutions allowing for both the perseverance of ongoing traditions and the incubation of new musical styles and practices. Roberts is even more precise in signaling those extra-musical sources of change when he writes, "In the long term, by far the most important event of relevance to this process was not musical but political. On March 17, 1917, Puerto Ricans were granted U.S. citizenship. Almost immediately, migration from the Island to New York got under way. . . . These new arrivals were to lay the foundation for the development, little more than ten years later, of an indigenous urban Latin style."[3]

More relevant as regards the community's life and music in these years before the advent of recording was the remarkable experience of Rafael Hernández and other Afro-Puerto Rican musicians during World War I. As recounted by Ruth Glasser in her excellent book *My Music Is My Flag*,[4] in 1917 Hernández and his fellow Black musicians from the Island were recruited by celebrated African American bandleader James Reese Europe into the army's most prestigious marching band, the all-Black 369th Infantry's "Hellfighters" Band, and toured with them in France to huge fanfare. The seeds of a Latinized jazz, already present at the inception of jazz itself, were evident in the creolized sounds of this historic military band. At war's end, Hernández and many others, including some of the most prominent Puerto Rican musicians of the early century, settled in New York, part of the swelling ranks of the Puerto Rican community migrating after receiving US citizenship. Major attractions for these musicians were the budding recording industry and the numerous performance venues based in New York. The composer of "Lamento Borincano," who went on to become the most illustrious of all Puerto Rican musicians, lived for a number of years in Mexico and Cuba before returning to his beloved Puerto Rico in his later life. But he composed many of his most celebrated songs in New York, and in 1927 his sister Victoria opened the first and best-known Latin music store on Madison Avenue and 114th Street in El Barrio. It is even said that Hernández actually composed "Lamento Borincano" at that address. Through the efforts and accomplishments of his sister—his most renowned musical group, Cuarteto Victoria, was named in her honor—and because of his active role in the musical life of the time, Rafael

Hernández's name is identified in a direct way with the New York Latino community and its music. His repertoire included many tangos, but unlike the tango craze, and later the "rhumba craze" of the 1930s, his music stands as a direct expression of community life, including that of its less privileged but most numerous inhabitants.

The first studio recordings of Cuban and Puerto Rican popular dance styles date from the mid- to late 1920s. Of greatest public acclaim were the *son* sextets from Havana, notably the Sexteto Habanero and the Sexteto Nacional led by the premier composer and bandleader of early *son*, Ignacio Piñero; the New York visits of the Habanero and Nacional groups in the late 1920s were major events throughout Latin New York, as in

FIGURE 2 Grupo Victoria (also called Grupo Hernández). New York, 1932. Standing, center, Rafael Hernández. Courtesy of Jaime Flores.

addition to recording they played to avid audiences at multiple venues. Of special importance for the Latino community was the presence and work of Puerto Rican vocalist and bandleader Manuel Jiménez, known as "Canario," and the various groups he organized for performance and recording opportunities. His musical tastes were broad, having been formed in the traditions of bolero and *música jíbara*, and he had been one of the original vocalists of Trio Borinquen. Canario made an influential recording of "Lamento Borincano," but his most enduring achievement was his prolific composition and recording of Puerto Rican plenas. Many of these remain standards of the genre despite the relatively sparse presence of plena in the subsequent history of recorded Latin music in New York until more recent decades.

Though the initial recordings of Puerto Rican and Cuban music coincided in time, and though by 1930 the Puerto Rican population in New York was more than double that of the Cubans, Cuban musical styles and presence typically eclipsed the Puerto Rican traditions for the duration of that history down to the recent past. The *son cubano* became the stylistic backbone of the major trends and eras to follow, from "rhumba" to *conga* and mambo to cha cha, Latin jazz, pachanga, boogaloo, and salsa; it even became the best-known and preferred style of many Puerto Rican musicians and audiences themselves. Native Puerto Rican styles, on the other hand, from danza to bomba, plena, and música jíbara, never really transcended their national and ethnic origins in a massive way and were only on occasion incorporated into those more widely diffused and commercially viable genres of Latin music. Thus, in the 1930s and early 1940s, Cuban music was spread through the success of Don Azpiazú's Havana Casino Orchestra and then of the highly influential bandleader and impresario Xavier Cugat, who came to New York around 1920 from Spain via Cuba. They brought this music, often in its watered-down, ballroom-style "Latin" form, to mainstream American audiences on Broadway, in Hollywood, and for years in New York's classy Waldorf Astoria Hotel and other swanky ballrooms of the time. Cugat himself described the artistic consequences of offering up music for the unknowing American audiences: "Americans know nothing about Latin music. They neither understand nor feel it. So they have to be given music more for the eyes and not for the ears. Eighty percent visual, the rest aural."[5]

The most familiar narrative of Latin music history tells of the ascendancy and prevalence of this tango-"Manisero"-Cugat lineage of the "Latin tinge," Cuban-based dance music diluted to suit the taste of largely white, middle-class, and non-Latino audiences, in ballrooms, in films, on the radio, and in the most marketable recordings. The focus is usually on the so-called downtown scene, the strongly Cuban-influenced, tropicalized face of the culture, which was clearly where the money and the glamor were to be found in Latin music and entertainment of the day. The success story reached its peak in the late 1940s and 1950s with that most visible of all the musically inclined sons of Cuba, Desi Arnaz, who played Mr. Babalú in New York and Los Angeles clubs, and Ricky Ricardo on his wildly popular television show *I Love Lucy*. Cuban American novelist Oscar Hijuelos tried with mixed success to capture this version of the mid-century New York Latin music scene in his 1990 Pulitzer Prize–winning novel *The Mambo Kings Play Songs of Love*. It is indicative of Latino racial and class experience that Desi Arnaz's Mr. Babalú is really a cover version, a white-face rendition of the signature act of that towering vocalist and inimitable presence reared in Afro-Cuban musical and spiritual traditions, the great Miguelito Valdés. This outright appropriation was of course only the most glaring instance of the racial exclusions and white skin privilege at work in the world of Latin music in those years. Countless stories tell of clubs restricting their bands to light-skinned musicians and their audiences to whites only (flyers would actually include the words "para raza blanca"), and bandleaders going along with such segregationist policies. Mario Bauzá had many memories of prejudice against Black Latino musicians, including by light-skinned Latinos; Bobby Capó recalled vividly how Xavier Cugat refused his services, saying "What a pity you are so dark."

GRAN BAILE

ORGANIZADO POR EL

CLUB AZTECA

PARA CELEBRAR LA

FIESTA DE LA RAZA

a beneficio de los damnificados de

PUERTO RICO

EN EL BALL ROOM DEL HOTEL PENNSYLVANIA
CALLE 33 Y SEPTIMA AVENIDA

Sabado 15 de Octubre de 1932
A LAS 9 P. M.

2 - ORQUESTAS - 2

ADMISION:

Caballeros: adelantado $1.00 . . . . Damas $1.00
"   en la Taquilla . . . $1.50

Con autorizacion del Puerto Rico Hurricane Relief Committee.
No es requirito traje de etiqueta.   Para raza blanca.

Tickets de venta en: Libreria Cervantes - 62 Lenox Avenue; Fotografía Torres - 224 West 116th Street;
Restaurant El Rancho - 57 Lenox Avenue; Constance Hand Laundry 104 W. 111th Street y en los princi-
pales establecimientos de Manhattan, Brooklyn, Queens, Bronx y Richmond.

Trianole Printing Company. 9 West 19th St., New York.

FIGURE 3 Poster for Columbus Day Dance at Club Azteca, 1932. Note, in small letters at lower right, "para raza blanca" ("whites only"). Jesús Colón Papers, Archives of the Puerto Rican Diaspora, Centro de Estudios Puertorriqueños, Hunter College, City University of New York.

The "uptown-downtown" dichotomy is thus more than a musical demarcation and only partly involves an aesthetic judgment. The "downtown" location did not preclude music of quality and authenticity, nor were the grassroots community settings in Harlem and the Bronx necessarily guaranteed to offer the best of Latin music. A major venue of this 1925–1945 period was the Havana Madrid Night Club, which opened on 51st Street and Broadway in 1938. The opening act itself was of some historic note, in that it featured the heralded female *son* group, Grupo Anacaona, with famous lead vocalist Graciela, Machito's sister, and accompanied by the legendary vocalist for the Sexteto Nacional, Alfredito Valdéz. The Havana Madrid remained a key venue for the "rhumba craze," its combination of forceful Afro-Cuban dance music and the usual "tropical" and "Spanish" ephemera lending it a quality all its own in Latin New York history. A similar magnetic role was played in the early 1950s by the Chateau Madrid, its house band led by the well-known conguero Cándido Camero and featuring musical luminaries, like illustrious Mexican singer Toña la Negra, from all over Latin America and the Caribbean. These two early mid-Manhattan venues, and others, anticipate the unparalleled fame of the Palladium Ballroom.

The "uptown" scene, on the other hand, comprised Puerto Rican, Cuban, and other Latino musicians and audiences more organically linked to the local neighborhoods and communities, which became increasingly Puerto Rican working class over the decades. Ironically, while the "rhumba craze" was in full swing and New York Latin music was achieving commercial success and a level of public visibility incommensurate with its sometimes negligible musical significance, the more grassroots music of the city's expanding Latino communities was actually experiencing a veritable renaissance of talent and production. Though the prolific Afro-Cuban community could certainly boast the unquestioned importance of such pre-1940s greats as flutist Alberto Socarrás, pioneering bandleader Mario Bauzá, and many others, the foremost Puerto Rican musicians of that period in all styles and genres came to live, compose, perform, and record in New York. Alongside Rafael Hernández, virtually all of the major composers of Puerto Rican popular song, from Pedro Flores and Plácido Acevedo to Noro Morales and Bobby Capó, were in New York between 1925 and 1945. Together they produced thousands of boleros, *sones*, and guarachas, many of which live on, their authorship often unacknowledged, in the songbook of twentieth-century Puerto Rican and Latin American music.

In contrast to the show-business, ballroom, and hotel lounge music of the downtown variety, and even to the generally light lyrics and ephemeral themes of the mambos and cha chas of the subsequent generation, much of this voluminous, primarily Puerto Rican output of the 1930s comprises songs, generally populist and anti-colonial in tenor, about Puerto Rican and Latin American politics, labor migrations, and the struggling New York Latino communities during the Depression years. Featuring themes of patriotism and nostalgia, making do in a hostile environment, and the ironies and tribulations of modern urban life, this expansive repertoire makes it possible to appreciate the diverse "representation of New York City in Latin music," as ethnomusicologist Peter Manuel demonstrates in a helpful study of song lyrics.[6] Like Rafael Hernández, prolific composers and bandleaders Pedro Flores and Plácido Acevedo wrote and performed scores of songs with strong social content, as well as many with infectious good humor in the vernacular idiom, which have remained dear to the hearts of Latinos everywhere and ever since. Flores's song "Despedida," for example, a moving reflection on the anticipated departure of Puerto Ricans to fight in World War II, was recorded in 1939 by the Cuarteto Flores

FIGURE 4 Pedro Flores (r.) with Piquito Marcano, New York, ca. 1935. The Pedro "Piquito" Marcano Collection. Archives of the Puerto Rican Diaspora, Centro de Estudios Puertorriqueños, Hunter College, City University of New York. Courtesy of Grego Marcano.

with Daniel Santos in the lead vocal and became the biggest hit of the period and another enduring Latin American standard. Another rich, and especially consequential, instance of this politically themed music is Flores's bitter lament for his colonized homeland, "Sin Bandera"; it was so gloomy in its prospects that it provoked the more sanguine Rafael Hernández to answer with "Preciosa," a paean to the Puerto Rican flag that also enjoys canonical stature in the country's songbook.

Hernández, Flores, Acevedo, and many other prominent musicians, like Davilita, Augusto Coen, and Pedro ("Piquito") Marcano, made up a rich and varied musical community with its own venues in East Harlem, the Bronx, and Brooklyn, most notably the magnetic Park Palace dance hall on Fifth Avenue and 110th Street in Manhattan. The "uptown" scene also had its own distinctive, locally based audiences more savvy of the musical idioms at the center of Caribbean and Latin American traditions than those of the flashier, more touristic downtown clubs. Yet even the uptown repertoire was not primarily indigenous Puerto Rican or Cuban forms, such as música jíbara, *punto guajiro*, rumba, bomba, or plena, nor the more jazz-oriented innovations of musicians like Socarrás or Bauzá or Puerto Rican Juan Tizol in their seminal roles in premier African American bands. Rather, their foremost though largely unheralded achievement was to bring such more broadly pan-Latino genres as the bolero and guaracha to their highest levels of mastery and to relate them to the lived social realities of their peoples and communities. In contrast to the downtown scene, "East Harlem served as a source of new musicians, a gateway for innovation from Cuba and elsewhere, and a place where more purely Latin styles were played, and a workshop for fusions of a very different nature from the Tin-Pan-Alley, mass-popular-oriented downtown versions."[7]

Yet despite its inroads into the mainstream of North American musical culture, and the robust volume, variety, and quality of musical production and consumption during those years, the pre-1945 chapter of Latin music history in New York is in retrospect all but overshadowed in relative significance by the transformative developments in the period to come. Indeed, it is not unreasonable to regard 1945 as marking not so much the "end" of a war and a generation but rather the propitious onset of modern-day Latin cultural history in New York, and that earlier period more a prelude to the main event. For when Mario Bauzá, percussionist Chano Pozo, and the all-time greatest of Latin orchestras, Machito and His Afro-Cubans, link up with master jazz pioneers of the stature of Dizzy Gillespie and Charlie Parker, and together mesmerize audiences in venues from the historic Palladium Ballroom to Carnegie Hall to the Cotton Club, we witness a transcending moment of modern-day musical innovation.

This special postwar collaboration, which coincided with the massive influx of Puerto Ricans from the island, witnessed the emergence of the first major Latin styles, mambo and Cubop, actually created and popularized in the United States. In those pivotal years we are clearly at a new stage in the historical narrative because some of the most seasoned and boldly creative musicians of the time succeeded in creating an intersection, or "marriage of love" as Machito called it, between Afro-Latin and African American music that would set the cross-cultural paradigm for Latin music ever after. And this "revolution" occurred, and perhaps could only occur, in New York City; it is profoundly reflective of Latino life in New York City as its Latino presence approached the proportions and maturity closer to what it has become in our own times. When talk is of New York Latin music, the post-1945 mambo era appears to be when it all got going, and then, with the pachanga, boogaloo, and salsa of the subsequent generation, Latino musical roots finally struck deep in the fertile soil of the New York diaspora.

From our present-day vantage point of the salsa and post-salsa generations, it takes a stretch of historical memory and imagination to harken back to the days of Rafael Hernández, the first-ever recording of "The Peanut Vendor," and the richly atmospheric but traditional sounds of the many trios, cuartetos, and big bands of the earlier decades. Happily, though, creative history is not about erasure and discarding; rather, it attests to continuities and re-invention. "Lamento Borincano" has enjoyed dozens of salsa versions and has even made its appearance in hip-hop, merengue, reggaeton, and other more recent musical styles and formats. Songs by Pedro Flores continue to inspire modern-day dance and Latin jazz bands, even boldly experimental ones like the Fort Apache Band and Grupo Folklórico y Experimental Nuevayorquino. And perhaps most memorably, and resonating through the decades of Latin music history, is the legendary Afro-Cuban singer Graciela. Her career extends back to 1930s Cuba where she sang with the world famous Grupo Anacaona, and her fame as the most distinguished Latina vocalist is rivaled only by that of her celebrated compatriot Celia Cruz, whose presence in New York she preceded by some twenty years. Until recently Graciela, Machito's sister and long-time vocalist in his historic orchestra, was still singing and making honorary appearances, a vibrant Afro-Latina New Yorker well into her nineties—what better testament to the endurance and resilience of Latino culture in New York through the decades and generations of constantly changing musical temperament?

But of equal importance to such continuities of individual creative achievement and influence is remembering that the earlier decades set the stage and dynamics of what was to come. Once a sizable and self-conscious Latino community formed its own musical life and infrastructure, as occurred in that period, then the relationship between that community and the American musical mainstream became the key for understanding the entire historical process. The uptown-downtown paradigm as evident in a contrast like that between "Lamento Borincano" and "El Manisero" continues to apply, with all its exceptions and blurring, to subsequent chapters of Latin music history. The story of New York mambo, and of salsa, cannot be told with the necessary interpretive rigor without that interwoven analysis. Contrasting sharply with the master narrative of each generation, the story of commercial ascendancy and mainstream success best known to the general public, there is the backstory, the vibrant musical life of the Latino communities themselves, where different musical practices and measures of achievement prevailed and where in many cases the most daring innovations of the time actually originated. What makes it big "downtown," where commercial and crossover imperatives rule, was usually conceived and incubated in the decidedly less glamorous, less propitious "uptown" settings—the small clubs, dance halls, and house parties right there in the neighborhood.

Mambo, Cubop, and Much More (1945–1960)

If there is an event that heralded a new generation of New York Latin music and marked off the earlier decades from the momentous ones to follow, it was the formation of Machito and His Afro-Cubans in 1940 and the bandleader's incorporation of his brother-in-law Mario Bauzá as musical director the following year. That band, actually a full sixteen-piece orchestra, reigns indisputably as the premier Latin band ever—as Al Santiago once said, "no ifs, ands or buts"—and even less arguably, the most influential. With the band's debut at the Park Plaza

Ballroom on 110th Street and 5th Avenue on December 3, 1940, and continuing with their first recording, the album *Machito and His Afro-Cubans* for Decca in 1941, they established themselves as history makers. Their first hit song, "Sopa de Pichón" ("Pigeon Soup"), struck a chord with the Latino population with its reference to their pressing economic straits; it even featured on timbales their hometown son Tito Puente, born and raised in El Barrio. A few years later, on May 29, 1943, the band made further history by occasioning the composition, under Bauzá's direction, of "Tanga," widely regarded as the first example of Latin jazz. That same year, when Machito was doing a tour in the military, his sister Graciela took his place as the band's lead vocalist and quickly became the foremost female singer in Latin music. Then in 1944, Machito and Bauzá added Carlos Vidal on congas, which marked the first use of the three-part percussion section (conga, bongo, and timbales). It was that instrumentation, especially when the percussion section was brought dramatically to the front of the orchestra by Tito Puente, which defined the format characteristic of many New York Latin bands thereafter.[8] And finally, the evening of September 29, 1947, saw the historic concert at Carnegie Hall when Bauzá arranged for Dizzie Gillespie to meet and team with famed Afro-Cuban percussionist Chano Pozo and the Machito orchestra to perform the debut of "Manteca," the foundational composition of Latin jazz or Cubop, jazz writer Gary Giddens would later call "one of the most important records ever made in the United States."[9]

By the following year, 1948, the Afro-Cubans were permanently installed as the house band of that venue of venues, the Palladium Ballroom on 53rd Street and Broadway, where for nearly two decades, till its closing in 1966, the Palladium would be the most celebrated home of New York Latin music. It became the mecca for the best Latin bands and dancers of the day, and when in the early 1950s the Tito Puente and Tito Rodríguez orchestras were added to the regular billing alongside Machito, the level of exuberance reached a boiling point. The creative rivalries among "The Big Three" and the remarkable stylistic variety within the same musical genres made for an electric atmosphere that drew in audiences of all ethnic and racial backgrounds. In Machito's words, that was "the most exciting era in Latin music." The many musicians and attendees who recall that experience all attest to the validity of Machito's judgment.

The story of the mambo era in New York is so rich in larger-than-life personalities, memories of exhilaration, inter-ethnic sharing, and creative innovations in music and dance that it has come to be told countless times and in many media. It is

FIGURE 5 Machito and Graciela perform at Harlem's Savoy Ballroom, ca. 1948. The Carlos Ortíz Collection. Archives of the Puerto Rican Diaspora, Centro de Estudios Puertorriqueños, Hunter College, City University of New York.

an indelible chunk of Americana by now, and a source of deep pride and fascination among Latin American and Caribbean peoples everywhere. Ironically, it is also a story that tends to be omitted from conventional accounts of popular music history in the United States and in Latin America. To name just one glaring example, Ken Burns's 2000 video documentary *Jazz* makes but scant mention of Machito and Mario Bauzá in its presentation of jazz history, even when covering the period during which the Afro-Cuban impact was paramount and seminal. But in the history of Latin music in New York the breakthrough of the Afro-Cubans and the invention of Cubop and mambo occupy center stage, as the period of those achievements and their influence stands as the apex, the before-and-after benchmark, of the entire narrative. And of course the broader implications of this ingenious musical fusion, of Latino and African American cultures converging and creating something radically new, go beyond musical expression and carry deep lessons of a sociological and political nature.

The musical era that began in the early 1940s and extended through the 1950s involved both continuities with the preceding period and major innovations and changes. The Machito band and other musicians emerging in this new stage continued to center their repertoire around the bolero, guaracha, and of course the Cuban *son*, and the differentiation between a "downtown" and "uptown" social context remained in effect even though the major groups were active in both settings. Important composers and bandleaders such as Noro Morales and Marcelino Guerra bridged the two generations, as did many of the venues throughout the city. The multi-ethnic excitement at the Palladium and other midtown venues of the period was in many ways an extension of the white, middle-class fascination with the earlier "downtown" acts at places like the Waldorf-Astoria and the Conga, and of the offerings of the Xavier Cugat band, with some of the personnel, including Machito himself, moving from one to the other; the "mambo kings," as they came to be known, found their greatest public visibility in the persona and show-biz antics of Desi Arnaz, a view underlined by Oscar Hijuelos's novel and the movie that followed. Demographically, the city's Latino population continued to grow and remained overwhelmingly of Puerto Rican origin. The Depression and then the wartime economy conditioned life before and after the beginning of the 1940s.

But perhaps the sharper dividing line between the periods occurs at mid-decade—John Storm Roberts signals 1946 as the pivotal year; it has to do with the end of World War II and the onset of the Puerto Rican mass migration, which swelled their population in New York to roughly a million by 1960. Musically, from that point on the mambo began to take hold as the powerful music and dance force that it was to become for a full generation and beyond, replacing the fading "rhumba" and conga crazes, while Afro-Cuban jazz came to the attention of a wider public in the same years. Or, to describe the generational shift in terms of historically grounded musical styles rather than that endless sequence of commercial fads, the transition is from the prevalence of the guaracha to the emergence of mambo; as Al Santiago explains it, "the guaracha supplanted the rhumba, and the mambo supplanted the guaracha."[10] Santiago's account of the change of musical generations in the mid-1940s as a "guaracha to mambo" shift is compatible in interesting ways with that of jazz historian Ira Gitler's idea of "swing to bop" in his book of that title.[11]

In the later 1940s and early 1950s, New York-raised Puerto Rican musicians like the two famed Titos (Puente and Rodríguez) and Charlie Palmieri began to emerge as the new leaders of the years ahead, reared by but ultimately replacing the largely foreign-born Cubans and Puerto Ricans of the prior decades. With good reason New York–based mambo has been called "the first Latin idiom largely developed in the United States."[12] Nationally, the same years brought a growing challenge to the perpetuation of Jim Crow and the beginnings of the civil rights movement. A space was thus opened for the unprecedented diffusion of a Latin style like the mambo to enter the pores of the larger society, as evident in the proliferation of mambo fusions in rhythm and blues, early rock and roll, and jazz during the 1950s.[13] That highly sophisticated fusion called Cubop or Afro-Cuban jazz thus had its corollaries on a much more widespread vernacular level in the music of the era, all corresponding to a loosening of the racial and cultural boundaries that had prevailed through the decades in American life.

The most immediate sociohistorical development to condition the course of New York's Latin music in that period was the massive migration of Puerto Ricans from the Island that took off in 1946–1947 and extended through the 1950s and early 1960s. This huge demographic movement, which was impelled by the changing economy on the Island and adjustments in the colonial relation, transported hundreds of thousands of working-class families into a metropolis in the throes of de-industrialization and the resultant loss of manufacturing jobs. The new wave of Puerto Rican migrants, which quickly dwarfed in numbers the entire previous population of Puerto Rican descent, found their new home in the most impoverished, marginal, and underserviced neighborhoods of Harlem, the Bronx, and Brooklyn— in many instances alongside African Americans in a similar social situation. The conditions were set for the intense intercultural jostling and exchange that ensued during those years and ever since, with the kinds of musical fusions developed by Mario Bauzá and others being a paramount expression of those societal circumstances—and Harlem-born Tito Puente, more than any of the other gigantic figures of the age, embodied in his own life and work that new generational reality.

However, the same class and cultural discrepancies implicit in the downtown-uptown dichotomy persisted and indeed were made even more pronounced by the social placement of the new arrivals, who rapidly became the large majority of Latinos in New York City. The Puerto Rican "gringones" (greenhorns) or "Marine Tigers" (after the passenger ship), as the fresh-off-the-boat and then first airborne migrants were variously referred to, were overwhelming poor, unskilled, and uneducated workers cast off as a result of the rapid industrialization process afoot in Puerto Rico under US government and corporate tutelage. They did not necessarily find their way easily into the existing Latino life, especially that of the often more privileged middle-class patrons of the midtown clubs and ballrooms. While some made their way to the Palladium, the Conga, and other upscale venues for their share of the mambo excitement, the majority had decidedly different resources and tastes, often preferring to stay in the neighborhood and share more familiar, down-home musical and dance styles.

There is thus an important backstory to the Palladium-mambo narrative of this pivotal era in New York Latin music, an overlooked uptown reality that contrasts markedly with the flashier, widely disseminated drama that tends to exhaust accounts of what was going on musically for Latinos in those years. Probing just beneath the surface we come to recognize, in accord with those who lived the experience directly, that vast numbers of Latinos in New York, especially those more recent arrivals who constituted the growing bulk of the population, were less aware of or taken by the mambo and Latin jazz, and preferred other, more familiar styles and settings for their musical life. At house parties and local clubs and nightspots,

Puerto Rican New Yorkers loved to listen and dance to boleros and guarachas played by guitar trios; they were transported by the sounds of Puerto Rican country music ("música jíbara") as performed and recorded by some of the leading exponents of that style; and their house parties and local events often included popular merengues by New York-based Dominican groups of the time. Such was the repertoire for the mass of working-class Latinos in New York during the mambo era. Without in any way diminishing the lofty historical importance of the internationally diffused mambo and Cubop innovations, it is essential to account for the stylistic predilections that also prevailed during the same musical and cultural era.

Affection for the broadly popular love songs by guitar-and-voice trios and quartets of course spans all of Latin America and the Spanish-speaking world, but over the decades that preference was brought to New York and other Latino communities by the Puerto Rican migrants from the Island. In the postwar years this is the sound that resonated from phonographs and radios in the city's Latino barrios perhaps more widely than any other, a continuation of the deeply held tastes from the Island and from the previous generation of emigrant life. The songs were by Rafael Hernández, Pedro Flores, and other composers of the 1930s and 1940s, some of whom lived, performed, and composed in the city; trios like the Trio Vegabajeño—the most popular among New York Puerto Ricans—the Trio los Panchos, the Trio San Juan, and others drew adoring crowds to the neighborhood theaters and concert spaces, in many instances sharing the bill with some of the illustrious mambo artists. Records put out by Decca, RCA, Verne, Ansonia, and other labels received constant radio play and were among the prized possessions of many of the tenement-dwelling families, who listened and danced to them while cleaning the house on Saturday mornings or at house parties on weekend nights. Romantic ballads alternated with playful, humorous guarachas and other songs in delivering cadences and catchy lyrics that many knew by heart and sang along to. Musically and lyrically, the music of the trios and small voice-and-guitar groups was a far cry from the mambo of the period, a contrast captured memorably in the well-known guaracha by Pedro Flores, "Este No Es Un Mambo."

The *décimas* and *aguinaldos* of Puerto Rican música jíbara root the musical experience firmly in the soil of the Island, projecting the deep patriotic sentiments often voiced in clear opposition to colonial imposition and oppression. Deriving from age-old Spanish and Moorish song traditions, and developing over the centuries in the Caribbean nation, música jíbara would seem inseparable from the social reference and musical styles of the Island. Yet over the course of the Puerto Rican migration this tradition has taken its place in the new urban setting of New York, and coinciding with the mass migration of the 1940s and 1950s many of its most revered practitioners have visited and even come to live, perform, and compose in the city. Foremost among them, Florencio Morales Ramos ("Ramito") and the other Morales brothers (Luisito and Moralito), Ernestina Reyes ("La Calandria"), Jesús Sánchez ("Chuito el de Bayamón"), Jesús Ríos Robles ("Chuito el de Cayey"), and many others lived and were active in New York during that period, their songs filling the tenement households and drawing crowds to popular neighborhood venues like the Teatro Puerto Rico and Teatro San Juan in the Bronx. Some groups, like the Conjunto Típico Ladí, were formed and enjoyed their entire careers in New York; they were founded by Puerto Ricans who had made the city their home, in this case renowned cuatro player and composer Ladislao Martínez ("Maestro Ladí") in the early 1950s. The fledgling Ansonia label, founded in 1949 by Puerto Rican Rafael Pérez, released many of the most popular música jíbara recordings of the period. Interestingly and perhaps surprisingly, more than other popular musical forms, the *jíbaro* repertoire included many compositions explicitly set in and commenting on life in the big city. Songs like "Un Jíbaro en Nueva York" and "Culpando el Subway" recount the tribulations of the mountain folk as they navigate life in these strange new environs, often in a hilarious way. But most of all they tend to be strongly patriotic and nostalgic, accompanied by a disdain for the values and lifestyles attributed to urban modernity in the United States. Ramito's songbook contains countless numbers in this vein, most memorably his "No Cambio a Puerto Rico" with its defiant refrain "I wouldn't trade Puerto Rico for twenty New Yorks."

Rarely mentioned in the history of Latin music is the immense popularity of the Dominican merengue among working-class Puerto Ricans in New York and other northeastern cities during the 1950s. Largely eclipsed by the more recent, post-salsa merengue boom of the 1980s, the love of merengue among New York Latinos during that earlier period, prior to the massive Dominican migration following the death of Trujillo, made that genre a mainstay of the repertoire alongside the boleros, guarachas, and música jíbara popular in those years. Some of the foremost *merengueros* of the time were active in or lived in New York, starting with Dioris Valladares who came to live in the city as early as 1936 and remained a presence in the Latin music world through the decades. In 1951 he joined with merengue players and composers Luis Quintero and Angel Viloria to form the Conjunto Típico Cibaeño. Other merengueros to gain avid popularity among mostly Puerto Rican New York Latinos were Alberto Beltrán, Joseito Mateo, and Luis Kalaf. Again, as with música jíbara, it was Ansonia Records that put out many of the merengue recordings made in New York during those years. As Mateo recalls, "It was Puerto Ricans who originally brought merengue to popularity, who gave their hand to merengue."[14] Merengue hits like Mateo's "La Ligadura," and the standards

"El Negrito del Batey" and "Compadre Pedro Juan" as recorded by various groups of the time, were favorites at house parties and neighborhood dances throughout Latin New York of those years, as was the ubiquitous "A Lo Oscuro," a hilarious party number which called for turning off the lights and seeing what happens in the dark. In the later 1950s and 1960s Puerto Rican plena legend Mon Rivera regularly included merengues in his repertoire, often blending plena and merengue, and recorded with Valadares, Viloria, and other merengueros.

Such were the tastes and musical preferences of many New York Latinos during the famed mambo era, and they constitute part of the erased history that persists under the sensationalist radar screen. For many of those Latinos, especially the swelling ranks of the recent arrivals, the Palladium was a distant reference, both geographically and in terms of class and culture; and the mambo was unfamiliar to them and carried minimal interest to communities that had their musical fill with their favorite *decimas*, boleros, merengues, and other popular styles and rhythms. This entire field of musical practice and consumption goes unmentioned and unnoticed in the predominant narrative of the era, with its typical effusion about the Palladium and the Cubop revolution. Again, bringing these obscured aspects to the fore should not detract in any way from the very warranted attention given to those major musical innovations and lived experiences; there can be no slighting of the revolutionary innovations of the giants, Machito, Bauzá, Tito Rodríguez, and Tito Puente. But recalling "uptown" musical tastes and practices during the 1950s does help to cast the age in which they occurred in a fuller, more expansive light, and take adequate account of community life and the musicality of the mass of disenfranchised who too often fall from view in favor of more spectacular, publicly visible events.

The community-level taste for trios, *jíbaro* music, and merengue is of course familiar to those who lived it, such that many New York Latinos from the barrios of those years will readily concur with an emphasis on the vitality of those genres and recognize the need for those correctives to the most prevalent narrative. Less visible even to many Latinos themselves, though, are two other untold stories of uptown mambo-era Latin music that need mention, especially if a view is toward what was to follow in the subsequent period of the 1960s. Significantly, both have to do with the racial dimension of Latino cultural life and the cultural relation of Latinos to Blackness. The first refers to the Club Cubano Interamericano in the Bronx and the role of Arsenio Rodríguez in the creation of the mambo; the second brings into view the largely forgotten multi-ethnic bands in 1950s Harlem, groups led by African Americans but which included Latin music in their repertoire and some Latin musicians among their personnel. An important corollary to the latter of these was the growing popularity of doo wop and early rock and roll among urban Latino youth; it is well established that many of the prominent New York doo-wop groups of the 1950s included Latino harmonizers, and that the style remained a powerful force informing future generations of Latin soul artists and fans.

The Club Cubano Interamericano was founded in 1945 on Prospect Avenue in the Bronx (now the South Bronx) to serve as a social club and self-help center for working-class Afro-Cubans and Puerto Ricans. As time went by it became well known for its dances and celebrations, where some of the most renowned Latin musicians of the time would come to its intimate environment to play and socialize. Among them, and serving as a kind of house band, was the group around the great Arsenio Rodríguez, the pioneer of the influential *son montuno* style. As musicologist David García recounts in his book on Arsenio, the Club Cubano was the preferred venue for Black Latinos in those days, who attest to feeling more at home there than in many of the other "Latin" venues including the Palladium. Rodríguez of course did play the Palladium often and to great acclaim. But as documented in García's well-argued study, Rodríguez offered up a very different kind of mambo and musical sensibility; and in those years he had a stake in claiming authorship of the mambo in his "diablitos" style, at one point even pressing Pérez Prado to acknowledge his creation of the genre as early as the late 1930s.[15] The music played, composed, and enjoyed at the Club Cubano during the 1950s is not included in the record of the mambo era, but it is needed as part of the story if the full account of Latino music of the time is to be complete. The central influence of Arsenio Rodríguez in the founding of salsa during the subsequent decade reinforces the need for such a historical corrective.

Finally, to further fill in the picture of the musical era, there was the direct, community-based musical interplay between Latinos and African Americans at the vernacular level. The club circuit of Harlem in those days included seminal bands that were led by African Americans but had white and Latino members and played active schedules right there in Harlem. Because of the diverse musical tastes prevalent in Harlem at the time, their repertoire had to include not only rb and later soul music, but also jazz, calypso, and, most prominently, Latin. These versatile groupings—the best known led by Joe Panama, Pucho Brown, and Hugo Dickens—proved to be important training grounds for a range of musicians who went on to significant musical accomplishments of their own. The Joe Panama Sextet had a long and successful life following its original years in the 1950s when, after Panama himself left the group, his place was taken by Gilberto Calderón, who came to be known as Joe Cuba, the renowned Puerto Rican percussionist and bandleader from

East Harlem; this was the origin of the Joe Cuba Sextet, which through years of great popularity always remained true to its Harlem birthplace by highlighting the connections between Latin and African American culture and musical genres. Pucho Brown's band, which took on the name the Latin Soul Brothers during the 1960s, was to gain wider visibility during the boogaloo years, when Pucho offered his pithy characterization of Latin boogaloo as "cha cha with a backbeat." Pucho and his band are still playing into the new millennium, a favorite among international fans of what is now called "acid jazz."

Perhaps most interesting of all as pertains to New York Latin music is the Hugo Dickens Band. While its founder and leader has fallen into near oblivion, his physical condition and whereabouts unknown even to his closest partners of the later 1950s period, a surprising number of musicians who gained prominence in subsequent years received their apprenticeship playing with Hugo Dickens and practicing at his home on Convent Avenue and 146th Street. Phil Newsum, the African American drummer who knew Dickens from their days at George Washington High School, was an original member of the band; he went on to play in various Latin bands of the salsa era, including most notably that of Larry Harlow, but also Eddie Palmieri's La Perfecta when he filled in for one of his lifelong idols, Manny Oquendo. Newsum and trumpeter-arranger Marty Sheller, another Hugo Dickens alumnus, remember vividly the many other graduates of that multistylistic grouping, such as Hubert Laws, Rodgers Grant, Arthur Jenkins, Pete LaRoca Simms, Bobby Porcelli, Bill Salter, and other stellar musicians of subsequent acclaim and achievement. They also recall, fondly and admiringly, that the musical director of the Hugo Dickens band was none other than Barry Rogers. They note that, within a few years, Rogers would team up with Eddie Palmieri and create the unique, hugely influential, trombone-centered sound of La Perfecta and all the salsa to come.

A related testimony to the ever-intensifying linkage between Latin and African American popular music is the active involvement of Latino youth in early doo-wop and the harmonizing groups from the streets of Harlem, the Bronx, and other working-class neighborhoods of New York and other urban centers. As one commentator writes, "In the early development of the street corner sound, especially on the Eastern Coast of the United States during the 1950s, Hispanics primarily Puerto Ricans, were the main vocalists found singing with Black and white ethnic groups. They were involved in many of the popular vocal groups. The Crests, featuring Johnny Maestro included Hispanics, Frankie Lymon and the Teenagers, Tune Weavers, Five Discs, Vocaleers, and the Wrens had members who were Latinos."[16] The influence of doo-wop on subsequent generations of New York's Latin music and culture, though barely mentioned in historical accounts, is pervasive, most obviously on the Latin soul and boogaloo movements of the later 1960s and beyond. Elliot Rivera, an English-language vocalist for the LeBron Brothers, emphasizes that many of the young singers in the boogaloo era were reared on doo-wop, as does King Nando of some shingaling fame during those years. A more unlikely though equally genuine testimony to that effect is evident in the remarkable "doo-wop rumba" on the 1981 album *Totico y Sus Rumberos;* in the track titled "What's Your Name?" this varied ensemble of New York-based rumberos move smoothly from the well-known doo-wop tune, sung in hilariously accented English, into buoyant *guaguancó*. The album's producer René López asserts that when he asked some of the musicians in the group what style of American music most influenced them in their earlier years, they answered that it was doo-wop. In another vein, when asked what was his favorite music growing up, leading Nuyorican poet Pedro Pietri showed no hesitation in answering, Frankie Lymon and the Teenagers.

Such are the most prominent untold stories and forgotten Latino musicality of the mambo era. With all the necessary correctives and qualifications, however, and all due wariness about the dominant meta-narrative, this transforming musical period, when New York's Latin music first goes international and enters

FIGURE 6 Tito Puente, ca. 1950. Courtesy of Izzy Sanabria.

the mainstream, is most indelibly marked by the crowning historic achievement of the mambo and Afro-Cuban jazz fusion. As for transcending creative personages, the generation preceding the onset of salsa is embodied in the looming presence of Machito at its onset and Tito Puente at its apex and transition to the musical and cultural achievements to follow.

Though he started in the early 1940s and his career continued on through the decades till his death in 2000, Puente is clearly a figure of the 1950s, the pinnacle of his creative achievement located squarely in that decade. He is the first towering innovator in the Latin field to come from the streets of Latin New York and to create music that emanates from that sociocultural matrix. As such, he stands at the cusp, the crossroads of the mambo at its peak and the first stirrings of salsa, that looming buzzword which—fittingly—signaled for him not the music he played but what he put on his spaghetti.

1

Pachanga Alegre

Later in his life, around 1980, the venerable Machito had occasion to ruminate on the turning points in the history of Latin music in New York. His thoughts would often turn to that moment some twenty years earlier when his generation first came to sense the advent of a new era. "Youth, as always, gravitates to new things," he said. "There were some lean times there, but then a young artist came along, with a fantastic dynamism, Eddie Palmieri. By that time his brother Charlie was already established with his charanga."[1] The illustrious bandleader, and doyen of Latin music in New York for decades, called to mind some of the other emerging names—Johnny Pacheco, Ray Barretto, Willie Bobo, Willie Colón—mostly young Puerto Ricans born and raised in New York City, who over the course of that decade went on to forge a new musical style and sensibility that came to be known as "salsa."

The historical moment Machito is signaling can be dated with some precision as 1960, and his reference to Charlie and Eddie Palmieri helps mark off neatly two key steps in that complex process of generational change. Individually and in tandem, the two Palmieri brothers, separated in age by nine years (born 1927 and 1936, respectively), contributed crucially to the new directions taken by the music in the transitional years to follow. It is important to note that with all its bold innovation this historic breakthrough also involved an unflinching allegiance to the prior generation and to the Cuban traditions that continued to reign supreme as standard-setters of New York Latin musical style. In the late 1950s and early '60s both Palmieris were coming into their own as influential bandleaders, Charlie with his hugely popular La Duboney and as musical director of the experimental Alegre All-Stars, and Eddie in the formation of La Perfecta, by broad consensus the most important Latin band of the 1960s. Of key interest to our "rising salsa" narrative, both Palmieris wrote and recorded songs using the word "salsa" in the early 1960s, Charlie in the title of his third album with his charanga orchestra La Duboney, *Salsa Na' Ma'*, with the chorus of its lead song "salsa na' ma', que cosa rica," (Just salsa, so delicious) and Eddie in the programmatic song "Ritmo Caliente" (Hot Rhythm) from his first La Perfecta album, with its repeated phrase "ritmo con salsa." Thus a full decade prior to the announcement of the "salsa explosion," at the dawn of the new musical generation, these two foremost pioneers were already, perhaps unwittingly, suggesting a catchy name for the emerging sensibility. As Max Salazar points out in his helpful article "Salsa Origins," the Palmieris' early use of the phrase coincided with a number of their contemporaries, such as Jimmy Sabater, Willie Bobo, and Cal Tjader.[2]

Such dramatic changes in the music, of course, correspond to transitions in the larger social and cultural history—in this case most saliently to the stage in the Puerto Rican and Cuban migration to New York, the formation and reconfiguration of communities, and their relation to other groups with whom they most directly interact. By 1960, Puerto Ricans had lived through more than a decade of massive migration to New York, experiencing the avalanche displacement of the later 1940s and through the 1950s that brought the total Puerto Rican diasporic presence to nearly a million people, already exceeding the population of

FIGURE 7 Charlie and Eddie Palmieri, ca. 1960. From *Latin New York* magazine. Courtesy of Izzy Sanabria.

San Juan. The overwhelmingly poor and working-class composition of those emigrants and their children defined their social location in the city's most marginal, underserved neighborhoods of Harlem, the South Bronx, and Brooklyn; their relative isolation within the city; and their growing proximity to and lively intermingling with African Americans and other poor people of color. That same historical moment saw the Cuban Revolution and the attendant changes in political and inter-community relations: after a century of remarkably close and mutually supportive solidarity between Puerto Ricans and Cubans in New York, the groups now followed increasingly divergent trajectories. The impact that these political shifts had on the music was profound, for once the "umbilical cord" to Cuba was severed, New York–based musicians and their communities were left largely to their own devices in the creation of new styles and traditions.

But turning to that specific point in history also calls to mind key places for the emergence of new musical forms and practices, special physical locations where change was incubating and finding early expression. As documented in important recent research, an impressive array of theaters, ballrooms, dance halls, nightclubs, and recording studios existed throughout the city in those years, all with stories of their own and all contributing to the larger narrative.[3] Towering above them all is the legendary Palladium Ballroom in mid-town Manhattan, still the mecca well into the 1960s, though a vast range of other venues, especially in uptown Manhattan and the Bronx, were also influential in scale and quality. Just to name some of the most prominent, there was the Park Palace, the Audubon Ballroom, and the Taft Hotel in Manhattan; the Hunts Point Palace, the Colgate Gardens, and the Tropicana in the Bronx; and the St. George Hotel in Brooklyn. There were also active recording studios on the west side of Manhattan where a steady stream of new releases came out on the Tico, Seeco, and other New York–based labels.

But as that and my own research attests and documents, it was a place called the Tritons Club, a very modest, small-scale social club on Southern Boulevard in the Hunts Point neighborhood of the Bronx, that seems to have been the cradle, a kind of incubator and point of origin, for key musical innovations of the upcoming generation. As urban folklorists Roberta Singer and Elena Martínez explain, "Few clubs have the [Tritons'] distinction of being so humble, unassuming, small, and undistinguished, yet so important in the creation and development of a music that became as internationally popular."[4] As many today still recall, the Tritons was in those years the most happening place of them all for the young Latino population, New York–raised Puerto Ricans creating new sounds and dance moves in tune with their own social realities. As one Tritons regular recalls, "I think it was the hottest after-hours club that I knew of in the Bronx at that time. And the greatest played there, from Patato to Mangual, to Pacheco to Barry Rogers to Eddie Palmieri, Charlie Palmieri. Everyone played in the Tritons after-hours."[5]

Located down the hall from a poolroom on the second floor behind the historic Spooner Theater and next door to the much larger and more prominent Hunts Point Palace ballroom, the Tritons witnessed and was home to decisive events in the music history. There Johnny Pacheco, a twenty-five-year-old Dominican New Yorker, took center stage with his charanga band and went on to introduce the pachanga, the new dance step that accompanied his fast-paced flute and violin rhythms and quickly became the craze.

The Tritons was where Charlie Palmieri's wildly popular charanga band La Duboney performed to enthusiastic local crowds before the historic recording *Pachanga at the Caravana*, which helped solidify the reigning status of the pachanga and spread the fever throughout the city and beyond. It was there at the Tritons that record producer Al Santiago first heard Johnny Pacheco and signed him up for the huge hit album, *Pacheco y su Charanga*, the first and bestselling recording in the extensive catalogue of Santiago's Alegre Records company. It was also at the Tritons during the early 1960s that the Alegre All-Stars jammed on Tuesday nights and congealed their inimitable descarga style so important for subsequent musical developments.

It was there, too, at the Tritons, that Eddie Palmieri linked up with trombonist Barry Rogers to begin a symbiosis that soon gave rise to La Perfecta, the most influential band of the whole generation. So strong was Eddie's attachment to the Tritons that he even decided to rent the club for a month, during which the budding band would gain their crucial formative experience. And finally, it was once again at the Tritons that Al Santiago first heard La Perfecta and contracted them for the first of their historic recordings on the Alegre label.

So, the obvious question follows, why the Tritons? What is it about this modest and unheralded location that made it such a magnet for local folk and musicians, and such a wellspring of creative innovation? Why the Tritons as a stage for so many historic encounters and collaborations? It was not the only stage or source, to be sure, nor the one with the brightest marquee lights or largest dance floor; yet the years of Tritons

FIGURE 8 Johnny Pacheco at the Tritons Club, Bronx, New York, 1960. Photo from the Joe Rodríguez Collection, Courtesy of City Lore.

at its peak—1959–63 or so—coincided with the ongoing glory of the Palladium years, not to mention the plethora of lively, well-publicized venues all over the city, including right there in the Bronx. But somehow amid all the glamor and glitter, it was the lowly Tritons that turned out to have been the place where the new musical currents of the time found their earliest expression, where they first took popular root and found adherents among a community of musicians and neighbors and dancers.

The building that housed the Tritons was centrally located in the midst of a bustling shopping center along Southern Boulevard and 173rd Street that made up the main commercial stretch in that section of the Bronx in those years; since the 1970s or so, that and the surrounding neighborhoods have come to be referred to as the South Bronx. The Tritons was situated on the second floor of the prominent and historic Loews Spooner Theater, which was itself surrounded by other lively establishments—a Woolworth's, a Schrafft's candy store, a Chinese restaurant, a large Thom McAn shoe store, the J&B record store, and the even more majestic Loews Boulevard Theater down the block. Former and current residents recall that most of the businesses were still owned by Jewish proprietors, so that in the immediate vicinity of the Tritons the main intergroup interaction was between Puerto Ricans and Jews, though there was also a strong Irish presence, most notably among the police officers.

Both of the huge theaters—the Spooner and the Boulevard—came to be purchased by the Loews movie house chain, and aside from showing movies they also hosted well-attended concerts by many of the great Latin orchestras and musical acts of the time. Thus, in addition to being a commercial center, the Southern Boulevard area was also something of an entertainment mecca, boasting right there on the same and nearby blocks the cavernous Hunts Point Palace ballroom (sometimes mentioned as the borough's counterpart to the Palladium), the Alhambra Lounge and the Campana, and within a few blocks the Caravana, the Tropicana, and the Tropicoro. All of these venues were close by, some within walking distance of each other, and they were in full swing during the early 1960s.

One distinctive feature of the Tritons was that more than any other venue it was local, created and habituated by people from the neighborhood. As mentioned, most of the musicians and those in attendance grew up and lived within a short walk of these venues. Being of the same age—in their mid-twenties— Tritons regulars in many cases had known each other since childhood—from the block, from school, through family ties and friendships. The local people who were the bulk of regular habitués to the Tritons favored that venue because it was so convenient and affordable. Many of the musicians grew up in or came to live in the neighborhood over the years, so that the surrounding area of the Bronx was a remarkable wellspring of talent and creativity among a tight-knit circle of friends and acquaintances. Its geographical proximity wasn't the only quality that made the Tritons such a favored spot for the musicians; they found its intimate, informal, familiar atmosphere conducive to experimentation and the rehearsal of their acts. They also appreciated the lively and skilled dance audiences that frequented the club, even when compared to the higher profile locations in other parts of the city. The Tritons had been founded by a local social club, and this added to its rootedness in community and its cohesiveness; contemporaries from that era often mention that chartered social clubs served as the foundation of the entire music field by congealing organically bound communities of listeners and dancers.[6]

The Tritons was started by the Sparks, a social club and neighborhood gang, at the core of which was a stickball team. The game of stickball has a lively history in its own right, one that is rightly associated with the musical world at a local level, especially during that period of New York Latino history. While not particularly admired for their athletic prowess, the Sparks were famous for throwing parties and dances, evidently their main and most prized activity through the years before setting up the Tritons Club. They were also successful in acquiring a charter and building a steady membership. The members agreed that they wanted a home base, a place to socialize and hang out and to throw a dance now and then. And since the gang was all male, the idea was to create a place where they could socialize with the debs and other young women. To that end, according to long-time Sparks president Herman "Pee Wee" López, five of the Sparks who could afford it—those whose fathers might have owned a bodega or a barber shop—put up fifty dollars each toward the rental of the space from the owners of the theater.[7]

Inside, the Tritons was an eminently simple place, its lighting sparse and its concrete block walls unadorned except for a large mural. Its modest floor space had an entrance counter and a bar area and some tables; there was ample room for the dance floor, with a small, one-foot-high wooden platform for the stage. The establishment had no liquor license for the first years but bringing-your-own was common practice, and there was an improvised cash bar functioning actively during most business hours. Drinks were cheap, and the cover charge on concert nights was only about $2–$3 depending on the musical attraction; on one unforgettable occasion when the feature was the two Titos (Puente and Rodríguez), Pee Wee remembers the entrance charge being as high as $10. In any case, it was much more affordable than any of the other places offering that quality of live music. At the beginning, only members with cards were admitted, but as the locale and its events became better known, its doors opened to the public. During its peak years, it was customary for the Tritons to be packed, to its approximately

200-person hilt, on most weekend nights. While as a social club it was supposed to close at 2:00 AM, it also became a favorite after-hours place, sometimes still going strong at five or six in the morning.

Like any other nightspot those days, the Tritons was generally off-limits for most unmarried young women, though many, mostly New York–born Puerto Ricans from the neighborhood, did frequent the place regularly and in large numbers. They knew there would be good music, and they loved to dance. To this day they speak of the excellent dance floor, especially smooth for the sliding and hopping of the pachanga, the dance craze of the time. They also remember fondly how comfortable and safe they felt in the friendly, fun atmosphere. One regular at the Tritons, Carmen Costas Vázquez, felt so at ease about the whole scene that she even chose to celebrate her wedding reception there on September 11, 1960, an evening she recalls vividly and with great fondness. She remembers dancing the night away in her wedding gown, surrounded by close friends and family, all to the tune of Johnny Pacheco's charanga.

The Tritons was not just an enjoyable place but in important ways also a safe space, a haven filled with a sense of camaraderie among friends and neighbors. According to present-day recollections there was a high level of physical and emotional energy, a lot of noise and some drinking going on, but no reported fights or acts of violence. Some even say that the police were glad that the Tritons Club was there because it kept the young people off the streets.

For let's not forget, despite the coziness of the Tritons, the streets were mean, and soon, over the course of the decade, were to get meaner. The neighborhood police precinct was after all the 41st, the infamous "Fort Apache," a well-known symbol of urban desolation and violent crime, especially as a result of the 1981 movie "Fort Apache, The Bronx." Indeed, some Tritons

FIGURE 9 Carmen Costas Vázquez wedding reception, Tritons Club, September 11, 1960. Courtesy of Sonia Lee Costas.

habitués tell of a traumatic moment when the police raided the club in the wee morning hours and arrested about forty of those present, including Pacheco and other musicians as well as many of the dancers and local residents, for alleged violation of the liquor and curfew laws. According to some, that fearsome event marked the beginning of the end of the Tritons' days of glory, and the establishment never recovered its prior attraction. In any case, though, the historical record will show this source of some of the day's most exciting creative riches was the most unlikely of geographic areas, the most "uncultured" of places to produce musical and dance innovations that swept fans and dance audiences across many cultures.

Johnny Pacheco had no doubts about being the originator of the pachanga craze, and that it all started in the Tritons Club. "I was the one that started the dance," he stated repeatedly, and went on to explain. "We call the music, the orchestra was called a charanga. And then I used to do the little hop with the hankie and people started watching me at the Tritons and that's where the dance started from, 'cause there was no dance. And that's what made it so popular, 'cause it was a very easy dance, and you hear the stomping of the people dancing, on the downbeat."[8] Tritons regulars confirm this origin, remembering vividly the intense moments when Pacheco and his singers would do those synchronized steps in the front of the stage and the dancers would copy them and join in, so that all separation between performers and dancing public broke down and it was like one unified movement to the music. From that starting point in time and place the new dance steps quickly spread to other clubs, most notably to the Caravana, the Tropicana, the Hunt's Point Palace, the Taft Hotel, and before long to the Palladium.

Al Santiago attests to this account of the creation and popularization of the dance step. "This is how the *pachanga* was created," Santiago said. "Somebody took out a handkerchief, they invented a dance and the people started following them. It's Johnny's creation."[9] In addition to the waving hankies and the "brinquitos" (little hops), Pacheco's reference to the "stomping on the downbeat" was also a strong feature of the choreography that some say the local Puerto Ricans added, deliberately or not, as a kind of trademark of the New York or Bronx style. Santiago goes on to explain how the new dance step came to be called pachanga. "Now Johnny had to give it a name. We called a meeting. I remember most of the people that were there: two people from Southern Music Peer International, Jorge García, Pete Rodríguez, Buddy (Rodríguez's manager), Federico Pagani, Charlie, Johnny and myself. We had this meeting with seven or eight people on a weekday afternoon, and the agenda was, what were we going to call this new dance? The famous dance promoter Federico Pagani said, 'Let's call this new dance the pachanga.' Most people went for *la pachanga*. So I was outvoted. I knew this was going to cause problems for the music industry."[10]

Santiago and others had reservations about use of the term because the word "pachanga" was not coined by Pacheco, nor was it first intended to refer specifically to the dance step. Rather, for one thing, "una pachanga" has long meant "a party" in Spanish colloquial usage; in some contexts it is often used in the verb form, "pachanguear," meaning to have a party or dance or have a good time. The word then took on its more specific modern-day reference in 1959 as the title of an extremely popular song by the well-known Cuban librettist, composer, and entertainer Eduardo Davidson. Indeed, the song "La Pachanga" as first performed in Havana by Orquesta Sublime and recorded by the most famous charanga band of the day, led by renowned flutist José Fajardo, generated a feverish craze in Cuba on the eve of the 1959 revolution. In a proverbial, wishful phrase, Che Guevara even spoke of wanting it to be a "revolución con pachanga." Right away the fever spread to New York, especially with the Fajardo recording of the song and its performance by none other than Orquesta Aragón at the Palladium and other prominent midtown venues.

In fact, pachanga bandleader Joe Quijano vividly recalls an occasion in 1960 when he and Pacheco shared the billing with Aragón at the Palladium and how they marveled at the dancers whose performances were an integral part of the storied band's engaging floor show. In particular, Quijano remembers that the famed singer and dancer Rafael Bacallao, who had recently joined Aragón after many years with Fajardo, embellished his cha cha steps with little hops ("brinquitos" was Quijano's word) and a skating glide similar to the moves introduced at the Tritons by Pacheco and his singers. According to Quijano, Pacheco didn't so much create the steps called pachanga as imitate and emulate Bacallao, and try them out with the crowd at the Tritons.

If Joe Quijano's version of events is accurate, then the trajectory of the pachanga dance would seem to have gone full circle, starting as a performance show at the Palladium, catching hold as a social dance at the Tritons, and then migrating back to the Palladium to be picked up by the seasoned mambo dancers of that storied venue. And the pachanga at the Palladium occasioned a sense of excitement of its own: the stomping that accompanied the hop-and-skating step famously strained the endurance of the Palladium floor, and the ceiling of the pharmacy located below the ballroom shook so much that the proprietors had to install pillars to avert a potential disaster.

This difference over the original authorship of the pachanga forms the background to an amusing story told by Al Santiago about a public exchange between Pacheco and Eduardo Davidson, who was well known to be gay. The first recording of Davidson's song, by the newly founded charanga Orquesta Sublime, was actually played as a merengue, which may explain why some sources—somewhat confusingly—identify pachanga as a combination of son and merengue.[11] Santiago continues, "A few years later, Davidson, who wrote 'La Pachanga', and Johnny Pacheco were at a radio station interview. On live radio, Johnny said, 'I guess you have to admit I'm the father of the pachanga.' So as talented as Davidson was, he came out of the closet and answered, 'If you're the father of the pachanga, I'm the mother.'"[12]

Whatever the parentage of "pachanga" choreography might have been, Pacheco's seminal role in involving the dancers and initiating the intense fad of the early 1960s is beyond a doubt. He was the matinee idol of the time, perhaps New York Latin music's first rock star in the modern sense of the word. No objection was occasioned by his unofficial coronation as the "King of Pachanga." And though slews of other pachanga-playing bands surfaced, and pachanga sounds proliferated in all genres and many musical venues of the city, Pacheco's is the name immediately associated with the craze that set it in motion—so much so that some even mistakenly assume that pachanga is a convenient verbal wedding of his surname, "Pacheco," and charanga.

Whether or not Pacheco took his cue from the imported Cuban model, what came to be pachanga dancing in New York also mixed in choreographic elements familiar to local audiences; sometimes the Charleston is mentioned, while merengue also comes up when the musical rhythms are discussed. Pacheco's Dominican background and musical beginnings (and his father's renown) playing merengue may also sustain the latter association, though contemporaries of that period all assert that people generally assumed that he was "one of us," a Puerto Rican New Yorker.

An even more serious cause of confusion regarding names and genres has to do with the terms "pachanga" and "charanga." Joe Quijano and Charlie Palmieri were so concerned about this mix-up that they wrote a song about it, "La Pachanga Se Baila Así," ("This is how you dance pachanga") which itself became one of the biggest pachanga hits. Opening with the often-quoted first line "Hay una discusión en el barrio" ("there's a debate in the neighborhood"), the song explains that "pachanga" only refers to the dance step, not to the music or the group, which is a charanga. One reason for the controversy was that Tito Rodríguez had come out with his very popular song "Baila la charanga," which talks of the "new rhythm" and even laces in an occasional flute riff to the otherwise non-charanga instrumentation. Quijano felt it was important to air this confusion publicly so as to be clear about the difference between the dance fad of the moment and the long-standing tradition of the charanga with its familiar flute-and-violin format. Though stemming from the danzón, charangas play a range of genres, most notably cha cha and other variants of mambo and son styles.

Pacheco himself joined in clarifying this important distinction, stating emphatically that "you don't dance a charanga, you dance with a charanga band. The pachanga was the dance." But when staking his claim as the innovator, he himself falls into the same over-identification: "I started the pachanga dance and the charanga craze." While the proliferation of the hop-and-hankie gimmick certainly lent great impetus to the public embrace of the charanga sound at that historical moment, the story of charanga in the United States goes back some years to the earlier 1950s and the group of the prominent Cuban band leader Gilberto Valdés, in which Pacheco himself played as percussionist. Though some claim that it was not really a charanga band because it didn't always include violins, and though it never caught on with a broad New York audience, this group is generally credited with being the first to introduce the flute sound.

The big moment for charanga in the United States occurred a few years later, in 1958, when Pacheco and Charlie first hooked up and recognized the potential for adding the flute as part of the conjunto format. Latin music historian Max Salazar captures the importance of this memorable encounter: "One night during October 1958, while Palmieri's small group was working opposite the Dioris Valladares orchestra at the Monte Carlo Ballroom at 137th Street and Broadway, he followed some piercing flute sounds to a room. There he found a tall, thin musician doing the piping. Palmieri watched and listened for a few minutes, then approached the flutist and said, 'Hi, I'm Charlie Palmieri.' 'I'm Johnny Pacheco,' said the other musician, shaking his hand. With these words the beginning of a new musical era was born."[13]

Recalling the occasion, Charlie remembers being immediately impressed with the flute sound behind a regular conjunto, a style of instrumentation consisting of guitar, *tres*, contrabass, *bongos*, three vocalists (who play hand percussion such as *maracas* and *claves*), and two to four trumpets. The piano and the *tumbadora* were later added by legendary tres player Arsenio Rodriguez. He looked into it and learned that Pacheco was playing the five-key wooden flute, the perfect one for a charanga. "The thought stayed in my mind," he says. "So when the trumpeter in my own band, Mario Cora, left to join Cortijo's band in Puerto Rico, I moved Pacheco, whom I had on battery, to fill the trumpet spot with flute. And that's when we started playing everything with a charanga feeling, 'charangueado,' but without violins."[14] Within six months the "charanga without violins" band started playing the Palladium, where this unusual sextet caused a sensation "because it was very different from what was happening in other orchestras at the time. So then we added violins and a cello, and that's how the Charanga Duboney got its start."

The transition was easy for Charlie because, as he often said, the danzón had long been his favorite kind of music. He knew and loved Fajardo, and the sensational Orquesta Aragón, Arcaño y Sus Maravillas, La Sensación, and others. Starting Duboney in 1959 was "like having a new baby," he claimed, "the most exciting thing in my life." "We were very excited," he went on. "We knew what the possibilities were, because it was so different from the rest of the music being played in New York. All of the bands were brass, and there wasn't a single charanga in the U.S. at that time. Though the first year wasn't as successful as we hoped we knew that we'd break through, and did so when we recorded the first album, called *Charanga*, with United Artists. [It later came to be titled *Echoes of an Era*.] And the rest was history."[15] Mentioning that Gilberto Valdes's group remained strictly in the tradition of danzón, had never recorded in the United States, and had disbanded years before, Charlie states that his Duboney was the first commercial charanga in the United States. He called it Duboney not because he loved Dubonnet wine, as some have assumed, but

FIGURE 10 Charanga Duboney at the Palladium, 1960 (Charlie Palmieri at piano, Johnny Pacheco on flute). David Carp Collection, Bronx County Historical Society.

because he had a special liking for the Orquesta Siboney, and because he had a friend from the neighborhood named Dubón. He put them together and made up a new word, which became famous and entered the annals of Latin music history.

That first album, a United Artists recording, met with little commercial success, but through 1959 the newfound charanga, with Pacheco on flute, attracted enthusiastic dance audiences in clubs throughout the city, including the Palladium, and was a regular sound at the Tritons. "It started to build," Charlie recalled, "at the Tritons Club, it started to build, which was good. It was regional, it was only in the Bronx that it was very popular." It wasn't long before the top-name bands—Machito, Tito Rodríguez, and Tito Puente—were playing and recording pachangas.

The initial euphoria was not to last long though. "But then Johnny and I started booking separately," Charlie recalled.

"'Look, I'll start my own group,' he said, and after about almost a year Johnny started his group." Though it was clearly only part of the story, Al Santiago importantly attributes this parting of ways to basic musical differences: "Charlie was into more harmony and a medium tempo and Johnny was into going *embalao* at a very fast tempo. Johnny was also into simplicity and he proved himself to be right. Charlie was into intricate arrangements, counterpoint and harmony. So they split."[16]

Pacheco's charanga quickly came to rival Charlie's in popularity, especially among younger audiences. At many venues around town Pacheco's band became an exciting new attraction, and at the Tritons he became a sensational draw of youthful audiences from near and far. Of course, Charlie Palmieri was widely beloved in the neighborhood as well and deeply respected everywhere for his musical prowess. But he was a good ten years older than most of the Tritons habitués, and while Pacheco was of the very same generation, his birth date in 1935 made him a direct contemporary of Charlie's younger brother Eddie, and of the club members and most of the usual Tritons crowd.

Some of the numbers from Pacheco's repertoire, such as "El Güiro de Macorina" and "Oyeme Mulata," drew special excitement at those live performances, yet had still not been recorded. But his recording breakthrough was not far off; as Pacheco recalls, "My opportunity came in 1960. It's ironic because I was trying to get the group recorded, but nobody wanted it. They said, 'That crap is going to die, forget about it.' But I never gave up. I went in a studio and did a demo with 'El Güiro de Macorina' and 'Oyeme Mulata' and went over to a guy who loved charanga, Rafael Font [a DJ on a radio station], and said, 'Coño, can you play this for me?'"[17] On hearing the demo Font recognized right away that it was going to be a hit. And sure enough, after that first radio play the station was flooded with calls from listeners trying to find out where they could get the record."

"It became an instant hit," Pacheco recalls, "and since Al Santiago had a record store [Casalegre], the people went over . . . and said, 'I want to buy that thing on the radio, "El Güiro de Macorina."' 'Who the hell is Güiro de Macori?' he [Santiago] asked. Nobody knew who recorded this thing. It was just a demo." When he asked around he was advised to stop in at the Tritons on a Tuesday night and hear the band play. "Ya gotta go to the Tritons. You gotta hear Pacheco." For Santiago, who said that at that point he had never even heard of Pacheco, the enthusiasm was immediate. "When I heard the band play the first few bars I said 'Wow!' So after the set I spoke to Johnny and he tells me, 'Man, I'm glad you want to record me because I've been to every record company in town and no one is interested.'"

Pacheco signed a contract with Alegre Records in 1960. "The contract wasn't worth the paper it was written on," according to Pacheco, "but since I shook hands on it, to me that was my bond." *Pacheco y Su Charanga, volume 1* turned out to be an unprecedented hit, by far the most successful release ever for Al Santiago and Alegre Records. "I opened my Casalegre record shop in 1955. We had put out forty-four singles but none of them had hit. We were able to break even on the 78 RPMs and 45s, but we didn't make any money. Alegre Records had no expenses because my retail store paid all the expenses." But that first Pacheco album, Alegre's first LP, sold like hotcakes, and in fact financed the recording company from then on. Promoter Richie Bonilla remembers seeing piles of the record stacked up at the entrance to the B&G record store on Southern Boulevard, even though their Latin section was situated toward the back of the store, and tells that it became a household item. Getting wind of the sensation, within three months United Artists approached Charlie Palmieri about recording "Hawaiian music, music from all over the world, as charangas." Charlie was not interested in that project, and at that point turned to his close friend Al Santiago and Alegre, which released his successful album *Pachanga at the Caravana* a year later. "And now," as he put it, "Charlie Palmieri was in business."

Alegre recorded five Pacheco albums over the next few years, many of them including extremely popular songs like "El Chivo," and "Acuyuyé." But the smash hit, the song that became the

FIGURE 11 Johnny Pacheco, *Pacheco y Su Charanga*. Permission Fania.

signature number for Pacheco and the pachanga craze, was no doubt "El Güiro de Macorina." According to Al Santiago, it was the ubiquitous Louie Ramírez who was the "major contributor to Johnny Pacheco's first charanga album in 1960 co-writing and arranging 'El Güiro de Macorina.'"[18] Like many of the other tunes on those albums for Alegre, it is a very fast-tempo, high-energy son with darting flute interjections, shifting violin lines, and sharp angular breaks and contrasts. Those qualities are what give the piece its "New York" feel, for it is otherwise a faithful rendition of a traditional Cuban charanga format very much in the vein of the adored Orquesta Aragón, Pacheco's musical role model. The lyrics also draw directly from Cuban phrases and choruses, with even the chorus "Dile a Macorina que me toque el guiro" resonating with the well-known verse from Arsenio Rodríguez, "Dile a Catalina que . . ." The text is made up of the playful quips and double entendres typical of the genre; in this case, the word "toque" means both play and touch, with "güiro" referring to the musical instrument but also, by suggestion, to the male sexual organ. The somewhat unusual female first name Macorina is also suggestive, as is her personality as a spectacular güiro player and "la reina de la pachanga." The contagiously festive neighborhood feel of the song, also present in the nearly as popular B-side "Oyeme Mulata," surely contributed to its immense popularity, especially in an environment like the Tritons Club and other local venues. The references to daily life are familiar to his audience, bearing as they do a resemblance to the lyrics of merengue, plena, and guaracha songs from the popular song traditions.

La Duboney, the other foundational band of the charanga breakthrough, is both more relaxed and more experimental by comparison. Their first album with Alegre, *Pachanga at the Caravana Club*, is explicitly playing into the wild dance craze, with six of the twelve numbers having the word "pachanga" in the title and nearly all of the selections exhorting to dance to the "new dance," "El Baile Nuevo," as one song is entitled. As Charlie said, "The tunes 'Son de Pachanga' and 'La Pachanga Se Baila Así' are the ones that put us in business."[19] As for musical differences, while Pacheco with all his exciting newness remains close to the Cuban script, Charlie Palmieri's repertoire in this and other Duboney recordings includes a wider range of genres set to the charanga format, including son montunos and American standards. Charlie's masterful piano is prominent, notably in his rollicking Charleston solo in "Charangona." Despite the commercial success of *Pachanga at the Caravana Club* and its central role in catalyzing the pachanga craze, Duboney perhaps reached its peak achievement in the slightly later album *Salsa Na' Ma'* from 1963; the title of the collection, and of its title tune, are obvious anticipations of the metaphorical term "salsa" introduced commercially a decade or so thereafter. That and other numbers, like "Tiene Sabor," "Doctor de Fama," and "El Yerbero," count as the finest achievements in the charanga/pachanga vein, and of Charlie Palmieri in his long and prolific career.

Pacheco's and Charlie's were clearly the central bands of the charanga phase in Latin music history, their output spanning the heyday years from 1959 to 1964. Between them, and with the recording facilities of Al Santiago, they defined the new musical sensibility in many regards. However, there were other important contributors to the emerging musical generation, and as mentioned, before long nearly all Latin musical artists were doing "pachangas" at some level, even if in many cases it involved little more than use of the word and some of the musical trappings. Most significant at a local level was vocalist, bandleader, and producer Joe Quijano, whose band La Cachana and Cesta label were dedicated to pachanga even though the group was not actually a charanga as it did not have violins. Quijano contends that his front line of two trumpets and flute was playing "the rhythm of the pachanga." And he is especially proud of having composed, with Charlie Palmieri, one of the biggest hits of the pachanga era, "Así Se Baila la Pachanga." The song took on programmatic significance in freeing charanga orchestration and music from the dance move, so that Quijano's band played it as a central piece of its repertoire and Charlie included it on *Pachanga at the Caravana Club*.

Also a frequent presence at the Tritons and on the pachanga scene was timbalero and bandleader Orlando Marín, who actually grew up in the same neighborhood and attained some acclaim for his leadership in the stickball leagues. While his big-band orchestra was not a charanga, the word "pachanga" is everywhere in his music of that period, notably on his best-known album, *Se Te Quemó la Casa* (Alegre, 1963). The title song was Marín's signature composition, some of its renown coming after the infamous "burning of the South Bronx" in the 1970s. The terror and excitement of buildings set ablaze found memorable expression in this evocative number of a few years prior; the recording begins and ends with the deafening blare of fire engines and the screaming neighbors witnessing the all-too-common inner-city disaster.

The pachanga era also occasioned the formation of numerous other charanga bands, two of the most important of them by major *congueros* (congo drummers) of Latin music history. Mongo Santamaría and Ray Barretto both founded their charangas in 1960–61 to ride the pachanga wave and they did so outside of the Alegre orbit. In different ways, both groupings anticipated stylistic developments of the years to come, more so perhaps than the charangas of either Pacheco or Palmieri even though those remained the recognized pillars of the style and movement.

Mongo's La Sabrosa, as his band was called, was formed after he parted ways with Cal Tjader, with whom he had played and recorded since 1957 when Mongo had left his seat on congas with the Tito Puente orchestra. In a historic shift, he and Willie Bobo had joined Tjader's band on the West Coast and recorded on the Fantasy label. La Sabrosa was made up of some of Tjader's former sidemen along with members of what had been the Chicago-based charanga Nuevo Ritmo, including master flutist Rolando Lozano and tenor saxman/violinist José "Chombo" Silva. Within a two-year period, La Sabrosa recorded five records, the best known of them the first, *Sabroso!*, which gave the band its name. Given the strong jazz experience of most of the musicians, including Mongo himself, and the jazz orientation of the Fantasy and Riverside labels, this was no doubt the jazziest of the many charangas of the day, and it became the best known among jazz musicians. Mongo's charanga phase came in the period between (and tends to be overshadowed by) the recording of his two biggest hits, "Afro-Blue" and "Watermelon Man," the first a 1959 standard of Latin jazz—especially with the heralded 1963 interpretation by John Coltrane, with whom the song is often identified—and "Watermelon Man," Mongo's chart-topping 1963 version of the Herbie Hancock tune that enjoys similar stature in the annals of Latin soul; indeed, that crossover hit anticipates the boogaloo era to emerge a few years later, if only because of its referencing of African American cultural trappings, as, for example, in Joe Cuba's mega-hit "Bang Bang." But La Sabrosa, marking his return to the New York scene after breaking new ground with Tjader in California and nationwide, enjoyed an avid following among charangueros. Songs like Mongo's own compositions "Para Tí" and "Guaguanco Mania" from the *Sabroso!* album demonstrate well the group's cohesion and consistent musicianship.

Charanga La Moderna was Ray Barretto's first band, formed after four years as conguero for Tito Puente (he had replaced Mongo). The 1961 *Pachanga with Barretto* on Riverside was the first LP in his long recording career. Chombo Silva also played with this grouping, as did another veteran of the Panart *descargas (jam sessions)*, trumpeter Alejandro "El Negro" Vivar. The second charanga album, *Latino!*, also with Riverside, contained one of Barretto's signature numbers and a mainstay of the "salsa" canon, the ubiquitous descarga "Cocinando Suave." The subsequent release, and the best known of his charanga LPs, was *Charanga Moderna* on the Tico label, which included the chart-topping hit "El Watusi," Barretto's bestselling song ever and also in its way anticipatory of the boogaloo era. Thus, as different from Mongo Santamaria's, Barretto's output of the pachanga days turned out to include two of his most popular songs, though neither of them is a pachanga in any but the broadest sense of the word.

For both of these major performers, and for others such as Tito Puente, Tito Rodríguez, or Orlando Marín, the charanga recordings were but a phase in their extended careers, and not the most productive or important one: for Mongo that generally came earlier, in his extremely influential 1950s albums *Tambores y Cantos, Yambú*, and *Mongo* highlighting masterful Afro-Cuban percussion, and for Barretto in the highly regarded releases with Fania starting in 1967, such as *Acid, Hard Hands, Together*, and *Que Viva la Música*. In retrospect, both Santamaría and Barretto seemed hemmed in by the charanga format, in part because as congueros, their own instrumental forte did not figure centrally in most compositions. Once the pachanga fever let up, both were soon headed in new directions more attuned to their musical sensibilities.

Indeed it was by then, around 1964, that the most insatiable taste for charanga had subsided, as both Pacheco and Charlie Palmieri dropped the flute-and-fiddle instrumentation in favor of more typical conjuntos. In part, the shift was due to difficulties identifying musicians on those two instruments, especially violin. For Pacheco, the change was also motivated by the demise of Alegre and his consequential decision to start Fania Records. Charlie attributed his own move away from the charanga style to the notable proliferation of charangas, and especially to his unbridled enthusiasm on hearing Orquesta Broadway. "I like to change things," Charlie said, "and when I realized there [were] as many as fifteen charangas in the city by that time, and especially when I got to know the marvelous Orquesta Broadway in 1964, I figured it was time to move on."[20] La Duboney officially disbanded in 1965. Formed in the early 1960s, Orquesta Broadway is still playing through the first decade of the new millennium and beyond, which makes it the longest-lasting New York Latin band of all time. Thanks to La Broadway, along with a few other important groups like Orquesta Novel and Típica '73, charanga has remained an essential stylistic flavor and tradition within the Latin music repertoire through the years. Though another wave of charanga revival came in the 1970s, it was the pachanga craze of the early 1960s, gestated in the Tritons Club and remaining identified with the Puerto Rican community in the Bronx, that gave impulse and novelty to the style on the New York scene. It was at that seminal moment that a new musical generation was born, a passing of the baton to the first massive cohort of New York–born Latinos.

It is important to bear in mind that the rapid ascendancy of the charanga style and the increasing presence of the flute part in Latin music of those years was directly attributable to the enthusiasm for a new dance step, la pachanga, by the community of fans and dancers. That same year, 1960, also saw the meteoric rise of the Twist, the first and most consequential of the many dance crazes marking the decade of the 1960s. Like the pachanga, and then the boogaloo, the Twist and its sequels were instrumental in marking off a specifically "youth" culture, a lineage that was perhaps initiated by 1950s doo-wop and rock and roll, and saw its fullest outburst in more recent music history with the advent of hip-hop. In Latin music, the pachanga thus marks the first generational divide in popular taste, with the young Latinos then coming to view the earlier styles like the trios and música jíbara, as old-fashioned, "hicky," what their parents listened to, and to consider the omnipresent mambo and cha cha as sounds to build on, and to move on from.

Al Santiago, a major catalyst of the charanga era and pachanga craze, was not content staying within the confines of a particular genre; he had a more expansive, way-out agenda in mind for his recording enterprise. Between 1960 and its demise in 1966, Alegre Records released an impressive eighty-five albums (after producing forty-four 78s in the preceding four years since its founding), and the catalogue reads like an inventory of the major new musical currents of those years. The repertoire ranges widely, from trios and jíbaro music to merengue, plena, son montuno, and of course an extensive and varied representation of mambo and cha cha chá. Both pachanga and boogaloo, the main two stylistic creations of the 1960s New York setting, also gained their primary impulse from Alegre. In addition to Pacheco and Charlie Palmieri, the artists recorded range from long-established acts like Johnny Rodriguez, César Concepción, Dioris Valladares, Mon Rivera, and Tito Puente to first recordings by some of the most significant up-and-coming bands, like those of Louie Ramirez, Orlando Marín, Kako (Francisco Angel Bastar), Richie Ray, Willie Colón, Pete Rodríguez, and, most consequential of all, Eddie Palmieri. Alegre Records has been referred to as the Blue Note of Latin music of that time.

The leader of his own band, the Chucku-ñu-ñu Boys, in the 1950s, Santiago has been called a visionary, a pioneer, and a genius. Reference is invariably made to his keen ear and his nose for emerging talent and promising new musical directions, however zany. He is also credited with innovative ideas in all aspects of

FIGURE 12 Al Santiago. @ Mary Kent. Courtesy of Mary Kent.

the music industry, from the technical dimension of new recording techniques to inroads in promotion and marketing, including opening up the Puerto Rican and Latin American markets.[21] His record store, Casalegre, which lasted through the years 1955–1975, served as a mecca for Latin music lovers and cognoscenti throughout the city. The Alegre label, after its relative obscurity in the late '50s, enjoyed prominent but not very profitable visibility for the first years of the 1960s. The subsequent hegemony of Fania and the establishment of the catchall term "salsa," is not thinkable without the groundbreaking achievements of Alegre.

Creative pioneer and entrepreneur though he certainly was, it could never be claimed that Santiago was a successful businessman, at least not over the long haul. His erratic, spendthrift ways are the most frequently cited reason, and he did go broke and sold Alegre to Tico by the mid-1960s. But a major contributing factor was in some important ways a virtue in disguise, as his musical preferences and predilections were not defined by commercial promise but by the value of innovation and creativity, as erratic as the outcome of such decisions may have been.

The most blatant example of this unusual (and ultimately suicidal) favoring of creative product over monetary profit is perhaps his choice for the label's second album. After raking in a small fortune for the sales of *Pacheco y Su Charanga* he found himself in a position to do whatever he pleased. But rather than following his debut blockbuster with another likely moneymaker by going with the fashion of the day, Santiago decided to produce a commercial bomb but artistic curiosity item, the Latin jazz album *Jazz Espagnole* by the idiosyncratic percussionist Sabú Martínez. "I knew it wasn't going to sell," Santiago said in retrospect. "In the first year it sold around 400 copies. I spent more money than it produced, and I also gave away a lot of copies so that they would play it on the radio."[22] If not profitable, though, *Jazz Espagnole* was eerily prophetic, especially when listened to in more recent times. Pioneer Latin music historian John Storm Roberts identified it early on as "one of the most solid recordings of Latin jazz ever produced,"[23] and by 1989 Santiago could proudly assert that "Sabu's album eventually became a hit with the underground culture and is considered a collectors' item."

The life of Louis Martínez—nicknamed Sabú by none other than Dizzy Gillespie—reads at once like a storybook tale of glory and a classical tragedy of human foibles. Born in El Barrio in 1930, he began playing professionally when he was only eleven years old after spending his childhood beating out rhythms on tin cans on 111th Street. The tragic side of his life (to dispense with that first) centers on his longtime heroin addiction, and the multiple attendant tribulations and pathologies that tend to cast him in a humiliating light in the minds of many who knew and dealt with him. But in spite of that sad and ultimately deadly reality—he died of a gastric ulcer in Sweden at the age of forty-eight—Sabú over the years played with a dazzling array of stellar musicians in both the Latin and jazz fields going back to the 1940s; to name a few, there were Charlie Parker, Duke Ellington, Count Basie, J. J. Johnson, Eartha Kitt, Horace Silver, Thelonious Monk, Charles Mingus, Mary Lou Williams, Lionel Hampton, Noro Morales, Edmundo Ros, Marcelino Guerra, Esy Morales, the Lecuona Cuban Boys, Miguelito Valdés, José Curbelo, and Joe Loco. Sabú also worked with vocalists Tony Bennett, Sammy Davis Jr., and Harry Belafonte, and recorded with Art Blakey between 1953 and 1958. But the apex of his career as a sideman came when he replaced Chano Pozo in Dizzy Gillespie's band in 1948.

Sabú debuted as a bandleader in 1957, when he recorded his first album, *Palo Congo*, on Blue Note; it has been called "an Afro-Cuban masterpiece," and with its inclusion of bomba and plena rhythms as well as rumba and palo, it anticipated by a full generation the turn to "roots music" in the Cuban and Afro-Puerto Rican vein which set in as of the later 1970s and early '80s. Unbeknownst to many subsequent listeners, the band on this recording is that of Arsenio Rodriguez, as are some of the compositions including the plena "El Choferito." *Jazz Espagnole*, which is now recognized as the highest of his achievements, is a veritable cornucopia of varied compositions in the Latin jazz spectrum, many of them anticipating the work of Fort Apache and Ray Barretto in the waves of Latin jazz of the post-Cubop generation. His collaborators, Marty Sheller on trumpet, Bob Porcelli on alto, and most of all Louie Ramírez on vibes and piano, contribute to what is really a timeless accomplishment. The album may not have added to Al Santiago's coffers, but with the passage of time it clearly stands as one of his most felicitous bets on music history. It certainly leaves subsequent generations with a clear idea of the creative boldness and lively imagination of this eccentric tastemaker of New York Latin music in one of its crucial stages.

But the most ambitious and long-standing of Santiago's experimental projects, though barely garnering more than a cursory note in music history, is no doubt the Alegre All-Stars. As the name indicates, it was a conglomeration of the leaders of the various bands that had recorded with Alegre, what Santiago referred to as the "Alegre family." So in 1961, once he had built up an impressive roster of bandleaders, vocalists, and instrumentalists, Santiago approached Pacheco and Charlie Palmieri, as well as the ubiquitous Puerto Rican percussionist Kako, veteran merengue bandleader and vocalist Dioris Valladares, bassist Bobby Rodríguez, esteemed tenor sax player/violinist Chombo Silva, vocalists Yayo El Indio and Rudy Calzado, and others of like stature in the Alegre stable. This first, twelve-member incarnation of the group also included the highly regarded trombonist Barry Rogers, who was invited in by Pacheco: Pacheco and Rogers had gone to Gompers High School together and played in the high school band.

As Santiago recalled years later, "When the idea of organizing such a group was presented to the bandleaders, vocalists and instrumentalists under contract to Alegre Records, the usual response was, 'It's a great idea but it won't work.' The biggest problem foreseen by all was the improbability of being able to bring these 'names' together because of different individual commitments. The solution was to pick an off-night during the week when all could be available and find a place where they could work as a unit while preparing for this LP; the night was Tuesday and the place was the Bronx Social Club, the Tritons."[24] Al arranged with Beco of the Tritons Club to reserve the place for ten consecutive Tuesdays. Once word got out of those sessions, the Tritons started drawing crowds on Tuesday nights.

"The Alegre All-Stars was my baby," Santiago said proudly. "I conceived it." Repeatedly Santiago identifies the inspiration for the project by referring to the well-known Cuban jam sessions or "descargas," *Descargas: Cuban Jam Sesions in Miniature*, released in 1957 on the Cuban Panart label, and inextricably associated with its creator, the legendary bassist Israel López, "Cachao." "I had heard the Panart release," he later recalled, "the Cuban all-stars with a trumpet, trombone, tenor sax and Peruchín on piano. Oh man, I heard this on radio; the hippest Latin jazz thing I had ever heard in my life."[25] He elaborated in a later conversation: "How loose, groovy, funky, swinging, and musically avant-garde. If they could put together a party studio band in Cuba and just jam, well so could we and of course we did." Chombo Silva, a regular with Alegre on violin with the charangas of both Charlie and Pacheco, had even played sax on the Cuban jam sessions. "Chombo told me that the Cuban musicians were invited to a party in which they ate, drank, and jammed for three days and nights. They knew they were being taped but they thought it was just for kicks."[26]

Santiago delighted in the prospect of replicating that jam-session feel and format: "I incorporated some of the Panart formula with the Alegre All-Stars 'modus operandi' to be. We had the party ambience with catering and bartender. We had invited guests, DJs, journalists, columnists and or course *los jodedores* [loosely, "party animals"] for more spice or should we say Salsa."[27] And then, interestingly, he mentions a significant difference from his all-Cuban model, reflecting the New York setting of these jam sessions: "We had variety in our ethnic backgrounds, our musicians consisted of not only Cubans but also Puerto Ricans, Dominicans and a golden long-haired Jew." (Note that with all its diversity the grouping included no African Americans and no women.)

The whole tenor of Santiago's experiment was also far more playful than that of his Cuban model; to give an idea of that goofiness, the list of personnel on the album cover includes entries like "Booze-getter: Juancho Feliciano Mercerón," "Bartender: Cecilio Carmona," and "Inspiration: THE CUBAN JAM SESSIONS (PANART)." But what most differentiated the Alegre All-Stars from the Cuban descargas was the level of informality and improvisation. While the Panart recordings provided the model of an "all-star" format bringing together exceptional instrumentalists having their own bands and not normally playing together, and emphasized spontaneity free of written arrangements, the Alegre project carried that aleatory, extemporaneous feel even further. "There was no written music," Santiago emphasized. "It was strictly improvised. There was no leader. I was like the supervisor. At first I really had no musical input other than suggesting a tune or two. The musicians worked it out among themselves. I heard them every Tuesday and I took them into the studio and we had a very easy time with the first album, because there was no written music." Not only were they playing free of charts, but the structuring of the pieces was minimal, relying on a rough outline of sequences under Santiago's very general direction. "Charlie would kick off a number by playing an 8- or 16-bar intro all by himself . . . setting up the tempo, the mood and the

FIGURE 13 Alegre All-Stars, first album, Alegre Records. Permission Fania Records.

feeling—then Kako would jump in with the always-prepared-for-anything rhythm section. . . . After the rhythm section advanced the tune forward somewhat I would encourage and cue Barry or Chombo to lay down a guajeo motif which the other would follow about 16 bars later."[28] Not totally arbitrary, to be sure, but freewheeling as a matter of principle.

The signature feature of the Alegre All-Stars recordings, which marks them off from others of the period and from its influential Cuban model, is the conspicuous inclusion of studio chatter. Nearly every tune on all of the five albums contains goofy banter among the musicians and other sound effects, indicating that they are having a good time and that the music-making is a part of a larger socializing experience. From shouts and raucous laughter to jokes and the very audible pouring of drinks, the musical track is but one of the auditory effects contained in the soundscape, the result being that the musical performance occurs within a lively, very human context. The lines between a recording session in a studio and a rehearsal at the Tritons Club, and between musicians and audience, are thereby reduced in significance, allowing for greater public participation in the musical process. Santiago himself and the musicians were of one mind about this technique, some of them extremely so. Vocalist Willie Torres, for one, whose playful exhortations can be heard in many of the tunes (though not on the first album), says that he decided to leave the group once they started trying to write things down: "Later I lost the feeling with the Alegre All-Stars when they started writing charts. The spontaneity went out of it."[29] As Santiago reported, "The All-Stars were an improvising group and Willie Torres would tell me off if I dared to bring in a sketch (not an arrangement, a sketch) to organize our intros and endings. He wanted us to strictly improvise, and for the most part we did."[30]

The irony of this eminently spontaneous, extemporaneous process is that the final recorded product was actually quite planned and deliberate. Music historian David Carp has contributed an insightful study of the highly creative work of audio engineer Roy Ramírez, in coordination with the unusually hands-on approach of producer Al Santiago. Ramírez speaks of the elaborate, time-consuming editing that went into each song, and Santiago explained, "The editing wasn't so much to shorten the number, it was because we were improvising. Let's say we would start, I would point to Chombo and tell him to play a guajeo and then the trombone would go off on it. By the time they got it together correctly they had already played like eight repeats on it or more, and I would take out all those fumbling intros and just use the solid playing."[31] Ramírez, whose prior work, importantly, had included post-production of comedy albums, proved to be especially adept at the inclusion of studio chatter effects. Having started use of this method on the Sabú Martínez album, he regarded such pastiche work as eminently creative and entertaining, and even speaks of it as a kind of collective aesthetic in its own right. "It's an ad lib session, you know, they're coming to jam so everybody's got input. So, you're listening to these inputs and you find it interesting, who comes up with what ideas. To me that's part of the aesthetic product, it's like watching a painter go through his process of painting."[32] The role of the engineer takes on such importance for Santiago that he goes so far as to list Ramirez among the personnel, along with the musicians, from the second album on. Evidently Ramírez would delight in surprising Santiago and the others when they heard what he left in. On one occasion he had asked Ramirez to eliminate some botched material, and "the next time I went to the studio I'm looking at Roy when his real devilish eye tells me, 'I want you to hear this,' and he had taken all these things and spliced them together the way you hear them now and we just cracked up."

To many in the music business, including Santiago's uncle, longtime bandleader and record store owner Bartolo Alvarez, this unique project was nothing short of folly. But again, from the beginning Alegre Records was not primarily intended as a moneymaking enterprise. "I never made any record for the mass listening audience. I made records, as arrogant and self-centered maybe as it may seem, because I enjoyed making them and I made them for my taste and if people liked them, wonderful, it was a plus. Thank God my retail store paid my rent and the grocer." As Carp rightly reminds us, Santiago was also banking on the huge commercial success of the label's first album, which sold an unprecedented 100,000 copies in six months and provided Santiago a cushion for his subsequent extravaganzas.

Santiago had one further decision to make before the release of the first album: whom to name as the leader or musical director of the Alegre All-Stars. Should it be Johnny Pacheco or Charlie Palmieri? He chose Charlie because they were very close long-term friends, but also because of what he called his "harmonic way of thinking."[33] His relation with Johnny Pacheco, on the other hand, his obvious other choice, was decidedly more business-like. Pacheco felt snubbed, probably with good reason given his huge popularity—and after all he had accomplished in establishing the status of the label, economic and otherwise. In any case, after that first album Pacheco left the Alegre All-Stars, never to record with them again. Indeed, he ended his relation with Alegre Records, and shortly thereafter founded Fania Records. This parting of ways obviously had deeper origins, reflecting as it did differing musical and commercial agendas. The divergence between Pacheco and Charlie, between Alegre and Fania, and the differences between the Alegre All-Stars and the Fania All-Stars, suggests a bifurcation of the musical history, and in particular two different narratives and programmatic intentions regarding what comes to be known as "salsa." All of these dynamic developments and interactions, including the seminal importance of the Tritons Club and of Al Santiago, contributed to the making of the most original, and eventually the most illustrious, of all of those local musical talents, Eddie Palmieri.

La Perfecta Fit

La Perfecta: From the Tritons to the Palladium

In 1960, Eddie Palmieri had decided the time had come to have his own band. He'd been at it for ten years by then, playing in one band or another, first on timbales and then settling into piano. He started with his uncle Chino Gueits's Orquesta Alma Tropical, and cutting his teeth in the ranks of Eddie Forrestier, Johnny Segui, Ray Almo, and Pete Terrace, by 1958 he made it to the big leagues when he joined the band of renowned vocalist Vicentico Valdés; then he moved to center stage playing with one of the giants of the time, Tito Rodríguez. He'd learned the ropes, especially with Vicentico's group, which included not only a wealth of talent and experience but deep knowledge of the Cuban traditions, especially as passed on to him by the group's bongocero and timbalero Manny Oquendo. Eddie's big brother Charlie, who had opened doors for him by passing on the piano seat to him in many of these groups, and who had finally set up his own successful charanga in La Duboney, was now advising him to get serious about his career and put together a professional band of his own.

It was a major challenge to him, and after leaving Tito Rodríguez in 1960 he struggled, playing with trios and makeshift bands at weddings, bar mitzvahs, anniversaries, anything he could get, while looking around for the right combination of instrumentalists to come up with something new and fresh. It turned out that the percussionists in Vincentico's orchestra, the galaxy comprised of Oquendo, Tommy López, and Mikey Collazo, had also moved on by then, so Eddie started by linking up with them. He was off to a promising start.

In those days, Johnny Pacheco was all the rage, having reached superstardom with his dynamic performances and the release of his bestselling album with the superhit "El Güiro de Macorina." Everyone was talking about it and about the jam sessions that Pacheco was holding at the Tritons Club every Tuesday night. Since he was living at that time with his in-laws on West Farms Road, a short walk from the Tritons, Eddie decided to stop in and see what all the buzz was about. The pachanga scene was indeed smoldering hot, but what most caught his attention was the trombonist, a tall, lanky Jewish guy named Barry Rogers. He had heard about him but was literally blown away by the remarkable rhythmic sense and fascinating fit between Rogers's unusual trombone part and the charanga and mambo songs they were playing. It was different, and new. So Eddie went over and introduced himself to Barry. He said, "I play here at the Tritons regularly; would you be interested in joining us sometime?" Barry said sure, and as of that moment at the Tritons a creative partnership was sealed that was to have seminal importance for the whole course of Latin music for over a decade to come. Without that remarkable symbiosis, what came to be called "salsa" would be a horse of a different color.

Eddie loved the Tritons. It was a very special place for him, especially in those years. He had grown up a few blocks away, on Kelly Street near the Intervale Avenue subway stop, and had been hearing about the local spot for some time. He would play there whenever he could pull a band together. It wasn't so much the money, but the convenience and familiarity of it. He must

FIGURE 14 Barry Rogers and Eddie Palmieri. Photo by Joe Rivera. David Carp Collection, Bronx County Historical Society.

also have heard that the Alegre All-Stars would practice there, and in fact what he recalls as Pacheco's jam sessions might well have been the Al Santiago experiment with Charlie leading and on piano.

In any case, once Eddie had managed to pull together the makings of his new group—with the powerful rhythm section from Vicentico's band, Barry on trombone, George Castro from Gilberto Valdés's early charanga on wooden flute, and the new-found young vocalist Ismael "Pat" Quintana—the aspiring bandleader felt he was ready to get going. He had the singer and he had seven men, now what they needed was work. But he knew they also needed a period of incubation, when the group could play together, become a unit, and work out the sound. They would need a congenial place with an informal atmosphere and lively dance crowd.

Where else but the Tritons? Eddie already knew Beco, having helped him deliver groceries in the neighborhood years back. The problem for Eddie was that he wasn't going to be able to pay the musicians with what Beco paid him for a gig. At that point he then borrowed $1000 from his mother-in-law—"the band really belonged to my mother-in-law"—and gave it to Beco in order to rent the Tritons for a month. He worked out a deal with another local friend whose father owned a liquor store: he'd get the liquor and they would split the profit. "It turned out we didn't make much money," Eddie recalls, "in fact we even lost some, and I never got the $1000 back (though I did pay my mother-in-law eventually). But at least the band was working constantly, I'm there every week, two or three days a week, and before you know it, we become a big hit in the Bronx."[1] Eddie recalls how quickly word of mouth in the street drew larger and more enthusiastic crowds to the Tritons, the Caravana and other clubs all over the city. "And then little by little we kept working until we got to the Palladium," he recalls. La Perfecta was such a draw there that the Palladium kept them on for the duration. "We closed the Palladium in 1966."[2]

The kind of band Eddie had in mind was a conjunto: four trumpets and a rhythm section. That was the format he loved. "Cuban style," he called it. His only problem was once again economic: in those days good trumpeters were at a premium, and fetched a high price. So he had to improvise and come up with some variation on that classical combination. The trombone was a good alternative, especially the way Barry played it, and then the flute was at the peak of its popularity because of the charanga vogue, so that could also help create a strong sound. Eddie would use the trombone on some nights and the flute on others. Then one night, "when we had the money," he used them both, and right away he knew it: "That's it, that's the sound, trombone and flute!" He then added another trombone, and brought the brass up front. It was like a charanga in a way, with the trombones replacing the violins, and also like a conjunto, but with trombones instead of trumpets. As Charlie famously baptized the new format, here was the "trombanga"!

The trombone sound was no doubt the signature and most influential feature of La Perfecta, though eventually it was Manny Oquendo's vast knowledge and experience, and his inimitable work on timbales and bongo, that served to anchor the band and bring out the best in all of the members. Between Barry and Manny the musical intelligence available to Eddie was unsurpassed, and Ismael Quintana's increasingly versatile and confident vocals were just what he needed to front up the new band. Eddie placed a lot of importance on the special fit of the entire band in unison. Even before the second trombone was added, and before Manny Oquendo replaced Mikie Collazo on timbales when he left to join the new Tito Rodríguez conjunto, Eddie said the band was "perfect." "Perfect, man. It was 'La Perfecta' before even being called that."

It was Al Santiago who came up with the name. The band still wasn't called La Perfecta after the first album, even though that was the title of the record. As Eddie explains, it was after that first album had been recorded, "and we're listening to Ismael singing one of his *inspiraciones: 'Son montuno es la perfecta, gavilán come pollo y nada más.'* In the Cuban version there are no *inspiraciones*, just *'Gavilán come pollo y nada más,'* but we added, for the coro, *'Palmieri con su conjunto,'* and then *'Son montuno es la perfecta.'* So Al Santiago heard that and said, 'Eddie, why don't you call the band La Perfecta?' And I said, 'Well, okay, so that's it, it's 'Eddie Palmieri y La Perfecta.'"

More controversial than the apt naming of the group was Santiago's repeated claim to have originated the idea of two or more trombones up front. Eddie himself disagrees, attributing the idea to himself and Barry and seeing it as a natural expansion of the breakthrough trombone-and-flute combination that already made them new and unique. But even more serious contention stems from the fact that Mon Rivera, the veteran Puerto Rican *plenero* and bandleader who also recorded with Alegre in those years, had been using multiple trombones prior to the La Perfecta recordings; his extremely popular album *Que Gente Averiguá*, later titled *Mon Rivera y Sus Trombones*, featured four trombones, and came out on Alegre at the same time as the first La Perfecta recording.

Though of some importance in the history of the music and one which evokes strong emotional allegiances, the issue of who was "first" may never be decisively resolved to everyone's satisfaction. But some commentators, notably David Carp, are more to the point in arguing that it is not so much who or when, but *how*. Even if it was Al Santiago who came up with the novel idea (and his creative boldness had few limits), or if Mon Rivera had indeed established the foregrounding of trombones in the new plena sound of the 1940s and 50s, it was Eddie and Barry who used the trombone in a new and distinctive way, thus initiating a style and sound which obviously caught on with the public and which reflected the musical influences at work in the forging of a musical taste reflective of the New York Latin community of that historical period.

The distinctiveness of La Perfecta's trombone line has everything to do with Barry Rogers, and his collaboration with the bandleader and other musicians of La Perfecta. For Eddie, Barry was quite simply a "genius," a word he uses sparingly and which he expands on by referring to his remarkable range of talents and areas of expertise. Eddie was awe-struck not only by Rogers' energetic interest in many traditions of world music and his self-taught multi-instrumentalism—he taught himself Cuban percussion and to play the tres—but also by his mastery of auto mechanics, photography, piano tuning, boats and sailing, and many more.

More pertinently, Barry's background experience on trombone in a range of bands and genres, and his very authoritative presence in any musical setting, meant that he injected a different and fresh sound to the conjunto and charanga formats in which La Perfecta was working. Barry had been playing in the Latin vein for some time, and had a longstanding interest in and affinity to Afro-Cuban percussion and dance music traditions, both modern and folkloric. In important ways, given that he worked with both Pacheco and with Charlie and the Alegre All-Stars, Rogers was one of the main links between Eddie's breakthrough and both the pachanga and descarga styles, which together comprised the immediate stylistic environment out of which La Perfecta was to grow.

But more than Latin, it was jazz and rhythm and blues that was the most familiar idiom to Barry Rogers, who had gained formative experience in the multi-genre bands active in Harlem during the 1950s. He was widely versed in the jazz idiom and was Eddie's main jazz mentor in those early years. Eddie was always the first to admit that his field was Latin and that throughout his early career he knew nothing about jazz. Even in more recent times, when he had firmly established himself in Latin jazz for more than thirty years, he asserts that he is not a jazz musician and doesn't understand it. But Barry would take him to performances by some of the masters, and Eddie remembers fondly the time when he traded a Celia Cruz album for Miles Davis's *Kind of Blue*. Even more consequentially over the course of time was that Barry first introduced Eddie to Bob Bianco, the esteemed teacher of many in the science of jazz harmony and Eddie's long-term adviser in things artistic, spiritual, and political. While the musical impact of Bianco's teachings were already present in the piano solos and structural conception of some of La Perfecta's output as of the mid-1960s, the political education was to take hold after the disbanding of La Perfecta and the onset of the charged radical protest atmosphere of the late 1960s and early 1970s.

Specifically, though, beyond his catalytic role in these and other regards, Barry Rogers played trombone and even served as musical director for some years with the seminal but largely forgotten band of Hugo Dickens. As previously mentioned, during the 1950s period, bands like that of Dickens and such other African American bandleaders as Joe Panama and Pucho Brown played fashion shows, cocktail sips, and what were colorfully called "chicken and booze" dances in Harlem and the Bronx. These groupings served as crucial incubators for many budding musicians who went on to successful careers and some note on their own: in addition to Barry Rogers, mention is sometimes made of Hugo Dickens graduates Pete Laroca Simms, Hubert Laws, Phil Newsum, Rodgers Grant, Bobby Porcelli, and Marty Sheller, among many others. Because of the varied musical tastes of their audiences, what was notable about these bands was their wide-ranging repertoire; as David Carp put it, "It was taken for granted that a musician working the 'chicken and booze' circuit would be able to play jazz, rhythm and blues, calypso, and Latin."[3]

Aside from his sheer power and impeccable timing, Barry Rogers's trombone was clearly defined by this eclectic, strongly African American background. For Rogers, and for many other trombonists at the time, the towering figure of J. J. Johnson was ubiquitous, and especially—in those very years—his trombone duos with Kai Winding. This was explicitly one of Barry's stron-gest influences, and the pairing of two trombones that became the earmark of La Perfecta may very well have been suggested by that historic example. Certainly that background, and Rogers's knowledge of the trombone in jazz history going back to the 1920s, would tend to differentiate La Perfecta's trombone parts from those of Mon Rivera, and as Carp also suggests, it may help to explain Palmieri's intense and enduring attraction among African American audiences.

There are interesting technical dimensions to the innova-tions and uniqueness of Rogers's trombone playing that fur-ther differentiate it from the Mon Rivera usage. As discussed by trombonists Marc Weinstein and Joe Orange, the latter of whom actually played with both of the bands in question, the first contrast has to do with harmony and chord changes, which tend to be less complex and varied in the more straightfor-ward Mon Rivera arrangements; La Perfecta charts show more intricacy and jazz influence. The other significant feature of La Perfecta's trombone parts has to do with range: while for Mon the high notes tend to hover around G above the piano's middle C, for La Perfecta it was higher, between F above middle C and the C a fifth higher. As Carp summarizes it, "Where Mon's trom-bone section leaves off, in terms of range, Eddie's begins."[4]

As all of the knowing commentators emphasize, what was special and unprecedented about La Perfecta in this regard is not only the idiosyncratic way that Rogers goes at his trombone work but bandleader and composer Palmieri's own remarkable sensitivity to the qualities of the trombone. After all, Barry Rogers also played with both Mon Rivera and with Willie Colón, and the contrast to La Perfecta still holds. In Joe Orange's words, "You can hear a lot of trombone bands where the writer doesn't understand the instrument he's writing for like Eddie did, and that's the difference. And you can even hear the awkwardness in the execution. Mon's is kind of rough because he didn't write for the upper middle register. His lines look easy on paper, but can be a lot more awkward than they look. But Eddie really knew where the sound of the trombone was, which is really in the middle to upper register."[5]

Thus, with all the awe that rightly goes to Barry Rogers, and the credit that is due him and Manny Oquendo for making La Perfecta the unique project that it was, it is ultimately Eddie Palmieri who made it all happen and whose unrivaled sense of how to build on and move beyond musical traditions enabled him to arrive at his guiding creative concept. There is testimony to the effect that Barry was already aware of Eddie's remarkable rhythmic sense by the time they first hooked up that night at the Tritons.[6] Eddie speaks continuously and reverently of the "structures" of Afro-Cuban music, the basic principles that nourish the musical execution and product no matter what composition or musical cohort is involved. While as a bandleader he placed a premium on securing the "best" player on each of the instruments and vocals, he also notes that once he arrived at the right "fit" for La Perfecta, or his later bands, he was confident that the music could be played to the utmost potential even with the inevitable changes of personnel and orchestration. He was to deepen this conceptual understanding over the course of his tireless career, and especially as he expanded his knowledge of both Afro-Cuban and jazz traditions.

At first the novelty of La Perfecta was the trombone and flute combination; no one had put them together before. But then it was decided that two trombones were needed to give the horn section more force working with the flute. The second trombone seat was varied at first, between Marc Weinstein and Joe Orange, and then Barry discovered Jose Rodrigues, a Brazilian musician who had been living in the Dominican Republic before settling in New York. Rodrigues turned out to provide the ideal counterpoint to Barry, in part because of his sheer endurance: Barry played so hard, and at such a toll on his lips, that he needed relief, especially as the numbers got longer even in their recorded versions. Both Weinstein and Orange attest to the special qualities of Rodrigues, and Eddie sings his praises to this day. The Rogers-Rodrigues duo set the standard for trombone work in the Latin genres, and their footprint was ubiquitous. The use of trombones was so pervasive in the music of the 1960s that Eddie recalls the pawnshops all over town suddenly selling them as fast as they came in!

The full band ended up being an octet: two trombones, flute, vocalist, and the rhythm section of timbales, congas, bass, and piano. Aside from a new sound, Eddie also had a new kind of lineup for the band in performance. He even compared the change with that introduced by Tito Puente when he brought the timbales and rhythm section up front for the first time; in his case, he brought up the trombones, flute, and vocalist, with the powerful rhythm section "in the backfield," as he called it, borrowing a phrase from football. He saw it as a kind of symmetry, four and four, a distribution of two layers, the front line and the rhythmic "backfield in motion." What added even further drama to the show was the way that Barry Rogers moved with his instrument, dancing with his trombone as he played, much as Pacheco had been known to dance with his flute.

In early 1962, as soon as Al Santiago picked up the word on the street and went to see the new band in action at the Tritons Club, he started telling Eddie he wanted to get them into the studio. He even arranged for an "audition" of the band at the Caravana Club, an event attended by Tito Rodríguez and Eddie's brother Charlie. In no time, Santiago had La Perfecta in the studio, where he recorded the first of three historic LPs on the Alegre label. Over the course of those three recordings, released in three consecutive years, one can follow the growth of the band as a unit and

FIGURE 15 La Perfecta at the Palladium, 1964. Courtesy of the Eddie Palmieri Collection.

the development of its distinctive sound. According to Santiago, the first two albums didn't sell well but the third was a big hit. All three contain some unforgettable songs, which have remained an active part of Eddie's repertoire through the years.

"My kid brother, Eddie Palmieri, is a nut." That's how Charlie begins his backliner notes to the debut album. What he meant was that Eddie always seemed to make it hard on himself, first by leaving Tito Rodríguez's prestigious band to form his own, then by (in Charlie's words) "Going against the tide and instead of organizing a Charanga, the popular sound of the day, he organized what I call a Trombanga, a band featuring trombones and flute." Actually, that first album, *Eddie Palmieri and His Conjunto La Perfecta*, comprises three different instrumental formats: first four trumpets and two trombones; then just four trumpets; and finally, on only four of the tracks, it was the trombone and flute combination. The steady shrinking in size and personnel came as a result of economic pressure on Al Santiago. The "trombanga" setup, though it was what Eddie had arrived at as new and just right, was actually the outcome of financial considerations as much as musical ones.

Though he had no interest in jumping on the pachanga bandwagon, Eddie did of necessity give a nod in that direction and acknowledged the popular pull of the reigning dance craze: on each of the first two albums several of the tunes are identified as "pachangas." On the debut release, in fact, the compelling first track, "Conmigo," is listed as a pachanga, as are the album's most enduring composition, "Ritmo Caliente," and the crisp version of the up-tempo Rafael Hernández standard, "Cachita." None of the numbers were played by charangas, as there were at no point any violins, but the rhythms are deliberately compatible with the novelty dance step in vogue in those years.

The varied orchestration on this first record, while done for extraneous financial reasons and somewhat confusing to the listener expecting a more uniform format, is nevertheless indicative of Eddie's intentions with La Perfecta. In all the subsequent LPs, both the other two on Alegre and the subsequent six for Tico, La Perfecta actually comprised what Eddie refers to as two bands in one, without adding or changing personnel: for any given number he had either a conjunto, with trombones and bongo, or what he calls "charanguea'o," that is, with the charanga feel, combining flute, trombones and timbales. As Eddie explains the transcending success of La Perfecta, all the other bands around at the time were either one or the other; he had the advantage of having two in one and being able to vary constantly between the two most popular formats in Latin music of the day.

The succession of La Perfecta releases evidences the peaking and then the waning of the pachanga craze and signals the emergence of the subsequent step in Latin music history. Based on genre designations alone, the second album, *El Molestoso*, has only two pachangas, while by the third, the 1964 *Lo Que Traigo Es Sabroso*, there are none at all. Again, that is the year when both Johnny Pacheco and Charlie Palmieri disbanded their charangas in favor of the conjunto format. The following, post-pachanga phase is generally referred to as *típico*," a term that Eddie is fine with and favors. Given his unwavering insistence that his intention is to be in strict accordance with Afro-Cuban roots and musical structures, his "revolution" will continue to be referred to as a resurgence of "típico" music. The problem with that ubiquitous term is that most other musical currents and practitioners of the time would make the same claim, and the word has been so widely and variously used in popular music history as to become almost synonymous with whatever the reigning musical style is.

The question of what is meant by "típico" becomes especially pertinent at this time because it is claimed by both Eddie Palmieri and Johnny Pacheco. Just as La Perfecta is coming into its own and establishing itself as the key band of the era, Johnny Pacheco is setting up Fania Records, the hub of Latin music production in that same era. As is known, by his own choosing Eddie never went with Fania and remained outside of what became the abundant and inclusive Fania stable. Though he did participate as an invited guest at the founding concert of the Fania All-Stars at the Red Garter in 1968, and recorded with them much later, in the late 1970s when Fania's star was already fading, the career of Eddie Palmieri is not an integral part of the Fania story. This bifurcation as of 1964 between the trajectories of Eddie Palmieri and Fania Records make for the central divide in the history of what came to be called "salsa"—that is, for Fania, but decidedly not for Eddie, who citing his towering forerunner and rival Tito Puente, never had any use for the word, at least to describe a kind of music. And in many ways, this complex difference is a reflection of differing meanings of the word "típico."

What Eddie Palmieri meant by típico is perhaps best gleaned from the music. In their first five albums, La Perfecta demonstrates a consistent power and originality from the beginning and a progression toward increasing cohesion, self-confidence, and creative boldness in stretching the limits of all genres and rhythmic traditions. On *El Molestoso*, when Manny Oquendo joins the band, the percussive center is in place and the interaction of the two trombones and flute establish the inimitable, unheard-of sound in such classic Palmieri compositions as "Lázaro y Su Micrófono" and "Sabroso Guaguancó" (originally by Sonora Matancera with Celia Cruz), and in the remarkable re-working of the traditional danzón "La Gioconda."

The third album, *Lo Que Traigo Es Sabroso* ("what I bring is delicious") is even more daring and fresh, a string of highly varied and consistently irresistible songs in many registers and tempos but with an unmistakable musical core. As "recording director" Al Santiago put it, *Sabroso* is just that, "delicious, because Eddie, Pat, Barry and the group are meat, gravy and nourishment (funk, salsa and drive). Volume III is the end of a three course dinner with Alegre."[7] Here Jose Rodrigues joins Barry Rogers as second trombone and the La Perfecta Alegre sound is there in full; from the opening title cut to the end, that duo shows itself to be peerless in the trombone-cluttered Latin field, the standardbearer for a whole generation. That first title song was an all-time favorite Palmieri tune among African Americans, behind only "Azúcar." Eddie recounts proudly the many times that an African American fan would sidle up to him and prod him with the title of that song, mispronounced of course as would be expected when blurted out by someone who has no idea what the words mean. But Eddie knew that, as with "Azúcar," it was about the flavor ("sabroso") and not the semantics. If anything is salsa avant-la-lettre, this is it.

But the highlight of this stellar album, and the signature tune for La Perfecta, was no doubt "Muñeca." This is the song—again excepting perhaps "Azúcar" and "Vamonos Pa'l Monte—by which Eddie Palmieri is best known to the world, and which stands as an all-time standard of the salsa canon. There is hardly a Latin act worth its salt that doesn't have a version of "Muñeca" as part of its repertoire. And it is vintage La Perfecta: the fresh excited voice of Pat Quintana; the Barry Rogers-Jose Rodrigues trombone duo—jokingly called the "roaring elephants" because of its sheer power—in full swing; the tight, powerful rhythm section; Eddie going "nuts" with his piano solos; a catchy melodic riff to hook and hold the audience; intriguing, slightly mysterious lyrics; and the most eminently danceable four minutes imaginable.

The song is about infidelity and forgiveness. An unfaithful male lover was caught with his pants down, or at least in the arms of another woman ("en los brazos de otra nena") and is now apologizing to his "doll" ("muñeca") and begging for forgiveness. Such is the gist of the lyrics and the sense that the casual listener takes to be the meaning of the song, especially as it trails off with the repeated chorus, "ay mi muñeca perdóname" ("oh my doll forgive me"). A closer listen though, and attention to the verbal and musical tone of the song, indicates that it is actually meant to be ironic, and intended to expose the pleading lover's insincerity and hypocrisy. As Eddie says, all we need is the violins. The trombones, the piano, the percussion are all saying it: "yeah, yeah, sure, sure, it didn't mean anything, just a momentary lapse? Bullshit!" According to Eddie, everyone loved this irresistible number, "until the women found out the guy was a stinking rat!" It was an open secret that the song was autobiographical. The very word "muñeca" is not always taken kindly by many women, for whom it is an infantilizing cliché of the worst order, and not a term of endearment.

"Muñeca" is, like most of Palmieri's recordings, an original composition, though he always qualifies that claim by explaining how he and Barry Rogers elaborated the concept and arrangements together, and how he worked closely with Pat Quintana on the vocal part. In this case he also borrowed some lines—"el amor y el interés se fueron al campo un día" (love and interest went to the countryside one day)—from a favorite by legendary Cuban vocalist Miguelito Cuní and the Conjunto Modelo, and worked on their execution with Quintana. Reflecting on the song's unprecedented popularity he points to the bass-and-piano intro that he perfected with unrivaled bassist of the period, Bobby Rodriguez, followed by the ominous groaning of the trombones. That was the hook, what make the song immediately recognizable as of the opening chords.

In the midst of recording this third album, *Lo Que Traigo Es Sabroso*, Al Santiago announced that he was going broke. Palmieri signed a contract for future recordings with Tico, a subsidiary of Roulette Records, which was owned by the infamous, Mafia-connected "hit man" Morris Levy. Before doing so he promised Santiago—and secured Levy's agreement—that he would go back to the studio and finish that album with Alegre, and in fact, since he kept his word, the band's fourth album and first with Tico, titled *Echando Palante/Straight Ahead*, was actually released earlier in 1964 than the third one with Alegre.

The switch from Alegre to Tico made for a big change, not the least of which involved Palmieri having to deal with the overbearing personality and mindset of Morris Levy. It also meant doing without the important presence of Al Santiago in the studio, a loss that surely took its toll in terms of creativity and a vast, lively knowledge of the music. The producer for *Echando Palante* and subsequent Tico recordings was Teddy Reig, whose long-term and influential experience in the jazz field did carry certain advantages. For as the La Perfecta releases progressed there was a steady lengthening of many of the tracks, such that they began to exceed the usual 2:45-minute length of single tunes by more and more time: while on the first two albums the songs remained around the three-minute length, in the third they are nearly all over four minutes. This was of concern because excessively long cuts had less chance of radio play. But Reig, having produced many of the jazz greats, and for years manager of the Count Basie orchestra, had no problem allowing for long tracks. While this became the central issue regarding the recording of "Azúcar," which clocked in at over 8:30, most of the cuts on *Echando Palante* were also over five minutes, and what turned out to be the jewel of the collection, "Café," lasted 6:32.

As an album, *Echando Palante* did not match up to the standard set by the Alegre releases, especially the consistently powerful *Lo Que Traigo Es Sabroso*. But "Café" is another of those timeless compositions and productions that has its firm place in the annals of salsa history. The lyrics of this relaxed-tempo though intense son montuno (a subgenre of the Cuban son), written by Eddie's cousin Roberto Gueits, tells the story of coffee and its centrality to the Spanish Caribbean cultural heritage. Its haunting chorus, "Café, tostao y colao" (coffee, roasted and brewed), has taken on nearly proverbial status, and the song succeeds in evoking the fragrance and taste of coffee in a nearly visceral way. Though the tempo is not typical of La Perfecta's repertoire, the band pulls out all the stops, with the trombone duet punctuating the steps in the song's meandering narrative. There is also here, perhaps for the first time in the band's output, a notable sense of social commentary, since the presence of the emblematic product is attributed to those attached to the land and working the plantations, not to the landowners or commercial traders. Here again, as with "Muñeca," La Perfecta produced a composition that has come to assume a canonical place in salsa history, capping off a string of four albums released within a three-year period that set the standard and stylistic modality for the musical production to follow, generally and increasingly subsumed under the name of salsa when that term came into currency nearly a decade later.

But in retrospect, those four albums appear like a buildup to the fifth, also with Tico, the 1965 *Azúcar Pa Tí*. Matching the achievement of *Lo Que Traigo Es Sabroso*, this collection is filled with gems, many of them—like "Mi Sonsito," "Cuídate Compay" and "Oyelo Que Te Conviene"—anthology pieces in their own

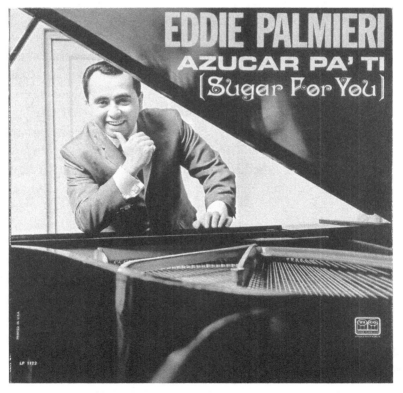

FIGURE 16 Eddie Palmieri y La Perfecta, *Azúcar.* Tico Records, courtesy of Fania Records.

right and an integral part of Palmieri's enduring repertoire. But it is the title song that made history like no other in Eddie's long career, and represents the artistic pinnacle for La Perfecta. Highest public recognition went to that composition in 2009 when it was inducted into the National Recording Registry of the United States Library of Congress.

Eddie, Barry, and the rest of the band placed great stock in "Azúcar." For several years before recording it they had been playing it in the clubs to huge acclaim—and to the point that they couldn't perform anywhere without the song being loudly requested by listening and dance audiences. The group felt so identified with it that they even decided against including it on the previous album so as to allow more time to hone it and ready themselves for a recorded version. Eddie tells that the highly influential disc jockey Symphony Sid was getting countless call-in requests to play the song before it was even available on record. And, happily, when they did bring it to the studio they faced no obstacle regarding the track's duration thanks to the encouragement of producer Teddy Reig. His response to Palmieri's concern that they wanted to record it as closely as possible to how they play it live was simply, in effect, "no problem, take as long as you want."

"Azúcar" may be viewed as the culmination of La Perfecta's achievement in many ways, not the least of which is that it actually combines the "two bands," the conjunto and the charanga formats and style, in a single composition. It starts off noticeably in the conjunto típico style and then shifts, with a switch in the guajeo (repeated riff) of the bass, to a more charanga feel, and then the piano part moves it into what can only be called jazz harmonics. That piano solo attracts attention because Eddie manages to hold his (stronger) left hand in the típico mode while ad libbing on the right. "People thought and said that there were two pianists," Eddie recalls. "They said that it was an overdub. But there were no overdubs, nor did I use another piano player. They thought of everything except that I did it alone, just me."

Eventually the song gets back to típico, but the piece as a whole remains wildly free-wheeling, perhaps the closest Eddie had thus far come to a descarga, but still retaining a well-plotted sense of structure and sequence. Though the composition is fully Palmieri's own, and among his proudest achievements, he is the first to point out that the collaborative input of Barry Rogers and Manny Oquendo is evident everywhere.

The towering stature of "Azúcar" within the Latin music pantheon rests largely on this recording, which Eddie considers the best among the various made subsequently, including the in-concert sequel version done at Sing Sing penitentiary for the historic *Live at Sing Sing* album from 1972. But even that premier studio achievement cannot match the energy or spontaneous synchronization of the countless live performances at venues all over the city and on the road. And, in Eddie's recall, none of those presentations were more memorable than the ones at the Palladium between 1964 and the great ballroom's closing in 1966. La Perfecta playing "Azúcar" at the Palladium was an event for the history books, and certainly a landmark in the story of Latin music of the 1960s.

It wasn't easy for Eddie and his band to get into the Palladium. With the "Big Three," Machito and the two Titos, still getting top billing and with the overnight stardom of the young boogaloo groups on the rise and soon eclipsing nearly everyone else, La Perfecta was hired only for one-night stands and short stays, nothing regular. To attract attention and eventually an ongoing contract, Palmieri had to resort to barking on the street in front of a rival dance spot down the block from the Palladium and drawing the clientele away from the world-famous ballroom.

What he did was rent the Riviera Terrace—later to become the second Cheetah Club and located next door to the jazz mecca Birdland—for Wednesday nights. That was when the Riviera Terrace had their shows and when the Palladium held the famed "celebrity nights," when they had the mambo show and attracted the likes of Marlon Brando, Kim Novak, Sammy Davis Jr., and other stellar guests. So every Wednesday for months in 1964 Eddie would be out in front of the Riviera Terrace barking, "Over here, folks! Not there, over here!" "There" of course meaning the Palladium, where the billing would be for Machito, or Tito Puente, or Charlie Palmieri, the big names.

Little by little he started to siphon people away from the Palladium, partly because the storied ballroom had already lost its liquor license, but also because more and more people knew about and favored the exciting sound of Eddie Palmieri and La Perfecta. The draw was getting so strong that Maxwell Hyman, the owner of the Palladium, started getting nervous, and went to José Curbelo, Eddie's agent by then, to complain about his losses. "That kid out there is crazy!" he'd say, and the crafty Curbelo would come back with, "Then you will have to book him!" Hyman even took it upon himself to go up to the Bronx to hear La Perfecta in performance at the Tritons Club. "And sure enough," Eddie recalls, "they gave me ninety gigs, ninety gigs at the Palladium! That ran for two years, all the way until it closed. In fact I closed the Palladium, in 1966."

It was in that period, between the waning of the pachanga craze in 1963 and the dawning of boogaloo in 1966, that La Perfecta was at its peak and established itself as the premier band of the decade. And it was at its Palladium performances that they were playing in prime form. Four nights a week they were there, often coming from gigs in other clubs throughout the city, from the Park Palace or Apollo Theater in Manhattan, or the Bronx Casino or Colgate Gardens in the Bronx, or the St. George Hotel or the 3&1 Club in Brooklyn. Wherever they went, La Perfecta drew crowds because their music was so impeccably tuned to the dancers, and because their sound was both in the vein of the great mambo era and new in a radical and daring way. They were, no doubt, the sound of the times.

The Palladium was open four nights a week those days, Wednesdays, Fridays, Saturdays, and Sundays, each night with its own specialty and primary clientele: Wednesdays drew a lot of Jewish people as well as the Hollywood crowd; Fridays it tended to be, as Eddie put it, "the Hispanic gamblers and their ladies, and the top drug guys, and the gangs"; Saturdays saw working-class Latinos, mainly Puerto Ricans from El Barrio and the Bronx; Sunday was famously "Black Night," because it was when African Americans came in droves. La Perfecta played all four nights, their music equally appealing to all four constituencies. But they were hottest of all on Sunday nights, playing for those adept, euphoric African American dance audiences who loved other bands, like those of Tito Puente and Joe Cuba, but whose favorite of all was La Perfecta. "You gonna give us some a-zoo-car, Eddie?" the African American audiences would plead as they filed in. He recalls vividly the frenzy that would set in with the trombone vamp at the beginning of "Lázaro y su Micrófono," and then again with the closing number, "Azúcar." They always closed with that because it was so long, intense, and demanding on musicians and dancers alike that after playing "Azucar" they were too exhausted to do anything but call it a night.

It was Sunday, May 1, 1966. The last night at the Palladium, the night it closed down for good, carries deep emotion and symbolism for the whole of Latin music. To this day people remember the sadness, and the shared sense that they were living a piece of history. Palladium owner Max Hyman and his wife seemed to be in a state of mourning, and the musicians and dancers carried on like there was no tomorrow, which there wasn't, at least in that revered setting. Some of the top bandleaders made it a point to stop by, not to play but just be present at that fateful hour. Even though many other venues would continue to accommodate that creative and festive energy, at the favorite of them all the party was over. "You could feel it in the air," Eddie reflects. "It was the end of an era."

The billing for that night was also laden with signs of the times. The headliner was Eddie Palmieri, followed by Orquesta Broadway, Pete Rodriguez, and Ricardo Rey. While La Broadway bore the standard of the charanga tradition, and La Perfecta also reflected continuities with the son montuno, mambo, and cha cha chá, the latter two names, Pete Rodriguez and Richie Ray, were a big draw to the younger boogaloo generation coming up and beginning to take the scene by storm. The sunset moment in the story of the famous ballroom marked a changing of the guard, the fading of the mambo age, whose decline was already first signaled in 1960, and the ascension of the young Turks into the limelight, however briefly. Eddie Palmieri's innovative sound was situated directly between these two directions, having built its identity on the shoulders of the mambo masters while at the same time refusing both slavish traditionalism and the crossover trends characteristic of boogaloo, shingaling, jala jala, and other faddish experiments of the day.

Though challenging economic conditions were setting in for them and other bands associated with the previous generation's tastes and predilections, La Perfecta continued playing in multiple settings as well as recording, mostly with Tico Records, though none of the albums following *Azúcar Pa' Tí* could boast much commercial success. The immediate post-Palladium period saw them taking up the *mozambique*, the first new rhythm to come out of Cuba after the Revolution. The idea for *Mambo con Conga Es Mozambique*, suggested to Palmieri by Manny Oquendo, wound up getting him into trouble with Morris Levy, whose notorious mob connections made him especially averse to visits by the FBI like those that occurred after anti-Castro protestors threatened reprisals at radio stations and the Feds came to Levy inquiring about this new "communist" music. The controversy subsided rapidly as a range of other groups also came out with their versions of the mozambique and use of the rhythm lost its political edge.

In 1966 and 1967, La Perfecta also recorded two highly regarded but poorly selling albums with Latin jazz pioneer Cal Tjader, the first of which, *El Sonido Nuevo*, even offered a kind of programmatic sample of the stylistic breakthrough achieved by Eddie and his influential band. Renowned cultural historian and mambo aficionado Robert Farris Thompson, in a prophetic 1967 article in *Saturday Review*, considered *El Sonido Nuevo* La Perfecta's "finest work to date . . . revealing the depth of Palmieri's instrumental resources."[8] Indeed, along with *Bamboleate*, the second release with Tjader, track after track exemplifies La Perfecta at their finest, though in historical terms both the Palmieri of La Perfecta and Tjader by this point seemed past their apogees of a few years earlier. The days of "Azúcar" at the Palladium were already behind Palmieri's group by then, as were, in Tjader's case, recordings of the immense popularity and nearly prophetic consequence of the 1964 *Soul Sauce*. Furthermore, the Palmieri-Tjader recordings were not really the result of intense musical collaboration, either in performance or even in the studio. Curiously, it turns out they never actually played together, either before or following the recording sessions: rather, the co-recordings were created by late-night visits Tjader made to the studio when he worked his vibraphone parts into the tracks.

La Perfecta's swansong was the *Champagne* album from 1968. Though standbys Barry Rogers, Pat Quintana, and Manny Oquendo were still in place, some of the personnel were already strikingly new: on different cuts Palmieri incorporated none other than premier vocalist Cheo Feliciano, formerly of the Joe Cuba Sextette, and trumpeter Chocolate Armenteros and bassist Cachao López, both of paramount stature in the history of Afro-Cuban music since the 1930s. As for the repertoire, the album includes two tracks, "Ay Que Rico" and "African Twist," which demonstrate that despite his vehement opposition to the boogaloo fad he was willing to try his hand at crossover sounds: the first of these is a shingaling, and starts with the playful exclamation, "Cómo, Palmieri en boogaloo?" while "African Twist" was composed and sung by African American rhythm and blues vocalist Cynthia Ellis. "Palo de Mango" is another example of Palmieri's creative variation on the boogaloo feel.

But by the time *Champagne* came out in 1968, the boogaloo star was already on the wane, so that Palmieri's reluctant participation in Latin soul crossover seemed more an ironic do-you-one-better gesture than genuine acceptance. Perhaps more indicative of things to come were the very disbanding of La Perfecta and the first concert of the Fania All-Stars at the Red Garter. By that point, many historical arrows were pointing toward the baptism of the music as "salsa," the Red Garter occasion serving as a kind of anticipation of the historic Cheetah concert of the Fania All-Stars in August 1971. Immortalized in the foundational film "Our Latin Thing" by Leon Gast, that moment is generally seen as the take-off point of the boom leading to the definitive coining of the "salsa" designation in the years immediately following. Eddie Palmieri did appear at the Red Garter as an invited guest, but it was the only time he did anything with Fania until years later. The irony of the pioneer and prime innovator of a cultural movement functioning outside the dominant narrative of that movement, which in the case of salsa history interfaces with that of Fania, signals the deep contradictions and contestations lurking just beneath the surface. In some ways that backstory has to do with the divergent paths taken by Palmieri and his equally influential contemporary, Johnny Pacheco.

Pacheco's Project: El Nuevo Tumbao and the Fania Formula

As the pachanga fever subsided, Johnny Pacheco moved in new directions, shifting from a charanga to a conjunto format and, of momentous importance, founding his own company, Fania Records. Wanting to strike off on his own, he not only left the charanga behind but also parted ways with Alegre Records and the Alegre All-Stars after their first recording. During the years 1963–64, as Eddie Palmieri's La Perfecta was gathering momentum and reaching the height of its musical innovations and popularity, Pacheco introduced his new band, which he called Nuevo Tumbao. The name of the conjunto was intended to be programmatic, the word "tumbao" indicating a strong turn to the típico Cuban sound in the style of Sonora Matancera and other seminal bands from Cuba. Gone were the violins and slashing flute solos, replaced by the traditional trumpet front-line and percussive sounds of the son montuno. Pacheco teamed up with Puerto Rican vocalist Pete "El Conde" Rodríguez, who would be his musical partner for some years to come, to produce that infectious típico sound. In retrospect, he attributes his major change in instrumentation in large part to his difficulty in finding good violinists, but his agenda was obviously larger than that.

The tight relation between the new ensemble and the label was clear: once again, as with his first pachanga album for Alegre a few years earlier, Pacheco's debut recording was also the opener for the new label, and it was a blockbuster hit: *Cañonazo* was Fania's bestselling LP for all the early years, until Joe Bataan and Willie Colón made their mark later in the decade. Indeed, of the first ten Fania releases, from 1964 through 1966, six were by Pacheco's band. As the familiar story has it, those early records were distributed by Pacheco himself from the trunk of his used

FIGURE 17 Johnny Pacheco y Su Nuevo Tumbao, *Cañonazo*. Courtesy of Fania Records.

Mercedes. Only Larry Harlow and his orchestra also had multiple recordings in the first three years. It wasn't until 1968, when not only Bataan and Colón but Ray Barretto started recording regularly on the label, and when the first incarnation of the Fania All-Stars held its first concert at the Red Garter, that the label took off and was on its way to becoming the predominant force in defining the new musical era of the 1970s.

Cañonazo is still a powerful contribution, capturing as it does the seemingly timeless perfection of the Cuban son montuno from the earlier decades. The resonances of Arsenio Rodríguez, Chappotín, Benny Moré, and other consummate innovators of the 1940s period are everywhere, and many of the tunes of the Nuevo Tumbao are remarkably faithful interpretations of the standards by Cheo Marquetti, La Sonora Matancera, Chappotín, and others. Song after song are displays of Pacheco's mastery of these varied forms of Cuba's incomparable dance music from its golden years, which had been his love since he left the merengue orbit of his apprenticeship playing with his father in the Dominican Republic. The album also includes some compositions that carried symbolic importance for Pacheco's career: "Fania" because it became the title he chose for his fledgling company, and the final cut, "Dakar Punto Final," because it anticipates his long-term relationship to and popularity in West Africa as subsequently attested to in his 1966 album *Viva Africa*.

The Nuevo Tumbao also contained the seeds of Pacheco's programmatically defined project for the Fania label and what he called the "family." *Cañonazo* is all Cuba, the songs filled with evocations of lush tropical landscapes, local references, and historical allusions to national heroes José Martí and Antonio Maceo. There is not a single mention of New York or life in the United States, nor much by way of jazz or other US styles in the music. As Pacheco reiterated in later statements, he was trying to "imitate" the Sonora Matancera sound and repertoire as accurately as possible.[9] At the same time he always also called attention to the "newness" of his tumbao, what he referred to as the "New York" feel, pointing to the foregrounding of the percussive section and the quickened tempo when compared with the original model. "We took the Cuban music and since we grew up in New York and had jazz influences, we modernized certain chords. Instead of being tonic and dominant, we made them more flamboyant. And the rhythm section is more pronounced when we perform."[10]

Despite such disclaimers, Pacheco's idea of "típico" is no doubt strongly traditionalist, averse to any significant adjustments to the original modality, and especially to any substantive influence of non-Cuban models. While the drive toward "típico" was the tenor of the times in the immediate post-pachanga years, Pacheco was perhaps the most orthodox in his insistence on non-divergence from the historical model. Rather than finding Cuba in New York, the music transports us to Cuba, retaining all the linguistic and musical trappings of the sound as developed in its native island setting. While this conservative sensibility was already evident in his block-buster pachanga stage, Pacheco's charanga being much closer to the Cuban model than any of the others, it was in his turn to the son conjunto that traditionalism becomes the predominant quality of the music. And just as he believed in sticking to the tested formula of the classic sound, so he saw his legacy as having introduced the "formula" for salsa. In more recent times, he unequivocally claims the authorship of salsa as a personal achievement: "I want to be remembered because of the basic formula for salsa that I created with El Tumbao. . . . One thing I believe is that once you have a formula, you don't change it."[11]

Pacheco, as co-owner and musical director of Fania Records and perhaps the most influential figure in defining the salsa generation, was not only traditionalist in his relation to the

Cuban background but was also faithful to his own stylistic formula over the decades: eventually he realized that the "nuevo"
he had originally attached to "tumbao" was inaccurate, so that
by 1977 he renamed his band "Pacheco y Su Tumbao Añejo." As
he explained, "Añejo means aged, like a good bottle of wine."[12]

However, while guided by this old-school sensibility, the
course of Fania, and for that matter of "salsa" itself, is not
defined or circumscribed by it. On the contrary, the Fania
catalogue and stable of musicians is remarkably eclectic, com-
prising everything from strictly faithful reproductions of
original standards and stylistic genres to the barely "Latin"
soul sounds of crooners like Joe Bataan and Ralfi Pagán—
and virtually every coloration in between on the Latin pal-
ette. Over the years, a stylistically multi-faceted bandleader
like Ray Barretto constantly sang the praises of Fania and
voiced his gratitude to the label for providing him a space to
do anything he wanted to, and the huge range of his own repertoire bears testament to that flexibility. Whatever critical
perspectives might be in order regarding Fania's gate-keeping
function and exploitative business dealings, the label must
also get credit for diffusing the New York–forged Latin styles
throughout the world and making "salsa" an indispensable
presence in world music.

To some extent Pacheco's fellow founder and head of Fania,
Jerry Masucci, whose love for Cuban music was only outstripped
by his gravitation toward the mainstream and attraction to
crossover possibilities, provided an effective counterbalance to
the deep-seated traditionalism of the musical director. While
Pacheco and Larry Harlow were upholding the típico banner,
Masucci tended to be the main force behind the push for crossovers and rock fusions and the like. Not that Pacheco didn't
also have his eye on the commercial prize and the American
dream; as he was later to say, after harvesting the fruit of Fania's

successes, "What was beautiful about salsa was its glamour. We had class: openings with Rolls Royces, big stretch limousines, big parties and shit like that. The office we had was fantastic. And the people were proud to see Latinos on a par with Americans."[13]

Whatever the ultimate verdict on the influence of Fania, of utmost interest for a historical assessment of the post-pachanga period is the glaring contrast between Pacheco's "new" sound with his Tumbao and the innovations of Eddie Palmieri with La Perfecta occurring in exactly the same years, both musical projects done in the name of "típico." While Pacheco's band reproduces the Cuban models in a way that is technically competent but overly imitative, La Perfecta weaves a striking and creatively novel musical fabric, using mostly original compositions and arrangements while remaining unflinchingly faithful to what Palmieri, Manny Oquendo, and the other band members knew to be the basic structures of the Afro-Cuban tradition. The result has been that La Perfecta was not only the most influential and important band of the period but has retained its dynamic power and relevance down to the present, as evident in the ongoing popularity of Palmieri's La Perfecta II since its founding in 2002. Pacheco's Tumbao on the other hand already seemed passé to many when it began and has had little if any staying power over the decades. Even in the annals of Fania history its appeal has long been overshadowed by the prominence of the Fania All-Stars, which along with his collaborations with Celia Cruz constitute Pacheco's primary musical legacy.

This contrast is of particular historical interest and importance because Eddie Palmieri, indisputably a founding pioneer of the 1960s musical generation, was never part of the Fania project, the principal conduit of this musical production worldwide and protagonist of the accepted narrative of the whole "salsa" phenomenon. The gap between El Nuevo Tumbao and La Perfecta, between the Fania "family" and the dogged individualist burning his own creative path, continues to color the salsa story. The two individuals with the most valid claims to be the originators of that musical modality have diametrically opposite views about its very naming: while Palmieri never tires of pointing to the distortion involved in throwing the many genres and rhythms of Cuban and Afro-Caribbean music into one pot, Pacheco believed that "we should call this salsa and cover the whole thing under one roof. . . . If we put everything under the name salsa, I think it's going to benefit all of us."[14]

3

Boogaloo Soul

In 1966, Pete Rodríguez and his band were playing the Sunday night dances at the Palm Gardens nightclub on 52nd Street, just around the corner from the Palladium. Wherever they played those days there would be a lot of African Americans, dancing and enjoying the Latin sounds. But they'd often ask him to put "a little bit of soul" in the music, just as they would ask Eddie Palmieri for some "azúcar," to make it more danceable for them and familiar to their tastes. At one point Pete was approached by two promoters from Harlem who asked him to write some catchy, Latin-flavored background music to help them in their pitches to get the African American public to go to the Palm Gardens. Pete, trumpeter and songwriter Tony Pabón, and the other band members came up with a demo, called "Pete's Boogaloo," that drew the immediate attention of radio listeners and attracted some to hear them live at the midtown club.[1]

"From that moment on," Pete recalls, "a certain excitement began to occur. We began to experiment with our new discovery at the Sunday night Palm Garden dances."[2] The band noticed that its African American followers would dance a different kind of step to the cha chas and son montunos that were the group's staple, and would call it "boogaloo." The term referred, literally, to the latest dance fad; following in the string of the Twist, the Hully Gully, the Monkey, and other crazes of the day, in 1965 it was the so-called boogaloo that was all the rage. The jerky,

angular moves of the dance were distinctive, as was the boisterous, rollicking sound of the soul party music.

It is generally assumed that the fad started with the single
entitled "Boo-Ga-Loo" by the Chicago soul act Tom and Jerry-o.
On its release in 1965, that 45 and the dance move that accompanied it gave rise to an overnight mania nationwide, and of
course it was hot among the African American dance crowds
at New York clubs. Listening to the original Tom and Jerry-O
single indicates clearly that many of the distinctive features of
Latin boogaloo—the handclapping, the energetic party exhortations, the nervous intensity of the vocals, the frequent use of
colloquial catchphrases, the insistent call-and-response sense
of collective participation—must have come directly from
there and other examples of what is termed "Chicago soul." It
is sometimes referred to as "light soul," perhaps influenced by
early Beatles and by Motown rather than the heavier Memphis
sounds of Aretha Franklin, Otis Redding, and James Brown.
In any case, the founding tune "Boo-Ga-Loo" is an undeni-
able source, whether direct or indirect, for the most distinctive
trappings of New York Latin megahits from "Bang Bang" to "I
Like It Like That"—minus, of course, the percussive and other
trappings of the Latin sound, including the frequent use of
Spanish or Spanglish lyrics. Latin boogaloo is thus a derivate, of
sorts, both musically and culturally, a ricochet off that African
American–based novelty sound of the moment. But by virtue
of creative adjustments and lively cross-cultural blendings, the
Latin version moves beyond its source and comes to create a
thoroughly new musical genre, the equivalent, at a vernacular
level, to Cubop in its time.

The idea was to find a rhythm that would fit those dance
moves, to match the Latin sound to the boogaloo dancing. It
wasn't long before the band—especially their main composer,
trumpeter, and vocalist Tony Pabón—came up with the song

"I Like It Like That," which put them on the map once and for all and went on to become an all-time Latin boogaloo classic. Pete Rodríguez y Su Orquesta became overnight rock stars in the Latin neighborhoods and started getting top billing in clubs across the city, including the Palladium itself. Indeed, they played on the closing night of that historic landmark on May 1, 1966, sharing the billing with Eddie Palmieri and Orquesta Broadway. As the sun set on one musical era it was clearly rising fast on another.

FIGURE 18 The Pete Rodríguez Orchestra, *I Like It Like That*. Courtesy of Fania Records.

The band's first two albums, *Latin Boogaloo* and *I Like It Like That*, came out in 1966 on the Alegre label, which by then was part of Tico. Once again, as with the first recordings of pachanga, Al Santiago played a key role, demonstrating his keen sensitivity to new and emerging styles and cultural sensibilities. Working for Tico at the time, he actively supported and fostered the upstart boogaloo musicians, over the objections of many of his direct contemporaries and long-term musician friends, and without contradicting his own commitment to típico. But despite Santiago's pioneering role, it was another giant of the recording world, George Goldner, who is most responsible for the recording and marketing of the Latin boogaloo sound. In 1965, Goldner founded the Cotique label, the name an inversion of Tico so as to establish the connection, on which he recorded many of the boogaloo artists of the day. Goldner himself was directly involved in identifying and nurturing them in what were generally debut recording opportunities. He had established himself in the popular music field by his "discovery" and initial recording of major doo-wop acts, notably Frankie Lymon and the Teenagers and Little Anthony and the Imperials, on his Roulette label. With Tico he had created the most important label for Latin music, from its founding in the late 1940s until Fania took over the Latin field by the early 1970s. The sequence of consolidations in the industry had Goldner selling Tico to Morris Levy, Al Santiago selling Alegre to Morris Levy where it became part of Tico, and then in 1974 Levy selling Tico and all of its constitutive catalogues to Jerry Masucci. This step-by-step centralization of the industry resulted in the Fania hegemony in the Latin music field and the branding of its various musical styles under the rubric of "salsa."

The Palm Gardens, one of the key settings for the emergence of boogaloo, was a venue of special significance, and not just because of its proximity to the Palladium. It was a huge, two-story space, accommodating over 1,000 patrons in its heyday and attracting entertainment audiences for decades going back to the early 1920s. Aside from its use as a ballroom, the first floor had served as a theater in earlier years, and in the larger upstairs space there were frequent union meetings and historic political speeches by the likes of Fidel Castro in 1955 and Malcolm X in 1964 and 1965. As for music history in the making, in 1957 John Coltrane performed there with Thelonious Monk, and on the days before Christmas, 1967, the Palm Gardens was host to concerts by the Grateful Dead.

Most important to the story of New York Latin music is that on March 28, 1968, the famous Cheetah Club moved into the Palm Gardens building. The Cheetah, which had opened on 53rd Street and Broadway on May 28, 1966, just weeks after the closing of the Palladium, made history when in 1971 it served as the venue for the Fania All-Stars, a concert that became the basis of the film *Our Latin Thing* and is often considered the birthplace of the so-called salsa explosion. The Palm Gardens, though—the Cheetah before it was called that—was the cradle of Latin boogaloo, and most especially at those Sunday night "Black dances." It is more than mere happenstance that in just that context, and during that same year, the Joe Cuba Sextette created its chart-setting boogaloo hit "Bang Bang," and in response to the same coaxing from African American dance audiences.[3] As Latin music historian Max Salazar astutely puts it, "Eddie Palmieri's recording of 'Azúcar' was the reason why Joe Cuba's, Ricardo Ray's, and Pete Rodríguez's bands were contracted to play the same venues."[4]

The boogaloo bands played the whole gamut of venues throughout the city, and once they took off commercially, they traveled frequently to Puerto Rico and Latin America. Indeed, pianist and bandleader Richie Ray recounts an identical story of adaptation of the Latin styles to African American requests while playing at the Basin Street East, another famed Manhattan nightclub, in 1966; it was there that he first heard of and saw the dance craze of the moment and would go on to compose, perform, and record some of the earliest and most memorable Latin boogaloo numbers. But the Palm Gardens was the most frequented and seminal of all the clubs for the inception of that short-lived but significant musical era.

Pete Rodriguez and his band were from the South Bronx, the same Hunts Point streets that were home to so many of the musicians from the pachanga period and earlier. Pete and his brothers, fellow band members Manny and Angel, were—"like a typical Latin New Yorker" as he said, and like his co-band leader Tony Pabón and his long-term bongocero and timbalero Benny Bonilla—born in El Barrio but raised in the increasingly Puerto Rican neighborhoods of the Bronx. They frequented the Tritons and other local clubs, having started out in the late 1950s as a fledgling conjunto struggling to get a start. Pete remembers that Eddie Palmieri brought together a small neighborhood group to play at his wedding in 1954. The group did not play the charanga or pachanga styles in their heyday of the early '60s, but remained a piano and trumpet-led cha cha and son montuno band until their moment came, in 1966. As Pabón tells it, "In early 1966, we kept getting repeated requests from dancers to add a little soul to the music. At that time, nothing similar to the boogaloo was being played by a Latin band, nor was the word 'boogaloo' used. Pete asked me to write music that would please the dance promoters. A week later, I heard Peggy Lee sing 'Fever.' I wrote a tune inspired by the bass lines of 'Fever' and called it 'Pete's Boogaloo.'"[5]

That history-making demo, which was included as the lead-off track on the group's first album entitled *Latin Boogaloo*, offers a representative taste of the new style in the making. Most of the composition is actually a straightforward son montuno highlighting piano, trumpet, and timbales instrumentation, but the lyrics immediately betray the novelty. Though in Spanish, the first lines are "Bailando el bugalú, yeah, el bugaloo galoo yeah." The very use of the word "boogaloo" (and it appears in every line of the brief song text) is probably a first in Latin music, and then its varying pronunciation between the Spanish "bugalú" and English "boogaloo," not to mention the repeated interjection of "yeah," all indicate a bilingual and bicultural circumstance. The musical language conveys the same message: beginning with the bluesy piano solo about a third of the way in, the Latin style is typically broken by interspersed African American sounds, most explicitly when the montunos are suddenly interrupted by boisterous handclapping, the jazzy and r & b piano and trumpet lines, and the street English shouting in the background. Here is where we can hear traces of the Peggy Lee bass line to which the composer alluded. The catchy soneo "Bailando bugalú" keeps coming back and helps retain that strong Afro-Cuban flavor, but by the end the boogaloo effect of handclapping and jazzy trumpet take the tune out.

The same back-and-forth interweaving of verbal and musical languages is what gives texture to the group's biggest hits, "Micaela" and the blockbuster "I Like It Like That." "Micaela" starts off establishing English as the primary spoken language of the performance with a somewhat corny spoken introduction of "Mr. Pete Rodriguez" (in heavy and almost exaggerated English pronunciation), with Pete then announcing in very colloquial terms, "And now from my latest basket of cheers, here it goes, baby!" Though the song's lyrics are again all in Spanish—actually taken from a familiar Miguelito Cuní tune—and the basic rhythm and orchestrations that of son montuno, the musical track this time begins with the handclapping and exclamations "ooh ah ooh ah," identical to the sounds best known from "Bang Bang" and certainly an influence in one direction or other, as it is not possible to determine which recording came first. Following this emphatically boogaloo-inflected beginning, the remainder of the track again alternates languages, with the contagious coro (chorus) "Ay ay ay Micaela se botó" anchoring the Latin sound, and the admiration for the dancing prowess of Micaela, "la reina del bugalú," resonating with the playful stories in some of the familiar pachanga megahits like Pacheco's "El Güiro de Macorina" and "Oyeme Mulata." Here the blending of the musical idioms is somewhat more intricate, the latter half of the song being an extended counterpoint between percussion-based montunos and handclapping, excited shouting, and verbal exhortations like "hurry baby, hurry momma" and "you want more? yeah!"

The balance is tipped even further toward the boogaloo and soul side in the group's biggest hit, perhaps the best-known boogaloo recording of them all, "I Like It Like That." In an earlier writing I referred to the song as "quintessential boogaloo,"[6] pointing to the rich r&b background to the lyrics and the special shifting role of the timbales between Latin and trap-drum formats.[7] Despite its sometimes corny lyrics, the original Pete Rodriguez version of the song—there have been many covers and interpretations—is a masterfully textured piece with infectiously catchy hook-lines and an irresistible joviality. It is guaranteed to liven up any party and to lend a party feel to any occasion.

The other major overnight boogaloo sensation, whose group is also credited with originating the style in New York's Latin music, is Richie Ray (Richard Maldonado Morales). Classically trained at piano from an early age and long-term collaborator with vocalist Bobby Cruz, Richie Ray and his band were natives of Brooklyn and were strongly identified with that borough. Indeed, as complemented by the influential presence of Brooklyn-based producer, promoter, and club-owner Ralph

Mercado, Ray helped put the long-neglected Brooklyn scene on the map of the city's Latin music. The spacious St. George Hotel and the famously jumping "3-and-1 Club" were but the best known of the many venues in the borough, which had long been home to sizable Puerto Rican and other Latino communities since the earliest years of the migration and settlement. Though direct contemporaries of the Pete Rodriguez band, and having turned to boogaloo under similar circumstances, Richie Ray y Su Conjunto created a quite different sound and experimented with distinctive kinds of fusion and crossover.

Though Ray had already recorded several albums prior to his boogaloo breakthrough, in 1966 he came out with two historic LPs with Alegre/Tico that contain all of his recorded contributions to the genre. Interestingly, he decided against going with Fania because in his estimation the company didn't have it together at that time. The first, titled *Se Soltó/On the Loose*, includes what he and others sometimes regard as the first boogaloo, "Lookie Lookie," a gentle, simple song with the refrain, "How I do the boogaloo." Sung in English with a slight Spanish accent, there is here none of the rowdiness of the Pete Rodriguez or Joe Cuba numbers. Only a carefully timed shift to a faster tempo in the latter part of the song veers at all from the sauntering pace of the piano, trumpet, and timbales and mild celebration of the new dance, learned in New York and conveyed to other places—in this case, "old Mexico."[8] What stands out strikingly in the Richie Ray version of the boogaloo is the sheer quality of the piano work, especially as contrasted with that of Pete Rodriguez, Johnny Colón, and other exponents of the genre. Ray pays tribute to one of his masters, Noro Morales, in his "Suite Noro Morales" on this album, and often expressed his reverence for Charlie Palmieri, two of the foremost pianists in the Latin music genre. Also featuring the confident vocals of Bobby Cruz and Chivirico Dávila and the masterful trumpet part by Doc Cheatham and Richie's brother Ray, the album contains some gems of the Latin canon, such as "Danzón Boogalú," "El Señor Embajador," and "Azucaré y Bongó."

Many of these songs, along with those of his second album from the boogaloo period, *Jala Jala y Boogaloo* (1967), have become standards of "salsa clásica"; indeed, the opener and title number of the latter collection, "Richie's Jala Jala," which comprises a heartfelt salute to Puerto Rico, has long been the theme song of the main salsa radio station on the Island. It also established the jala jala as the Spanish language offshoot of the boogaloo repertoire, as was in other ways the shingaling. Both albums display an impressive range of stylistic options, from guaguancó (a subgenre of Cuban rumba) and son montuno to inventive jazzy versions of danzón, Puerto Rican bomba, and Cuban mozambique. In "Colombia's Boogaloo" the band salutes that country where they came to be idolized for many years by serving as ambassadors of the boogaloo style: "Colombia tiene su bugalú, yeah yeah."

What the two albums demonstrate is that while the boogaloo craze helped to jumpstart the group's career (and that of their main contemporaries), and though many songs contain the word in their lyrics or titles, the typical earmarks of boogaloo, like English words, party noises, and handclapping, constitute only one aspect of their overall production. Richie Ray and Bobby Cruz went on to successful salsa careers and became widely admired, especially in Puerto Rico and Latin America, though they are likely to remain best known for their association with Latin boogaloo. No sooner did the craze take off than the band transcended its local and apprentice status to gain a place at the lofty Palladium and other prominent venues, where they shared the billing with giants of the stature of Tito Puente, Tito Rodríguez, and Eddie Palmieri. The rapid hype, and the widespread disparagement of boogaloo among the tastemakers and gatekeepers, have tended to eclipse and obscure the accomplished and fresh offerings of a skilled young band.

The other two of the best-known boogaloo bands, those of Johnny Colón and Joe Cuba, stem from and were based in El Barrio, the historic Manhattan neighborhood of the Puerto Rican community. The diverse home turfs of the four groups—two from Manhattan and one each from the Bronx and Brooklyn—attest to one important difference between the boogaloo craze and its predecessor by a few years, the pachanga. While the pachanga was rooted in the South Bronx and incubated in the small clubs of the Hunts Point section, the boogaloo was an all-city phenomenon, the expression of the up-and-coming Nuyorican generation throughout the city and beyond, and more integrally connected than was the pachanga with the cultural expression of other youth from the neighborhood. This broader reach and point of reference may explain why it was the midtown Palm Gardens rather than a smaller local venue that saw the concoction of the new style.

Of the best-known boogaloo bands, it was perhaps that of Johnny Colón that has least successfully stood the test of time. While one song, "Boogaloo Blues," was a spectacular overnight hit and an integral part of the fever when it came out on his album of that title in 1967, it is the only composition by which the group is widely remembered, perhaps because it disbanded within a year. Nevertheless, "Boogaloo Blues" with all its musical shortcomings remains a valuable cultural document of its times, and there are good reasons that it stands as an anthem of sorts for the whole boogaloo experience. As I have pointed out, the music industry had more to do with the fashioning of the composition in this case than any response to the dancers, but here more than in any other of the boogaloo classics, the Nuyorican youth experience is related to the countercultural tenor of the late 1960s.[9] Only the Lebrón Brothers, with their first album entitled *Psychedelic Goes Latin* and their song "Let's Get Stoned," signal the involvement of that generation of young Latinos in the "sex, drugs and rock 'n roll" excitement of the times. With its chorus "LSD got a hold on me" and repetition of the phrase "let's be free," "Boogaloo Blues" uses the discursive space opened up by the crossover style to refer to aspects of the youth culture often erased from the historical record. In addition, Colón adds to the Latino-African American intercultural connection by bringing out not just the r&b and soul dimensions, but with Colón's piano work, the deeper relation to blues and jazz. His partners and band members Tito Ramos and Tony Rojas, Harlem street-corner harmonizers, assure a strong soul sound as well, so that the characteristic influence of US Black musical culture on the forging of a boogaloo style is evident.

The main legacy of Johnny Colón's efforts, aside from the song itself, is his valiant initiative to found and maintain the East Harlem Music School, which has helped keep culturally informed music instruction available to youth in El Barrio. Colón also deserves credit for his bold outspokenness in recounting the troubling conditions behind the "assassination" of boogaloo by what he called the "Coalition" of promoters, radio DJs and resentful bandleaders who orchestrated the sidelining of the inexperienced upstarts from the musical limelight.[10] The subsequent musical careers of Tito and Tony were of some note as well; after breaking with Johnny Colón they formed the TNT Band and had some minor Latin soul hits on their album *Meditation*, notably the title song and their popular "Mr. Slick." Here perhaps more than in "Boogaloo Blues" they were able to articulate in a more grounded way the intense Black-Latin fusion at play in the cultural experiences of working-class Nuyorican youth in Harlem.

But the most prominent, representative, and enduring of the East Harlem boogaloo bands was that of Joe Cuba. The Joe

Cuba Sextet was actually the band that created, performed, and recorded the bestselling and most popular of all boogaloos, namely "Bang Bang," "El Pito," and a few others. Compared with the other boogaloo groups, this band had a much longer life span and musical range than boogaloo. The sextet, all of whose members had grown up in El Barrio during the 1940s and '50s, first came together in the mid-1950s as an incarnation of the Harlem-based Joe Panama band, and by the end of that decade the group had become well known in many venues for their fiery fast mambos and slow love ballads, many of them with English lyrics. In fact, Joe Cuba's group, and its vocalists Willie Torres and Jimmy Sabater, is generally considered the first Latin band to sing in English, over a decade before the boogaloo and Latin soul made it common practice.[11] They are also the first major band that, from the outset, and perhaps because of their strong roots in East Harlem, contributed to linking the core Latin styles with the cultural expression of African Americans. The issue of race and Blackness is, explicitly or by implication, often at the forefront of their work—as evident, for example, in their popular number, sung by Jimmy Sabater, "Y Tu Abuela, Dónde Está?"; the song's title and subject matter are based on the proverbial response to the denial of African ancestry common in Puerto Rican culture: as the well-known saying would have it (to paraphrase), "you claim to be of pure Spanish ancestry, but where are you hiding your (Black) grandma?"

The sextet had an early hit song in "Mambo of the Times" from the mid-'50s and modest successes with their early-'60s album *Steppin Out*, which contained the paramount Latin soul classic "To Be with You," composed by Willie Torres and immortalized in the version sung by Jimmy Sabater. It also included the forceful son montuno "Salsa y Bembé," sung by the rising star of the group, premier vocalist Cheo Feliciano, and prophetic because of its early use of the word "salsa" in the title. Many consider their 1963 album *Vagabundeando (Hangin Out)*, with Cheo in top form in nearly all the cuts, their crowning artistic achievement. But it was in 1966 that they reached the peak of their commercial success with the megahits in the boogaloo mode. Interestingly, despite the group's canonical status, none of their songs actually use the word "boogaloo" in either titles or lyrics, and "El Pito" even pre-dated the emergence of so-called Latin boogaloo by a year or so when it appeared on the 1965 album *Estamos Haciendo Algo Bien*. The only specifically boogaloo album was *Bang Bang Push Push*, and even there only a few of the eleven selections are boogaloos by any stretch of the term. Indeed, "Bang Bang" stands out as such a vintage example of the stylistic modality and social circumstances of Latin boogaloo that that song alone establishes the group's paramount place in the history of the genre. The unprecedented sales of that single and of "El Pito" added further to their prominence, each of those songs rising high on the Billboard charts and setting sales records for New York Latin music to that time.

As previously mentioned and analyzed, "Bang Bang" epitomizes the boogaloo circumstances by being composed in response to African American dance and musical tastes at the Palm Gardens ballroom. In this case, even more than with Pete Rodríguez or Richie Ray, the songs are actually celebrations of the cultural convergence between New York Puerto Ricans and African Americans during those years of the escalating civil rights movement.[12] And the studio session and recorded product was an attempt to emulate or enact the atmosphere and creative moment of the song's live performance.

The production of "El Pito," the band's other signature hit that actually preceded "Bang Bang," is equally interesting, and not just because of the whistles that the band would give out at live performances as a playful gimmick to get the dancers and listening public involved. Sonny (Joe Cuba's nickname, itself a nickname for Gilbert Calderón) recounts in colorful terms how the song was made. The piano vamp is based on a melody taken from Tito Puente's "Oye Como Va" and then used by Charlie Palmieri as a sign-off; the refrain "I'll never go back to Georgia" was from a line by Dizzy Gillespie in "Manteca"; and the sound of whistles in the song were provided by composer/percussionist Heny Alvarez. The whole composition was put together hastily in a recording session just as the allotted studio time was running out. With pianist Nick Jiménez playing the vamp over and over, Sonny recalls, "I got Heny Alvarez, Willie Torres, Jimmy Sabater and the singers doing the coros and I said, 'Go in the booth and sing the chorus, "Así se goza." Make all kinds of noise, stomp your feet, clap your hands. This is going to be a party record.'"[13]

"'El Pito' was created in the studio," Sonny continues. "I call it a studio hit. It was done by guys who went impromtu. It's a Frankenstein tune, because all the parts came out of nowhere."[14] Nobody expected the unprecedented success of the song. Like Ray Barretto's "El Watusi" of a few years earlier, it was really a B-side that caught on and went viral. The method of production brought out and benefited from the unschooled (though highly seasoned) nature of the band personnel. "We always kept doing things over and over till we got what we really wanted, what I call a bastard sound. It wasn't orchestrated by any particular composer or anybody who was really musically inclined, because we all did it by ear. In other words, we all took all the notes off the top of our head and put them together and that's where we got that sound from."[15]

What this improvisational, on-the-spot, collective method of composition illustrates is that an important aspect of the boogaloo style is its descarga quality. The improvisational pastiche effect is the result of jamming and making things up on the spot, either in live performance or in the studio. In that sense the Joe Cuba experience is perhaps the most faithful continuation of the work of the Alegre All-Stars: here again, experienced musicians get together and play spontaneously, without arrangements and charts, the result counting for its effect on the very roughness and jocularity of the recording moment left intact, though in a deliberate way. Composed of the patchwork alternation between and among musical languages and rhythmic concepts, many boogaloo songs, and the very aesthetics of boogaloo and Latin soul, illustrate this descarga sensibility and can best be appreciated as part of that lineage within the Latin music tradition. In fact, Willie Torres, who had been a vocalist with the Alegre All-Stars until they chose to start using arrangements, moved back to the Joe Cuba group (he had been part of the original group in the 1950s) for precisely that reason: he preferred the informal, improvisational mode as being most in tune with his jazz-inspired and jamming creativity.

Though he and his band members were a decade or more older than most of the other boogaloo musicians, Joe Cuba articulated the meaning and aesthetic sense of that elusive style in clear and appropriately goofy terms, slyly mocking without being dismissive. "Boogaloo is a simple Simon rhythm, so to speak. And it's an Americanized sound that you can beat out with your fingers. It's not a Latin feel. In the boogaloo you're playing on the backbeat. That was one of the keys to our success." The legendary, irreverent bandleader explains why he and his group were ideally qualified for playing Latin music while grounding themselves in an "American" musical aesthetic. "The American-born were the proponents of boogaloo. Latin bands couldn't play it as well. You had to have the American influence to get into that bag. I'm 'Rican all the way. My bones are 'Rican, my food is 'Rican. But I was born with the American Hit Parade."[16]

Playing in the boogaloo mode came naturally to the bicultural Harlem-raised group, who grew up with both the vernacular Latin

FIGURE 19 The Joe Cuba Sextette. Courtesy of Izzy Sanabria.

and African American styles as their everyday musical diet. Indeed, it was so natural to them that they found it difficult to explain the specific musical components and principles of the style. As Sonny put it, "I still don't understand the boogaloo musically, and I was very successful with it. I can play the hell out of it, but there really was no musical aspect in it. It was like a lyric and a flow, a crossover type of feel where the rhythm and blues mixed with Latin rhythms."[17] Despite the difference in age and musical experience between them and the other well-known boogaloo practitioners, the Joe Cuba Sextet was no doubt the model, both musically and as bearers of a cultural style, of that sixties generation, and came to exert the greatest influence on the upcoming groups.

Of the bands that built on the foundation laid by the four major groups (those of Pete Rodríguez, Richie Ray, Johnny Colón, and Joe Cuba), the Brooklyn-based Lebrón Brothers are the most fascinating and have had by far the greatest longevity of them all. The original group of five brothers and some friends was literally born of the boogaloo era, recorded three albums in that mode, and then went on performing and recording through the years; they are still touring internationally, are avidly accessed on the Internet and in live performance, and are planning further releases. They make no claim to be the "first" to play boogaloo but rather built on the breakthrough hits and readily identify the Joe Cuba Sextet as their major influence. Their own compositions, though original and creative, are replete with allusions to and traces of the better-known boogaloo tunes.

The Black, working-class Lebrón family moved to New York from the city of Aguadilla, on the west coast of Puerto Rico, in the early 1950s, settling in the impoverished neighborhood of Williamsburg, Brooklyn. Most of the six children were either very young on arrival or were born in New York; the oldest sibling, Pablo, was raised on the Island and was active, there and after arriving at seventeen, as a singer in a trio. His strong tenor voice, reared in son montuno and bolero, graces many of the most successful of the group's songs, and his presence was key to assuring the use of Spanish lyrics and a ready knowledge of the Afro-Cuban and Latin stylistic traditions. The other brothers, José, Angel, Carlos, and Frankie, each learned and became proficient at a different instrument and sang coro. The group also included friends who added other valuable components, notably Elliot Rivera and Jack Soul for the English vocals and lyrics, and African American sax player and songwriter Gabe Gill, who served as a kind of senior mentor for the whole effort.

Prior to breaking into the boogaloo scene and market, the brothers and friends sang doo-wop and r&b, opening in many venues for some of the stellar groups of the times. They got their break one night in 1967 when they opened for Johnny Colón, who introduced them to George Goldner and Cotique records. Goldner had a good initial impression of the group and liked their sound, but he objected to their singing only covers of other people's repertoire and felt they needed their own songs. They scheduled an audition for a week later, and immediately set to work on their own compositions. José Lebrón, the group's pianist, assumed primary responsibility and came up with seven of the eight tunes for the first album. Goldner was delighted with the new repertoire and promptly produced their debut album, *Psychedelic Goes Latin*. The initial release was followed in 1968 by *Brooklyn Bums* and in the following year by *I Believe*.

The first two of these albums contain what must be regarded, in retrospect, as some of the most accomplished and innovative examples of the boogaloo genre, building as they explicitly do on both the son montuno and doo-wop traditions, while reflecting intelligently and in eminently danceable formats on the style itself. The very first number, "Summertime Blues," was their breakthrough hit and sets the standard with its contagious appeal to the funky Latin improvisations and easy alternation between Latin and r&b languages. "Tall Tale," also from *Psychedelic Goes Latin*, recounts a miniature history of 1960s dance fads and places boogaloo and shingaling (used interchangeably) in that lineage. The blending of Latin and funk here is seamless, the tune's slow-to-medium tempo hitting a relaxed groove for dancers of either style. The repertoire varies, including some memorable love ballads in the style of "To Be with You" and sung by accomplished vocalist Pablo, as well as some countercultural rock and roll narratives (in the manner of "Boogaloo Blues") in the compositions "The Village Chant" and "Let's Get

Stoned." There are also resonances of Pete Rodriguez/Tony Pabon's "Micaela" and Richie Ray's "Lookie Lookie" in "Mary, Mary," and of Joe Bataan's social message in a song like "Money Can't Buy Love" from *The Brooklyn Bums*.

Over the intervening years the Lebrón Brothers have produced a steady stream of albums, more than thirty in all, twenty of them on the Cotique label. In the process they have amassed dozens of songs, especially popular in Colombia, England, and a broad international market. They long ago left the boogaloo mode behind, finding, as José puts it in retrospect, that there was only so much that could be done with that limited set of techniques, creating songs instead within a very broadly defined "salsa" idiom.[18] Among that prolific output, they are and will likely remain best known for their album and title single "Salsa y Control." The recording was released in 1970, just as Fania was consolidating its predominant position in the creation of the salsa category, and on the early death, in April of that year, of the group's producer and main sponsor in the industry, George Goldner. The release of "Salsa y Control" also followed the marginalization of everything having to do with boogaloo within Latin music, including radio play, performance billings, and record promotion, and the Lebrón Brothers were easily dismissed as just another boogaloo band. As was their experience generally, the group found that their work was promoted unenthusiastically if at all, and as a result sales and exposure were not what they could have been.

But "Salsa y Control" and the move of the group beyond boogaloo provide valuable insight into the emergence of salsa and the period just before the baptism of the term in the early-mid 1970s. The song "Salsa y Control," though catchy and enjoying a huge fan following, is a fairly straightforward dance tune based on a son montuno rhythm and swing with a strong percussive grounding and confident vocal improvisation. Its fascination is the use of the word "salsa" to characterize a kind of music, and the pairing of that term with the word "control." Alternating with synonymous phrases "sabor" and "la llave," the song's lyrics establish a kind of balance or dialectic between jamming and organization, between freedom and structure, a concept that becomes axiomatic when considering the guiding principles of a salsa aesthetic. The tune's composer José Lebrón tells that he initially didn't want to record the song, which was such a free-wheeling descarga that it seemed to him still unfinished.[19] But then he was convinced that it should be in the album and would be a hit, so he set to giving it greater coherence and formulated the idea of "control" as a dimension of the music-making that serves to counterbalance the sense of freedom and unbridled spontaneity. So suggestive was the notion that Angel Quintero Rivera—perhaps not making the direct association—titled his important book on "tropical music" "salsa, sabor y control."

The Lebrón Brothers were also important to an understanding of the boogaloo phenomenon because of issues of race: they were the only explicitly Black band, their membership and following being overwhelmingly of African descent, whether Latino or African American. While they did not describe themselves in terms of Blackness and are quick to point out that the band also had lighter-skinned members, that reality was a central conditioning factor in the social experience of the family, and it also had a bearing on their musical tastes and fortunes. On various occasions they faced discrimination, at times overt, as when they were turned away by the management of the Casablanca Club because they would attract "beer-drinkers and not whisky drinkers"—in other words, the "wrong kind of people."[20]

Though they are not generally disposed to raise the issue, their marginalization within the music industry might well have something to do with their racial identity and humble social origins, as they were at no point included within the Fania family,

FIGURE 20 The Lebrón Brothers, ca. 1968. John Storm Roberts Collection, Photos and Prints Division, Schomburg Center, New York Public Library.

even as "poor relations." As Izzy Sanabria reflected on the Lebrón Brothers in a 1979 article, "The Lebron Brothers were a reflection of that time. Dark-skinned and bi-lingual, they represented the Rican with an afro. The Rican that was caught between two worlds, 'Black' and 'Latin.' The very things that made them successful, their funk and feeling, held them back and made them undesirable in certain clubs. . . . The Lebron Brothers never conformed to the standards of club owners who resented the prietos (Blacks) con afros."[21] Some of this experience may find expression in their highly popular song from 1982, whose title tells it all: "Sin Negros No Hay Guaguancó." Interestingly, the song's lyrics include in their naming of the Afro-based musical genres not only the Cuban rumba guaguancó but Afro-Puerto Rican bomba and plena as well. In any case, the deep irony of the Lebrón Brothers is that as early proponents of the word "salsa" to describe the music, they barely even draw a mention in the master narrative of salsa history.

Latin Soul Lives On

"The Boogaloo may have been killed off, but Latin Soul lived on."[22] As well-known Latin music historian Max Salazar explains in his valuable article "Afro-American Latinized Rhythms," Latin boogaloo was but one relatively brief though important episode in the larger story of the crossovers and fusions between New York's Afro-Cuban based Latin music and a range of African American musical styles, what John Storm Roberts suggestively refers to as "the Latin-jazz-R&B fusion."[23] The boogaloo mode flared up in 1966, was all the rage in 1967 and '68, went rapidly on the wane, and by 1969 was history. Latin soul, on the other hand, if understood expansively as all intersections of "Latin" and African American vernacular musical styles, boasts a long tradition ranging back to earlier in the twentieth century and proceeding to the present; it spans many musical styles from jazz at various historical stages to big band and show tunes to doo-wop, r&b, rock and roll, disco, and hip-hop. In diverse and complex ways, this sequence and spectrum of stylistic changes and innovations is ultimately expressive of the social interaction between US Latinos and African Americans in the New York setting.

Within this larger trajectory, which reached a watershed in the period of Cubop during the 1940s, it is also helpful to mark off Latin soul from Latin jazz, both historically and in terms of musical practice and style. Latin soul, which may (or may not) be viewed as a subset within the Latin jazz continuum, refers to the vernacular dimensions of both the Latin and especially the African American traditions, generally grounded in community and popular dance cultures, often practiced by self-taught or "unlettered" musicians, and more directly conditioned by current musical tastes and commercial interests. Latin jazz, on the other hand, involves the generally more "sophisticated" (for lack of a better word) musical practices and stylistic repertoires of trained Latin and jazz musicians and audiences, whose artistic innovations tend to transpire at a greater remove from the mass audiences of localized communities and popular tastes as defined by the music industry and as manifested in its string of short-lived fads and crazes.

It is a precarious demarcation, to be sure, as the boundaries are always porous and both traditions share strong roots in the blues and the Cuban son, swing and mambo, bebop and cha cha chá, respectively. If we are speaking, with Salazar, of "Afro-American Latinized rhythms," the two bleed into each other and form part of one rich, multifarious story. But the fusions orchestrated by Mario Bauzá and Dizzy Gillespie, for instance, or by the members of the Fort Apache Band, are different from the cha cha- and son montuno-inflected doo-wops and shingalings of the mid-sixties upstarts from the inner-city barrios. Latin soul refers to that cultural intersection in the vernacular register, and if we take soul in its more circumscribed sense, to that crossover as it played out when soul music and funk prevailed in African American popular music, that is, the 1960s and early 1970s. The use of English lyrics in Latin songs is surely an indicator of that shift, which began as early as the 1940s; became more common in the 1950s, with the Joe Cuba band and his longtime vocalist Willie Torres breaking the ground in this respect; and then becoming ubiquitous during the 1960s. From the African American side, the flirtation with the "tropical" sound evident since the 1930s then culminates in the torrent of "mambos" and "cha chas" of the 1950s. Nat King Cole's beloved Spanish-language versions of countless American and Latin standards made for a towering influence along this line of the so-called Latin tinge, as did, in the Latin to African American direction, Pérez Prado's hyped-up mambos and Tito Puente's virtuosic percussive feats on the timbales and vibes.

Latin soul in this historically more focused sense starts in the early 1960s, with Ray Barretto's smash hit "El Watusi," Mongo Santamaría's "Latinized" version of Herbie Hancock's "Watermelon Man," and Willie Torres's Latin soul ballad "To Be with You" generally considered the primary pre-boogaloo examples of the vernacular Latin–African American fusion. All three of these recordings, along with the early albums of percussionist Willie Bobo, another Latin soul proponent, date from the beginning years of the decade, which coincides directly with the first use of the generic term "soul music." It was during the charanga-pachanga phase of New York Latin music, the first "Nuyorican" generation (before it went by that name, of course), that the intense interaction took hold, as examples began to proliferate in both directions. While Johnny Pacheco's torrid pachangas from the beginning of the decade evidenced little African American influence, Charlie Palmieri's charangas did more so, and Ray Barretto's and Mongo Santamaría's were in some instances patchworks of Afro-Cuban and African American musical languages—not to mention Eddie Palmieri's revolutionary "trombanga" sound culminating in "Azúcar," with its immense appeal to African American dance audiences, or perhaps even more relevantly, the enormous popularity of Joe

Cuba's strongly African American inflected cha chas and bole-ros even prior to the boogaloo years. Bearing perhaps strongest testimony to that intercultural sharing in Harlem and other Black and Latino neighborhoods of the time, as mentioned earlier, were the versatile Harlem bands, led or constituted by African American musicians but including Latin music promi-nently in their repertoire, with Pucho Brown, Hugo Dixon, and Joe Panama standing out as the most frequently mentioned examples. Significantly, Pucho Brown named his band, which over forty years later is still playing regularly, the Latin Soul Brothers.[24]

By 1965, as the momentum of the civil rights movement continued to build, the social rapprochement between New York's Latinos and African Americans at a local level increased accord-ingly, as evident in the greater frequency of shared cultural and entertainment venues and occasions including the "Black dances" at the major clubs and ballrooms. The mutual influence was tangible and direct, stemming from the performer-audience and music-dance interplay, and the adaptation was more than just fitting the music texture to choreographic movement—as recounted by Tony Pabón, Richie Ray, and Joe Cuba—but was obviously one of musical familiarity as well.

Strictly speaking, then, Latin boogaloo was music that evi-denced those identifiable qualities, as was the case in the rep-ertoire of a wide range of musicians and bands, including many who openly disavowed or disdained everything that went by that name. Eddie Palmieri, Tito Puente, Charlie Palmieri, Joe Bataan, Tito Rodríguez, Ray Barretto, Machito, Johnny Pacheco, Willie Colón—they and many other non- or anti-boogaloo per-formers all played and recorded their boogaloos and shingal-ings. Indeed, some of them are considered among the finest examples of the style, most prominently the song "Ay Qué Rico" by Eddie Palmieri, often called the best boogaloo ever (though it's actually a shingaling) even though Palmieri openly and disdainfully attacked the style as a fatal setback for Latin music. (Famously, he once quipped, "Boogaloo sounds like something you find in a Frosted Flakes box.") As long as it shows those recognizable signs, as in "Bang Bang" and "Micaela," it's a boogaloo. On the other hand, one can speak more broadly of a "boogaloo era," meaning that any and all examples of Latin music of those years showing the influence of African American vernacular song styles is part of boogaloo as a kind of cultural sensibility.

In this sense then, Latin soul of the time was part of "boogaloo" whether it demonstrated any specifically boogaloo traits or not, including of course the many soulful Latin ballads by artists like Joey Pastrana, King Nando, and Ralfi Pagán. Joe Bataan and Willie Colón, both of whom (for different reasons) declined to identify with boogaloo per se and as a designation, are sometimes grouped with the boogaloo artists of their early years. The term "boogaloo" became the point of gravitation for that brief interlude, the brand name that struck a chord and became the magnet for any musical endeavor that sought commercial success or popular enthusiasm.

But in spite of the enormous sway that the boogaloo fever held over Latin music of the immediate era, Latin soul should not be subsumed under that fleeting banner even when thus historically circumscribed. It is clearly a much larger, multigenerational process, one not contingent on short-lived branding and fad designations, and which both preceded and survived the life span of the craze itself. This is not to demean or diminish the significance of Latin boogaloo, for even though it was for various reasons a flash-in-the-pan phenomenon, it helped to bring the rich creative field of Latin–African American musical cross-fertilization to the forefront of contemporary possibilities, and in this sense it paved the way for its immediate successor, salsa. If it can arguably be said that without boogaloo there would have been no salsa as we have come to know it, critical emphasis needs to go to Latin soul as an integral and foundational dimension of what is meant by salsa in the years since the term gained currency. As we will see, it was that dimension of late 1960s Latin music that came to be sidelined by the típico orthodoxy of the Fania formula and its larger project.

Around 1973 Joe Bataan called it "salsoul," thus fusing the most familiar generic terms for Latin and African American vernacular music, salsa and soul, in a single catchy neologism. Though his name inevitably comes up whenever talk is of boogaloo, and he has even been prominently and affectionately called "Boogaloo Bad Boy,"[25] Bataan flatly disavows the term, considering it a demeaning reduction of an expansive cultural and musical field of expressive possibilities to a commercially (and perhaps racially) laden catchphrase, and of the creative experiment itself to a kind of Latin bubblegum music. He was strongly on the side of his contemporary boogaloo musicians in standing up to their powerful adversaries and didn't agree with established promoters, DJs, and bandleaders. But he was aware of how it could be so dismissed if extracted from its wider historical context. As we shall see in subsequent chapters, "Salsoul" was taken as the name of a record label, best known for its many disco releases in the later 1970s, but whose catalogue came to incorporate a wide range of genres including Bataan's own music of that period. It never caught on as a recognized term for Latin soul but does capture the experience in a more inclusive way than boogaloo. It is perhaps especially apt for Bataan's own location on the Latin–African American continuum, since his starting point and musical stronger suit is clearly r&b and soul music, with the Latin features adding another quality to the central trunk so as to capture that essentially bicultural cultural reality. It's salsoul: soul, in a sense, wrapped in salsa.

The Joe Bataan story is a familiar one, without ceasing to amaze. On the one hand, it is idiosyncratic—his father was Filipino, his mother African American, and he grew up among Nuyoricans (New York Puerto Ricans) in El Barrio. Yet it is at the same time archetypal—he was a street gang youth, served prison time at age fifteen, was a self-taught piano player and vocalist, then had a star-studded musical career that has brought him an avid worldwide following for nearly fifty years. This young, strident Afro-Filipino Nuyorican came up musically in the midst of the boogaloo era, and after a stinging initial rejection by Al Santiago and Alegre signed with Jerry Masucci and Fania Records for his first LP in 1967. His cover of the Impressions' 1961 r&b hit "Gypsy Woman" brought him immediate fame and at that point the most sizable record sales in the Fania catalogue, exceeded then by his classic 1968 LP *Riot!* The latter title, and many of his most beloved songs like "Subway Joe," "Ordinary Guy," and "What Good Is a Castle," demonstrate a degree of social commentary and attentiveness to contemporary political conditions and struggles unknown in much Latin music of the day. The title song "Riot!" for example, with its blaring police sirens and sounds of inner-city upheaval, evokes the urban uprisings of the later 1960s.

Bataan recorded eight albums with Fania, though he never was at home in the salsa field nor an integral and accepted member of the Fania stable. (Repeatedly he emphasized that his example as a bandleader was Eddie Palmieri.) Indeed, he wasn't even invited to the first Fania All-Stars concert at the Red Garter in 1968 (even though several non-Fania Latin standardbearers from Tico Records like Palmieri and Tito Puente were), nor in fact was he ever included in any other All-Stars configurations. As we shall discuss further along, by 1973 Bataan left Fania and turned to the newly forming Mericana (renamed Salsoul) label for his subsequent releases. His dissonant relation to the Fania

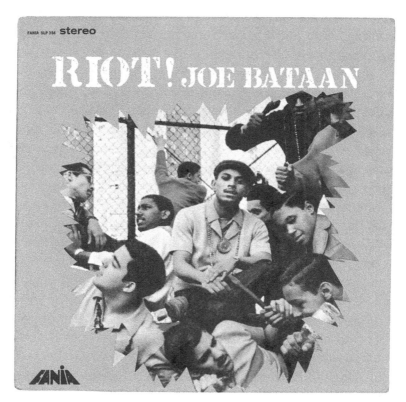

FIGURE 21 Joe Bataan, *Riot!* Courtesy of Fania Records.

project and outsider status among its roster of stars, despite his continuing commercial and popular success, indicates a major rift in the emergence of what came to be called salsa. And it was a divide that was not about ethnic difference—after all, Fania mainstay Larry Harlow and fellow all-star Barry Rogers were Jewish, not to mention the company's founding owner, Dominican Johnny Pacheco. Rather, the difference had to do with divergent musical concepts and intentions. It was also about ethical integrity and Bataan's streetwise wariness of commercial exploitation and refusal to be deprived of his contractually stipulated earnings. He recounts proudly that he was the first big-selling Fania artist to make the break, though of course not the last. But more about those divergences later.

Although he has enjoyed a long career extending to the present, in his beginnings Bataan helped define New York's Latin sound at the end of the 1960s, the period between boogaloo and salsa, without himself fitting neatly into either of those playlists. His songs were an integral part of the soundscape of those years, being adored by many working-class Nuyorican and African American youth at the time of the emerging Young Lords and Nuyorican cultural movements; in more recent years he has enjoyed his status as a featured "oldies" artist, wildly popular among Chicano audiences in Los Angeles and "acid jazz" fans internationally, especially in England. Like the Lebrón Brothers and more than any other repertoire and sound of the time, Bataan embodied and captured the social life of the struggling communities and the ordinary poor folk who rarely make an appearance or are given voice even in the most popular and politically conscious musical expression. Only in the rubric of Latin soul, in a lineage from Mongo Santamaria and Willie Bobo to Joe Cuba, Joey Pastrana, and Jimmy Castor, does Bataan consider himself truly at home. He also helped carry the Latin soul tradition further through his identification with Latin disco and the Latin hustle during the 1970s, and even boasts a very early rap recording with his 1979 hit "Rap-o Clap-o." Tellingly, this post-Fania part of Joe Bataan's career, which I return to in the final chapter, remains largely unexplored in the annals of Latin music history.

If Joe Bataan holds the uncontested title of "King of Latin Soul," that of the anointed "Queen of Latin Soul," the one-and-only La Lupe, may raise more questions. Lupe Yoli, also called La Lupe or La Yiyiyi, surfaced as a major name in

New York Latin music of the 1960s when first introduced by Mongo Santamaría in a range of performances and the 1963 recording, *Mongo Introduces La Lupe*. It was her collaborative recordings with Tito Puente in the following years that brought her unprecedented recognition and notoriety for her thrilling, daring shows in many New York venues. La Lupe was of course most famous for powerful boleros about her dramatic relationship with the "Mambo King," some of them like

FIGURE 22 Lupe, *Queen of Latin Soul*. Courtesy of Fania Records.

"Puro Teatro" and "La Tirana" written specifically for her by the renowned Puerto Rican composer Tite Curet Alonso. She enjoyed an unusually diverse repertoire and range, singing everything from guaracha, mambo, bolero, guaguancó, plena, cumbia, and more, as well as boogaloo and Latin soul with a thick but endearing Spanish accent.

In 1967 at the height of the boogaloo era she was labeled the "Queen of Latin Soul," probably by the record producer for Tico Records Pancho Cristal, but according to other accounts, by Tito Puente himself. On two albums from those years, *La Lupe Queen of Latin Soul* and Tito Puente and La Lupe, *The King and I*, La Lupe belts out wrenching versions of "Fever" and the boogaloo "Streak-o-Lean." The productions generally lack the excitement and expertise of the better-known recordings in the genre, but the mood typical of the most popular party boogaloos is very much there, and captured in her energetic, bilingual voice. Whether or not the royal title is justified, since she is obviously not directly representative of the Latin soul experience, La Lupe's recordings certainly bear witness to the ubiquity of the stylistic mode at that time and the expansiveness of those emergent musical categories. La Lupe demonstrates that it is possible for a bold newcomer and relative outsider to join in and contribute to the style.

La Lupe's turbulent life and sad ending after being eclipsed in the Fania stable by Celia Cruz are the stuff of legend, and indeed of several film and theatrical projects of recent years. Her role as one of the very few female artists of the 1960s Latin scene is inadequately analyzed, much less her efforts to cross over from a deeply Cuban background to the African American fusions and interactions of the boogaloo era.

4

Revolt in Típico

Willie Colón was a little too young to be a boogaloo musician, though that brief era served as a kind of springboard for his long and successful career. Born in 1950 in the South Bronx, he was still in his mid-teens and just getting started when the slightly older members of the Richie Ray, Pete Rodríguez, and Johnny Colón bands took the Latin music world by storm. And Joe Cuba and most of his sextet were old enough to be his father. Even the Lebrón brothers, who were not yet of age to be among the first boogaloo breakthrough groups, had a couple of years on him, and Joe Bataan (b. 1942), with whom he shares that street-tough image and social awareness, was old enough to choose not to ride the boogaloo wave. Willie's early albums do include a few boogaloos ("Willie Baby" and "Skinny Papa" come to mind), and the sounds of r&b and doo-wop are present throughout his early recordings. Musically, the strongest and most enduring resonance was not so much Latin soul but Eddie Palmieri's La Perfecta, and especially the signature trombone front line; the sound of Barry Rogers and Jose Rodrigues are there from the opening notes of the first cut, "Jazzy," on his first album, *El Malo* (1967), and remain a strong presence throughout his work.

Thus Willie Colón may well be considered the first lifelong salsa musician. The start of his career coincided precisely with the waning of boogaloo and the final rush toward that supposedly new style, and its naming as "salsa," some five years hence.

Between 1967 and 1972 he came out with eight LPs in rapid succession, and taken together, they do much to define what is meant by that controversial catchall term. Along with Joe Bataan and Ray Barretto, he was no doubt the biggest catch for the Fania project, all three of them signing on to the label in 1967 just as it was about to take off and eclipse all other recording options. Over his forty-five-year career, nearly all fifty and counting of Colón's recordings have been with Fania.

The early Colón albums in particular evidence a prodigious and original project that established itself by virtue of its stylistic distinctiveness and thematic coherence; the titles alone—*El Malo, The Hustler, Guisando, Cosa Nuestra, La Gran Fuga,* among others—indicate the unifying image of organized crime as played out in the "mean streets" of El Barrio, and the "bad boy" who inhabits that underworld. One indication that he chose to buck the boogaloo trend was that with few exceptions his lyrics were in Spanish, though an undertone of Spanglish always seems to linger just below the surface. In tune with the post-boogaloo spirit he averted the complete crossover appeal by going for típico, with only occasional traces of the backbeat, handclapping, and party exhortations that were so much the earmarks of boogaloo.

A major influence on Colón's style, including his opting for Spanish lyrics, was no doubt the presence of his long-term vocalist and "partner-in-crime" Héctor Lavoe, who joined the group for the second album, *The Hustler,* on the suggestion of producer Johnny Pacheco. Already on that recording came the band's explicit refusal of the boogaloo mode in the track "Eso Se Baila Así," which pronounces repeatedly "Bugalú no va conmigo" and "Báilalo tú," most likely reflecting Island-raised Lavoe's non-identification with the characteristically New York–grounded tastes and predilections of many young Puerto Ricans of the time. Indeed, the ongoing reference to and interaction with Puerto Rico, much stronger than among other New York musicians of those years, clearly had to do with that fascinating symbiosis between Colón and Lavoe, who between them embodied the complex Island-diaspora interaction. But even on the debut album, before Lavoe made his appearance, the dialogue with Puerto Rico began, most notably in the track "Borinquen," a ceremonial "dedication" of the preferred Afro-Cuban guaguancó to the musicians' beloved homeland. The abiding irony of voicing heartfelt patriotism in stylistic modes of a neighboring country, true of much New York–based Puerto Rican music including what comes to be called salsa, finds memorable expression in this early composition of Willie Colón. And a few years later, in their hugely popular and commercially successful 1971 Christmas album *Asalto Navideño,* this Island-diaspora interplay forms the thematic crux of the whole collection.[1]

FIGURE 23 Willie Colón, singing at mic with José Mangual (l.) and Héctor Lavoe, Izzy Sanabria in background. Courtesy of Izzy Sanabria.

While the influence of La Perfecta is pervasive, the early Colón sound is not a mere re-play of that historic band. To begin with, it is a pale imitation, with little of the inimitable virtuosity and bold originality of the Eddie Palmieri sound. Most obviously, Colón's two-trombone front line (himself and either Angel Matos or Joe Santiago), as engaging as they usually are, is simply no match whatsoever for the unique, masterful Barry Rogers and Jose Rodrigues duo, an unfair comparison of novices with past masters, but one that needs to be made nonetheless. Whereas La Perfecta's "trombanga" shows remarkable subtlety and impeccable modulation, the Colón version is simpler and frequently makes up for shortcomings in musical execution with sheer volume and brashness. This is not to say that it is mere mannerism and failed effort, as many of the most enduring Colón-Lavoe compositions, with Pacheco's seasoned guidance, owe their powerful effect to the daring exploits of that very trombone stylization. In some instances it appears that Mon Rivera may have been as strong a presence as La Perfecta in creating that distinctive, swinging, multi-trombone effect. Beyond that, while Nicky Marrero on timbales and African American pianist Markolino Dimond do more than hold their own, they do not yet have the experience or creative daring of Manny Oquendo or Palmieri himself on those instruments. Most important of all, of course, is Eddie's idiosyncratic musical concept, his unmatched sense of Afro-Cuban musical structures and how to ground unbridled experimentalism in those solid, time-tested traditions, which are simply not part of the Colón project however ambitious and original in its own right.

Despite these relative drawbacks to Colón's upstart band, there can be no doubt as to the freshness and imaginative eclecticism of his style, nor the appeal of his adventurous, often jocular and mischievous anti-heroic persona. His relation to both Afro-Cuban roots and to jazz clearly lacked the depth of both

Palmieri and Barretto, his two major counterparts in pioneering the salsa sensibility, but he ventured further than either of them in musical terrain. After his first few albums he began to include lesser explored rhythmic sources, most notably those of a Ghanaian children's song in his first mammoth hit, "Che Che Colé," on *Cosa Nuestra*, the Panamanian dance style "la murga" in his blockbuster of that title on the Christmas album, and the very strong influence of Puerto Rican jíbaro music in much of his work starting most pronouncedly with *Asalto Navideño*. Though many of these forays amount to strands of those rhythmic languages attached to the more familiar Cuban stylistic anchor, they do represent a widening of the musical palate and a connecting to many musical cultures in tune with the cosmopolitan New York setting from which these varied sounds spring.

For the first ten years of his trajectory, represented by fourteen albums, the ruggedness of the neighborhood and the street-tough central sensibility of the songs, captured by such titles as "El Malo" or "The Hustler," were the hallmarks of the Willie Colón group. The most immediate source of this imagery is to be found in the popular gangster movies like *The Hustler* and *The Godfather* that were the rage among young inner-city youth at the time. But the musical lineage to which the theme belongs is clearly that of "guapería" in the Afro-Cuban tradition, notably in some of the best-known songs of Arsenio Rodríguez, and in Barretto's pervasively influential megahit "El Watusi," to which direct reference is made in several of Colón's songs, most notably "El Titan" from the *Guisando* album. Another strong parallel for the forbidding neighborhood setting is Piri Thomas's autobiographical novel *Down These Mean Streets*, which was published in 1967, the same year as Colón's debut *El Malo* album. The coincidence is more than fortuitous, since the entire era of "salsa" occurs in the very same years as the Nuyorican literary and cultural movement and needs to be understood as part of the same artistic sensibility of the years around 1970. The foregrounding of that social reality is true of the most representative cultural expression of those years, as is the radical political impulse characterized by the advent of the Young Lords Party and other activist organizations.

It is important to grasp this bad-boy image and ghetto backdrop in the Willie Colón repertoire as a literary trope and dramatic persona, from all accounts much at the initiative of empresario and graphic designer Izzy Sanabria rather than as primarily autobiographical or descriptive in intent. Of course, his music from the start reflects the downgrading of the Puerto Rican and African American neighborhoods in the later 1960s and '70s, and Colón makes no secret of his own origins on 139th Street and his street credibility. Clearly his intention was at least in part social criticism and a portrayal of real-life conditions; that intention continues to be manifested as late as his 1975 album *Se Chavó el Vecindario!/There Goes the Neighborhood* which he did with Mon Rivera, and which included some of the veteran plenero's most influential songs, most notably the plena standard composed by Mon's father, "Aló Quién Llama?" But it is also evident from the ironic, fun-loving tone that he and his Island running-buddy were mainly just goofing around and playing on what they knew to be a widely shared fascination with crime figures and sensationalist violence, whether of the organized mob or inner-city street gangs.

These were after all the years of the so-called blaxploitation books and wildly popular films like *Shaft* and *Super Fly*, followed shortly by *The Godfather*; as is clear from the album cover showing the band hovering over a pool table, *The Hustler* was a direct reference to the 1961 Paul Newman film classic of that title. Though the world according to the early Willie Colón albums may well be charged with reinforcing sensationalist stereotypes of the New York Puerto Rican community—the impact of *West*

Side Story and the Capeman were everywhere, to mention the most obvious sources—the creative intention and probably most powerful effect of this imagery and personification had to do with a kind of "outlaw aesthetic," a will toward transgression and transcendence of the oppressive immediacy of social reality by means of sarcasm and creative expression. Songs like "El Malo," "Guisando," "El Titán," and "Te Están Buscando," all built on that theme of crime and police pursuit, illustrate that the lyrics are often speaking more about dancing and music-making than actual violence and illegality. The tough-guy language in "El Malo," as in the chorus "Echate pa'llá, que tú no estás en ná," ("step aside, man, cause you ain't into anything") is modified by the variant "Si no sabes bailar, que tú no estás en ná" ("if you don't know how to dance, you ain't into anything").

Perhaps even more memorable than the gangster themes of these compositions is the colorful Puerto Rican colloquialism and folkloric references present in most of the lyrics. Though nearly impossible to translate into English and at times barely comprehensible even to Spanish speakers, these features from everyday speech surely have done much to endear the music to its most immediate fan base, the Latino and Latin American audiences. The 1970 *Cosa Nuestra* album is particularly strong in this regard, as in such memorable numbers as "No Me Llores," "Te Conozco," and "Sangrigorda," while the narrative ballad "Juana Peña" even seems to anticipate some of the popular compositions from the highly regarded and huge-selling albums Colón did a few years later with Rubén Blades, such as "Pablo Pueblo" and "Pedro Navaja." The defining role of Lavoe's colloquial Spanish in the performance of these songs is obvious, as are the historic compositions of the revered songwriter from Puerto Rico, Tite Curet Alonso, in much of Colón's repertoire. While he helped decisively to establish Cuban son and guaguancó as the taproot of what is called salsa as of the early 1970s, Colón was also more than any other exponent responsible for centering the New York Puerto Rican community as the demographic base of the music, the geographic and social home setting for the entire cultural movement of which salsa was a part.

As is evident from its title, *Asalto Navideño* (Christmas Assault, 1971), Colón's fifth album is obviously carrying forward the theme of street crime and violence of the first four, and anticipating the next four to come, *La Gran Fuga* (The Great Escape), *El Juicio* (The Verdict), *Lo Mato* (I'll Kill Him), and *Crime Pays* (title in English). But the difference is that in *Asalto Navideño* attention turns to the relation between Puerto Rican culture in New York and on the Island. The word for the violent act of mugging, "asalto," is the same as that used for the centuries-old cultural ritual of "invading" the house of friends and neighbors in order to bring Christmas cheer; appropriately, the album cover shows Colón and Lavoe in Santa Claus hats attempting to rob a Christmas tree. That is, in an ingenious way the haughty attitude of the Nuyoricans toward Puerto Ricans on the Island is undermined, while at the same time tribute is paid to the expansive cosmopolitanism of the diasporic experience in New York. This complex ambivalence and two-directional critique, all in the context of the culturally laden Christmas rituals, finds its optimal expression in this contagiously popular musical medley—for many the all-time favorite Willie Colón album—with the familiar salsa Cubanism ("el tumbao") set into active dialogue with the familiar cadences and tonalities of jíbaro music. Most remarkable is that the frolicking party atmosphere is in no way dampened by the quite serious dialectic of tension and harmony between the main cultural zones of Puerto Rican life. Colón's trombone and Lavoe's irresistible nasalized vocals are joined by the emblematic cuatro playing of master Yomo Toro, who remains unparalleled in his ability to move imperceptibly between the traditional chords from

Puerto Rican aguinaldos and décimas to the highly percussive sounds of Afro-Cuban son, while also including strong traces of jazz and rock.[2]

Willie Colón's eclectic but remarkably coherent body of early recorded work, from his debut in 1967 until the historic Cheetah Club concert of the Fania All-Stars and the parting of ways with Héctor Lavoe starting in 1972, did more than any equivalent output to set the tone for the ascendant "salsa" sound. Though his subsequent collaboration with Rubén Blades achieved even greater commercial success—their 1978 album *Siembra* is on record as the best-selling salsa album of all time—and had an expansive Latin American and international reach, it was the string of gangster releases that marked the standard for the Fania narrative of the entire musical era, as is clear from the name of the foundational Fania film, *Nuestra Cosa (Our Latin Thing)*, after one of Colón's album titles and the epithet of organized crime in tune with his central metaphor.

Though the label "Mr. Salsa" is most commonly associated with the ubiquitous Izzy Sanabria, if any bandleader of the time may be regarded as such, the leader of the salsa "gang" would have to be Willie Colón.

But the full picture of emergent "salsa" by that name only comes into full view by considering his most important contemporaries, one within the Fania fold, Ray Barretto, and the other the perennial outlier who towers above them all in terms of sheer musical prowess and originality, Eddie Palmieri. While the influence of La Perfecta is everywhere on the early salsa practitioners including Colón, by the time we get to the 1968–72 period Palmieri is already taking the music in exciting new directions of his own. And while Colón, Barretto, and others do address social realities in their music of those years, it is Palmieri who creates some of the most imaginative and powerful political songs in the history of New York Latin music.

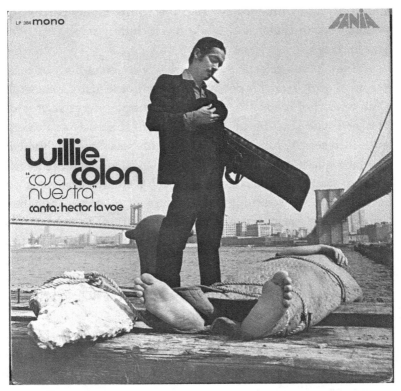

FIGURE 24 Willie Colón, *Cosa Nuestra*. Courtesy of Fania Records.

When Ray Barretto signed with the Fania label in 1967 he was already exploring new possibilities. After his initial epiphany on hearing "Manteca" while still in the army in Germany, he had begun his musical career playing congas with jazz groups, then did his stint with the José Curbelo band, and went on to reach a new level in 1957 when he replaced Mongo Santamaría in Tito Puente's band. In the early 1960s he got his start as a bandleader with his Charanga Moderna, making his mark with the fluke megahit "El Watusi." While continuing to sit in on conga with various jazz and soul bands, he changed from the charanga format to a conjunto with trumpets (though he initially retained the violin parts) and recorded five albums with United Artists during the mid-60s. The last of these, from 1966, was *Latino Con Soul*, and the title is indicative. Along with some driving son montuno cuts, notably his enduring "Fuego y Palante," the selection includes a boogaloo/shingaling ("Can You Dig It?"), an unusual, slow boogaloo-like soul number "Boogaloo con Soul," and even a plena, "El Picor." The mingling of soul, jazz, and son montunos is what then prevails in his Fania recordings, at least for the first few years.

The first and perhaps best known of them all was *Acid*, an album noteworthy for its eclecticism and range. Here the balance is tipped toward the soul and jazz side of Barretto's palate, with straight-ahead English-language soul numbers like "Mercy Mercy Baby," "A Deeper Shade of Soul," and "Soul Drummers" alternating with típico sounds as in "Solo Te Dejaré," and with somewhat longer Latin jazz cuts like the title number and the 8.5 minute closer, "Espiritu Libre." These latter two, extended free instrumentals with consistent bass-and-güiro lines and intense trumpet solos, are perhaps the most powerful, anticipating as they do such trademark Barretto compositions as his "Cocinando" and his version of "Tin Tin Deo" from slightly later albums. But it is in the opening selection, "El Nuevo Barretto," announcing his new program, that the interaction between Latin soul, jazz, and conjunto is at its most active, with a rapid shifting between and among the generic languages without a loss of expressive coherence. Barretto often commented on having a leg up on many of his contemporaries when it came to fusions and crossovers, and here and in his subsequent albums we have the most telling evidence. Complementing his stellar instrumentalists, in Adalberto Santiago, who remained with him until the band's breakup in 1972, and Pete Bonet, he boasted a pair of vocalists who assured him a full bilingual and bicultural range, his varied compositions sounding equally fluent with the English soul and the Spanish son montuno lyrics.

The final cut from *Acid*, the remarkable conga-led descarga "Espiritú Libre," is of further interest because it occasioned a poem by the pioneering Nuyorican poet Victor Hernández Cruz, dedicated to Ray Barretto. There followed a fascinating and generally unknown creative exchange between these two major Nuyorican artists. Hernández Cruz's first book, *Snaps*, published by Norton in 1967, was also the first published book

FIGURE 25 Ray Barretto. *Acid*. Courtesy of Fania Records.

of Nuyorican poetry, as that movement came to be called a few years later. There he included his poem "Drum Poem" (Free Spirit), which emulates or reverberates with the Barretto composition as a kind of sonorous word-sound painting, the visual image on the page and the poem's acoustic effects re-creating the conga jazz force of the musical experience. A few lines from that work illustrate well Hernández Cruz's intentions, and his admiration for the revered conguero and bandleader:

watch ray   watch ray
good & strong   moving moving
moving
now
& forever   moving like the
earth
moving like rain/summer streets
summer
your fingers bleeding
bleeding   your eyes closed
eyes closed   bleedy conga
listen
listen
hear hear hear   everything
everything[3]

When the book came out, the boogaloo and Latin soul-loving poet made it a point to give a copy to his favorite musicians. He brought one to Eddie Palmieri when he played a dance at the Psycho Room, and he brought one to Ray Barretto at the St. George Hotel in Brooklyn. Barretto was evidently so taken by the poem dedicated to him that he composed a follow-up musical response (for his transitional 1969 compilation *Head Sounds*) that he gave the same title as the Hernández Cruz poem and in which one of his musicians reads from the poem. He also reproduced the poem itself as the back cover of the album. The episode, which remains an important memory for Hernández Cruz to this day,[4] is a rich illustration of the cohesion and simultaneity of the new artistic generation, as the Nuyorican reality finds more and more interesting and interconnected lines of creative expression. As we shall see, similar interactions with the music are evident as regards the vibrant political movements of the day.

After *Acid*, a similar mix of cultural and musical languages persists through the next three albums—*Hard Hands, Together*, and *Power*—though with each one the soul side increasingly gives way to a prevalence of montunos and guaguancós, such that by *The Message* from 1971 all selections are in Spanish and in the típico vein. This readily traceable shift reflects not only Barretto's own personal predilections and the "Latin pride" sensibilities of those years, but significantly corresponds to the priorities of the "Fania sound" as it arrived at its formula for what "salsa" is supposed to be about. *Hard Hands* does include some powerful típico pieces like "Mi Ritmo Te Llama" and "Ahora Sí," though even the most engaging of these, "Son Con Cuero," does contain an expansive conga solo and a coro blending in the boogaloo reference: "son, cuero y bugalú." But the standout compositions are no doubt the title opener, "Hard Hands," and the programmatic "New York Soul," where the conga and cowbell work blends so organically with the exhortations to the bandleader and the refrain line "Afro thing, Latin Swing, more than rock and roll, New York soul." The sound is very much of the times, but the centrality of Barretto's forceful conga part lends a special quality, in the direction of both Afro-Cuban roots and jazz, to what would otherwise be a predictable Latin soul language.

The most resonant of Barretto's Fania albums of the late '60s—if not musically, at least politically—is the 1969 *Together*,

FIGURE 26 Ray Barretto. Courtesy of Izzy Sanabria. John Storm
Roberts Collection, Photos and Prints Division, Schomburg Center,
New York Public Library.

as its overtly and implicitly political content gained favor among
young Puerto Rican militants, including the Young Lords Party,
in those heady years. Former Young Lord Mickey Meléndez,
author of the historical chronicle *We Took to the Streets,* attests
to the deep significance that he and others found in the philosophical son montuno "Hipocresía y Falsedad," which cautions
against the treacherous backstabbers and traitors that lurk
in their path.[5] And in an obituary for Barretto in the *Village
Voice,* ex-Lord Pablo "Yoruba" Guzmán refers to the racial lessons in "De Dónde Vengo" ("where do I come from?") with its
questioning of the biblical creation story of Adam and Eve: if
they were white and were the original ancestors of all humans,

"porqué es negra mi piel?" ("why's my skin black?"). The narrative voice announces that he is Black ("soy niche") and that he has no explanation as to his own racial origins: "no me explico de dónde vengo yo." As Guzmán put it, the song "gets to the essence of the 'y tu abuela, dónde está?' ('and your grandmother, where is she?') controversy among some light-skinned Puerto Ricans who somehow thought the slaveship skipped their family."[6] Both "De Dónde Vengo" and the final cut, Barretto's version of the Gillespie-Chano Pozo classic "Tin Tin Deo," formed part of the soundtrack of the 1973 documentary about the Young Lords, "El Pueblo Se Levanta." The title track, with which the *Together* album opens, is a Latin soul call for multi-racial unity that also found support in the progressive movement of the day.

Barretto's political sympathies were expressed not just in his music but also in his personal convictions as well. According to Guzmán, "In late 1969, Ray was the first of the 'name' musicians to seek out the militant group I had helped form, the Young Lords Party, and ask if he could do anything to help. It was a big deal when his great band played a gig at 110th Street at a benefit for us ('Some of the Cuban cats in the band, though, ain't too crazy about this,' Ray said. 'They think you guys are too much like Fidel.')"[7] As with Eddie Palmieri, the social conditions and political movements of the time provided a vital context for the music of Barretto and others, which resulted in songs with a social conscience years before Rubén Blades composed and sang his world-famous political salsa in collaboration with Willie Colón. Too little attention has gone thus far to what can only be called political salsa, which has been overshadowed in the historical narrative by the ascendancy of Fania Records and the commercial diffusion of the bands and recordings as hot dance music devoid of social content. And it is important to note that the political theme is generally part of the convergence of the Latin and African American musical traditions, especially in the Latin soul dimension that tended to get minimized in the impending Fania prescription.

This connection between expressive style and social conscience is evident in Barretto's subsequent album, perhaps his most deliberately political release, the significantly entitled *Power* from 1970. In line with the general direction of Barretto's music over these years, the prevalent stylistic mode of the collection is strongly típico, especially the best-known track "Quítate la Máscara," which proudly announces "mi nuevo guaguancó." But "Right On"—the radical movement's phrase of the day—is one of the final examples of a Latin soul sound in his repertoire, with powerful trumpet and percussion interplay, while the album's closing title cut is an extended instrumental featuring intense soul and jazz trumpet and piano parts along with a vintage conga solo. It seems that the "power" is in the very music itself, with no need for lyrics pronouncing political engagement in verbal clichés. This composition, which has gone largely unmentioned in the discussion of his work, represents Ray Barretto at full throttle, a crowning achievement of "salsa power."

Despite its promising title, the band's next album *The Message* shows little of this energetic fusion quality, with the recording's two most popular tracks, "Se Traba" and "O Elefante," relying on novelty twists on the típico sound and thematics: in the first the stuttering effect and in the second a search for Barretto in the wilds of Africa in a tune reminiscent of "El Watusi" but lacking its freshness and of course the appealing charanga format. Here all of the tracks are in Spanish and in the son montuno and bolero modes, impeccably executed because of the quality of the band but lacking in that soul and jazz dimension, and the political and social reference point, of the previous recordings.

The "message" seems to be, in the context of Barretto's prolific output of these years, that there is no message.

But the crowning achievement of the Barretto project of these years is the band's last album together, the 1972 *Que Viva la Música*. The recording's featured ten-minute cut alone, "Cocinando," would make it a historic release, as that inimitable instrumental went on to become a virtual anthem of salsa when it was used for the opening soundtrack to Fania's foundational concert film *Our Latin Thing*. That medium-tempo highly percussive Latin jazz track is everywhere when anyone talks of salsa, the constantly repeated words "cocinando suave, cocinando" seeming to be a kind of recipe for how to prepare the spicy musical repast. But in addition to this unique tour de force, the entire album is a showcase of the Barretto band at its irresistible best. From the opening title track in glorious praise of the music— "que viva!," as though it were "la revolución" or "Puerto Rico libre"—to the sign-off guaguancó "Alafia Cumayé," this "swan song" of the band has been referred to as "one of the brightest jewels in the Fania crown, and a key document of the New York salsa explosion of the '70s."[8] Worth mentioning is also the inclusion on this album of the band's intriguing version of the Arsenio Rodríguez classic "Bruca Maniguá" and another big hit, the son montuno "La Pelota." The slow-tempo bolero "Triunfó el Amor" is no doubt one of the outstanding successes in that genre, demonstrating once again the remarkable versatility of Barretto's long-term lead vocalist Adalberto Santiago.

The departure of Santiago and four of the other key band members just after the release of *Que Viva la Música* was a traumatic blow to Barretto, as he has never failed to recount. It marked a clear hiatus in his career, though he at no point ventures an explanation for the abandonment; for that, it is necessary to compare the musical output of the new band Típica 73, which his former bandmates formed after leaving him. As heavy an emotional setback as it was for him in terms of self-confidence, he immediately demonstrated his prowess as a bandleader with his very next release, from 1973, *Indestructible*. Having regrouped with the highly regarded Tito Allen as new lead vocalist and Edy Martínez on piano, Barretto got up off the mat and came out with some new hits, most famously the catchy novelty piece "El Diablo" featuring outbursts of eerie devilish laughter and a refrain about the playful spirit of it all, "el espiritu burlón." Though not equal to *Que Viva la Música*, *Indestructible* counts among Barretto's most impressive achievements and remained unmatched over the following years until his *Barretto* album of 1975, and then *Rican/Struction* from the end of the decade.

Clearly, despite his personal disappointment on the loss of his band, Barretto felt confident within the supportive home provided by Fania Records, where he delighted (as he repeatedly stated) in the freedom he enjoyed to do whatever he wanted with no evident restrictions of a commercial or aesthetic kind. After the dissolution of his long-term group he went on to dedicate himself to his work as musical director of the Fania All-Stars, which was soon to be regarded as the "most important salsa band of all time," the key forger of the Fania project during its days of wine and roses. But aside from the specific Fania context, Ray Barretto's contribution to the emergence of the new musical sound—some call it salsa—was significant though in retrospect difficult to pinpoint. He clearly lacks the bold experimentalism of Eddie Palmieri, and the attitude and dramatic flair of Willie Colón, and the business acumen of Johnny Pacheco, Jerry Masucci, or Larry Harlow. But of all the major players, Barretto unquestionably brought the deepest and most seasoned connection to jazz and affinity to African American culture, including its vernacular musical expression, as key ingredients of the musical innovations ahead. What is curious is that his

Fania affiliation seems to have downplayed those very aspects of the new Latin music just as it was incubating, replacing deeper musical and cultural connections with a decidedly more superficial, commercially motivated crossover trend divorced from the historical and social grounding of that ongoing cross-cultural process.

The breakup of La Perfecta in 1968 hit Eddie Palmieri hard, to the point that he felt he might be "going bananas," as he puts it. The writing had been on the wall of course, an early signal perhaps being the closing of the Palladium. Then with the meteoric rise of the (for Palmieri) detested boogaloo craze, that most exciting and influential of all the top bands, the one that had long seen itself and been seen as the guiding sound of the new generation, felt eclipsed by a trend that seemed such a musical step backward. In its last album together, the 1968 *Champagne*, La Perfecta even had to stoop to including their own shingaling, "Ay Qué Rico," and a straight-ahead soul number with a gimmicky pop title, "African Twist," which featured the inexperienced female African American soul vocalist Cynthia Ellis. It must have been Palmieri's ultimate humiliation that those two cuts were the hottest numbers on the entire superb album. It shouldn't have been a surprise, though, since "Ay Qué Rico" and the album in general featured guests of the towering stature of Israel "Cachao" López on bass and Chocolate Armenteros on his unique trumpet, not to mention the peerless vocalist Cheo Feliciano. No other band of the time could boast such a lineup, similar in stature to La Perfecta standardbearers Manny Oquendo, Barry Rogers, and the others.

Losing La Perfecta, his unique, history-making team, for a full six years during dramatically changing times left a vacuum for Palmieri, just as his creative juices were flowing with new energy and his voracious imaginative powers reaching out in new directions. The only members of the group who stayed

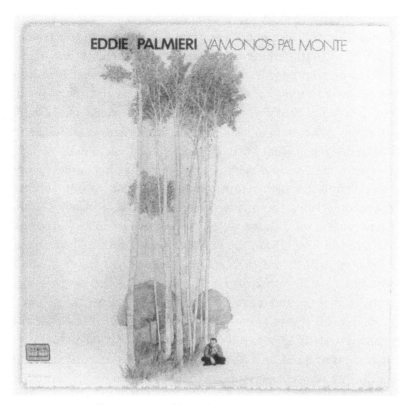

FIGURE 27 Album cover: Eddie Palmieri, *Vamonos Pal Monte*. Tico Records. Courtesy of Fania Records.

with him were Ismael Quintana on vocals and Jose Rodrigues; Barry Rogers and Manny Oquendo were gone, though they would rejoin him occasionally in the years ahead—most notably Rogers—for some of his major subsequent albums from the mid-1970s like *Sentido* and *Sun of Latin Music*. He had to start from scratch and put together a whole new ensemble. Many fans feared that it might be all over for him as the leader of the Latin music pack, that the Eddie Palmieri years had ended. He too experienced anxiety and self-doubt, as he still vividly recalls his

nightmarish experience at a hotel in Caracas when it was dawning on him that the band was definitely not going to survive.[9]
But rather than sinking into despair, that moment was also a
kind of epiphany for him; he woke up to realize that his music
would have to move in new directions to stay in tune with the
times. It was at that point that his idea for "Justicia," the historic
title song of his next album, first occurred to him, as well as an
initial inkling of what his next band would look like.

Palmieri quickly dispelled any fears that his career would
collapse and that he had nowhere to go, as his next four albums,
released within a three-year period, all stand as classics of the
Latin music canon: *Justicia, Superimposition, Vamonos Pa'l Monte*,
and *Harlem River Drive*. These were quickly followed by *Live at
Sing Sing, Sentido*, and *The Sun of Latin Music*, the latter of which
won the first Grammy for Latin music in 1975. This powerful
comeback indicated that La Perfecta, monumental achievement though it was, was not all that Palmieri had to offer and
that his artistic agenda did not depend on that particular con-
figuration of musicians however compatible and copacetic. His
guiding musical concept remained in place, and his ability to dis-
cover promising innovative paths assured that his compositions
would have a continued high quality and level of fascination. The
stylistic and thematic diversity of his emerging repertoire demonstrates both his consistency with ongoing musical projects
and principles and his bold move into new fields and sounds.
Though the personnel of his band tended to vary more than in
earlier years, there was nevertheless clearly a new core in place
soon, consisting of Nicky Marrero on timbales, Andy González
on bass, Chocolate Armenteros on trumpet, and a new, remarkably young percussion section. So young, in fact, that the last
tune on *Superimposition*, "17.1," indicates their average age at
the time. All traces of the charanga format are gone by now,
even the two-trombone front line that had been La Perfecta's

signature elaboration and transcendence of charanga. In general, the switch was back to a more typical conjunto setup, the feature now being the trumpet-trombone interactions between Chocolate and Jose Rodrigues. The very young Marrero could hardly fill Manny Oquendo's boots, but he had an energy of his own that perhaps meshed even better with the new constellation of players. The band was called simply "Eddie Palmieri and Friends."

Justicia and *Superimposition* were worked on and came out almost simultaneously, and each indicated one of the two main qualities of the new, post-La Perfecta project. While the first of these albums attested to Palmieri's growing social conscience and work on developing political lyrics and musical agenda, *Superimposition* evidenced his ongoing effort to combine Afro-Cuban foundations with a jazz-oriented aesthetic. Both of these initiatives were fostered and catalyzed by Palmieri's longtime mentor Bob Bianco, whom he referred to as a kind of savior figure. When he found himself in the doldrums and was lacking in self-confidence he would go visit this close friend in his apartment in Queens where he would get lessons in jazz harmonies and in political economy that proved invaluable to him in his awakening to new creative possibilities. According to Palmieri, Bianco considered himself most of all a saloon singer, who would croon standards in local neighborhood bars in exchange, evidently, for drinks, as he commonly had to be dragged home unconscious in the wee hours of the morning. But this unassuming character was also a fount of wisdom, about jazz, the social philosophy of poverty and injustice, and about life in general.

It was Palmieri's other mentor, Barry Rogers, who first introduced him to Bianco, sometime around 1964–65. For Rogers, it was part of his extended effort to familiarize Palmieri with jazz and the potential for its endlessly rich juncture with Afro-Cuban traditions as demonstrated by the previous Cubop breakthrough.

Rogers was the one who made sure that Palmieri was exposed to Charlie Parker, Thelonious Monk, Miles Davis, McCoy Tyner, and other jazz giants, all of whom came to influence his tireless musical development. Having gotten to know Bob Bianco, Rogers figured that Palmieri would have much to gain from his acquaintance. And he was right: under Bianco's supervision the bandleader studied intensely and began to apply the Schillinger method to his experiments in jazz harmony. In addition, thanks to intense discussions with Bianco, Palmieri came to attend the Henry George School in Manhattan and learn the rudiments of socioeconomic analysis as set forth in books like George's own classic *Progress and Poverty* (1879) and Phil Grant's *The Wonderful Wealth Machine* (1963). Palmieri to this day waxes on about the many social and philosophical lessons he learned from Bianco, who actually taught evening courses at the Henry George School. These are popular teachings for general public education purposes, offering up a kind of populist anti-capitalist economic analysis, with a sharp criticism of the tax system. It was decidedly non- (or even anti-) Marxist thinking, and Henry George's theories fell under the withering criticism of Lenin himself at one point. But Palmieri found what he learned at the school very appealing, perhaps because it validated his own well-known reluctance to pay taxes, considering taxation a form of thievery. It also seemed to be in line with the politics of the Young Lords Party and other radical movements of the day, with which he felt an affinity and solidarity. Former Young Lords members like Mickie Meléndez and Pablo Guzmán attest to the many occasions when Palmieri collaborated with them by playing benefit concerts and fundraisers.

Most interesting, of course, is how Palmieri managed to infuse these political views into his music and thereby create some of the most powerful and aesthetically engaging political songs in Latin music. Over the course of several albums

of the period, and as part of his regular performance repertoire, Palmieri included a string of thematically inter-related
compositions bearing a straightforward though not always
elaborated message of social criticism and utopian projection
out of the miserable real circumstances of his working-class
Puerto Rican and Black community. These songs—"Justicia"
and "Everything Is Everything" from the *Justicia* album, the
title cut and "La Libertad/Lógico" from *Vámonos Pa'l Monte*,
the entire *Harlem River Drive* album, and "Condiciones Que
Existen" from *Sentido* (1973)—form a thematically unified
cluster, while the *Live at Sing Sing* LPs from 1972 carry political significance because of the performance venue itself and
because of the poetry reading by ex-Young Lord Felipe Luciano
included as a track on the album. Taken together, these compositions stand at the center of the salsa canon while at the same
time diverging on many counts from what is considered salsa
in its mainstream form. They do demonstrate clearly that what
is called salsa is not only dance music with little social content but also includes a strong political voice in tune with the
vibrant movements for social change prevalent in those days.

Palmieri is proud of having used his music to project these
progressive ideas, even though they did get him into trouble
with record boss Morris Levy (the owner of the Tico label) when
the FBI investigated Levy. But he was also emphatic in pointing out that the music was still basically dance music. He did
not want to compromise the immense social and political power
inherent in the choreographic dimension of his compositions—
and of popular music generally. He was less interested in getting across his political message at the expense of that energy,
which had always been his foremost guide in structuring and
performing his work. Taking a cue from the title ("Revolt") of his
song best known by its subtitle, "La Libertad/Lógico," he aimed
at inciting what he called "Revolt con Swing," a combination

of political and kinetic energy that conveyed the sheer power of his band itself. Along with his canonical "Vámonos Pa'l Monte," "Revolt: La Libertad/Logico" is arguably his consummate achievement in this vein, a veritable masterwork of political salsa. Several Young Lord Party militants assert that they remember it as their "anthem." Along with some of the Barretto songs already mentioned and some favorite patriotic numbers by such well-known nationalist "trovadores" from the Island as Ramito, Danny Rivera, El Topo, Ralphy Leavitt, Roy Brown, and Pepe y Flora, Eddie Palmieri is no doubt a key component of the soundtrack of the late '60s–early '70s period in Latin New York radical politics.[10]

"Justicia tendrán, justicia serán, en el mundo los desafortunados," "the less fortunate will have justice, will be justice, in this world." With those resounding words Palmieri heralds a new theme in Latin popular music, broadly announcing a clamor for justice for the oppressed of the world and thereby making it immediately and abundantly clear that there is life after La Perfecta. The song "Justicia," though perhaps outdone in a musical sense by subsequent political compositions, is no doubt the most famous of all and sets the agenda for Palmieri's whole political concept. His lyrics make it clear in whose interest he is singing, with "los desafortunados" being later named as "los discriminados" and "los perjudicados," those suffering the damages of social injustice and discrimination, the reference becoming more explicit at the very end when mention is made of "justicia pa' los niches y los boricuas" ("justice for Blacks and Puerto Ricans").

In line with his "revolt con swing" intentions, the song proceeds to locate the source of the clamor for justice in the music itself, and specifically in the almighty drum: "con el canto del tambó, del tambó, la justicia la reclamo" ("with the song of the drum, of the drum, I call out for justice"). As so often in Palmieri's extensive repertoire of original compositions, the drum is the protagonist, since the percussive dimension of the music is what defines the structure and texture as a whole. Indeed, the musical text itself is so memorable and danceable in its own right that the very meaning of the lyrics may well have been overshadowed for many avid listeners. The defiant signature trombone opening, the blaring brass in counterpoint with the vibrant percussion of his young band, and of course the aggressive yet modulated piano attack as only Palmieri himself was capable of performing all give enormous force to the message of the song. By the lengthy descarga toward the end, when all hell breaks loose, the entire composition in every aspect seems to be conspiring in this clamor for justice and appeal for a new world free of tyranny and where all are like brothers and sisters, and happy. The utopian strain is contained in the repeated response to the wretched "condiciones que existen," Palmieri's term for the prevailing social reality that he used as the title of one of his slightly later songs.

The other Palmieri tune with an explicitly political content is "Revolt: La Libertad/Lógico," which he explains was a direct sequel to "Justicia." On a trip to Venezuela in 1970, a journalist asked him, perhaps half jokingly, who is the child or offspring of "justice," "¿Quién es el hijo de la justicia?" Palmieri blurted out his answer immediately, "freedom, of course," "la libertad/lógico." He placed the forward slash between "libertad" and "lógico" so as to avoid misunderstandings and make clear that he didn't mean "la libertad lógica," "logical freedom," which is grammatically correct and the more common usage. But with the slash and the "o" ending, the word "lógico" is being used as an adverb ("of course," or "logically") and not as an adjective modifying "libertad." In other words, it's not that "liberty" is logical, but that it's "logical" to fight for your freedom. The song articulates a strong resistance to any infringement on that freedom and any treatment that is unjust, the chorus repeating "no, no, no no me trates así" ("no, no, no, do not treat me that way"). And here, more than in "Justicia" where the talk was of prejudice and discrimination, the cause of the inequality is clearly identified as economic; several times in the latter part of the track the word "económicamente" occurs, and is accompanied by "esclavo." In line with his education at the Henry George School and with the Marxist leanings of the Young Lords, Palmieri believed the root of the enslavement of our times is to be found in the prevailing economic conditions and structures. Thus, it is only "logical" to ground the struggle for justice in the cause of those enslaved economically, a reality that afflicts all who live under the existing conditions. That reality is enforced by the state, enemy number one for Palmieri in the spirit of this and others of his songs about revolt. Indeed, here the music evokes a sense of foreboding and imminent revolt from the very opening bars of haunting piano and conga, followed by an ominous outburst of brass: something is happening (it seems to be announcing), and it's not good. As it turns out, our very freedom is in jeopardy, and we must speak out against that kind of treatment. That outcry is implicit in the music itself, in the forceful percussion, including piano, and the combative trombone and trumpet duets. Once again, "revolt con swing."

"Revolt: La Libertad/Lógico" is the opening track on what is arguably the most famous of all of Palmieri's fifty-plus albums, *Vámonos Pa'l Monte*, from 1971, one of his last recordings on the Tico label. By far the best-known track on that historic selection is the title piece, which features the virtuosic organ playing of none other than the masterful Charlie Palmieri and the unmistakable trumpet of Chocolate Armenteros. The song is a call to flee to the mountains in order to get away from the stress and suffering of modern urban life. It appears less overtly political than "Justicia" and "Revolt," its message sounding more Rousseauian in its love for nature, and perhaps nationalist in its longing for the mountains of the homeland so common in Puerto Rican songs of patriotic nostalgia, rather than a clamor for justice or an activist protest against modern-day economic slavery. But as the song's edgy and defiant musical text makes clear, the pitch to head for the hills to party ("vámonos pa'l monte, pa'l monte pa' guarachar") is actually an exhortation to protest the suffocating, dehumanizing conditions of modern capitalist society with its forever imminent economic disaster ("aquí en las grandes ciudades . . .? la congestión,. . . dicen que poquito a poco se acerca la depresión, y no se ha gozado, nos tumba el vacilón, el vacilón" ("here in the big cities? congestion . . . they say that little by little depression is approaching, and we haven't been able to enjoy ourselves, it wipes out our good time, our good time"); other lines are "este mundo está travieso, y aunque eso me importa a mí, yo no puedo controlarlo," indicating the individual person's inability to control or have any say in the disjointed social reality. The narrator is happier, enjoys himself more in the mountains, because it suggests a better world for human life; "guarachar," "el vacilón," "contento," "feliz"—words indicating the joy of partying and having a good time—are set in jarring contrast to the dullness and misery of the filthy urban reality in which he and his audience find themselves. Puerto Rico over against New York? It can be taken that way, and no doubt the young Puerto Rican militants embraced it as an affirmation of their patriotic feelings toward the ancestral homeland, sentiments that were shared by Eddie, Charlie, and the other musicians. But the contrast is broader and deeper than that, having to do with the wide critical view made clear by Henry George in his discussion of "progress and poverty," the title of his famous book. It is to Eddie Palmieri's ultimate credit that he was able to wrap such a gloomy portrait of modern conditions in such a majestic musical fabric, which serves to articulate the intended political message.

Aspects of Palmieri's social vision recur in some of his other, less familiar tunes, such as "Everything Is Everything" and "Condiciones Que Existen," all of which tend to stay close to the Afro-Cuban foundation of the music and yet constitute bold and experimental adaptations of son montuno and guaguancó. The other rich source of political insight, though, is in an album that is from the same year (1971) as *Vámonos Pa'l Monte* but which veers off sharply from that root: the controversial, often over-looked *Harlem River Drive*. While always attributed to Palmieri, this recording is actually a collaboration between him and bari-tone sax master Ronnie Cuber, who brought in some of the Aretha Franklin band to join forces with members of Palmieri's group at the time. In the best sense it is a fusion album, dif-ferent from his other work even in being released by Roulette, more of an r&b and soul label, of which Tico was a subsidiary soon to reach the end of its tether under Morris Levy and to be sold to Fania. Most of the songs, all in English, were composed by a highly regarded African American songwriter, Calvin Clash, better known by his nickname, Snooky. It was Snooky, who had lived the life of the mean streets and had done prison time, who named the project which became the title of the album, and wrote the lead-off "Harlem River Drive" (Theme Song). Jimmy Norman, the veteran lead singer on most of the cuts, explains the reason for that title, and it had all to do with poverty and social inequality: "In reality, Harlem River Drive was a dividing line, a highway where all the rich people just zip past the ghetto, and here we are, just watching them go by."[11]

The restless dynamic sound, driven by the electric piano and guitar, ample use of wa wa pedals, Charlie Palmieri on organ and Ron Cuber on his baritone sax, was sheer funk, but Palmieri made sure it was underpinned with strong Latin percussion and that it fit the structures he was such a master at working with. He explains that it didn't all occur to them once in the studio but that "the concepts were already in my mind." "[We] knew it was going to be really *heavy* on the rhythm section, because I was bringing in the deep guys, the conga, timbal, bass. It was going to be quite really authentic Latin rhythm, driving, and the [brass] arrangement was going to be complimentary to that, swinging. Except that we brought in the soul musicians, and plus it was gonna be sung in English, so the combination of all of that, I already conceived what it would sound like.... It still falls in with the structure, and I knew that it would work."[12]

He could hardly go wrong with the quality musicianship he had around him, complementing the top soul and jazz players like Cuber, Bernard Purdie, Cornell Dupree, Gerald Jemmott, and the Aretha Franklin Singers with a variety of standouts from the Latin field including Manny Oquendo, Barry Rogers, Andy González, and Nicky Marrero. With good reason, the recording has been called "the ultimate Latin soul album."[13]—and this despite the less-than-accommodating studio conditions for the dead-of-winter recording sessions: it seems Morris Levy had just acquired a new studio and had not yet put heat in it, so that the musicians had to wear gloves and overcoats when they weren't playing, and Palmieri talks about the out-of-tune broken down piano he had to play on.

It is in this album, too, that Palmieri gives clearest voice to the lessons in political economy he had learned from Bob Bianco and the Henry George School. In fact, he even had Bianco actively involved in the project: he played guitar on several tracks, sings on others, and helps with the arrangements, especially on the most important number on the recording, "Idle Hands." While all of the selections carry a strongly political message about war, poverty, racism, and other themes—most strongly in Snooky's reflections in the 10:37 narrative "Broken Home"—it is "Idle Hands," written by Marilyn and Ira Hirscher and "coordinated" (in Palmieri's words) by Bob Bianco, that the themes of poverty and progress are struck in the most direct way. In a sound that resonates with Marvin Gay's *What's Going On*, Curtis Mayfield's *People Get Ready*, and other politically outspoken soul sounds of exactly those years, "Idle Hands" is an eloquent outcry against the injustices and irrationality of modern society, all rooted in the reality of rampant poverty amid unprecedented individual and corporate wealth. The song begins: "You all know the story, how it all began. It took five days, and then came man. All the land was free, and so were we. No slavery to lead to poverty, no poverty to lead to slavery. Idle Hands." What follows is an indictment of the "whole political mess," as Palmieri refers to it when commenting on the song, "the state, taxes, killing, denying the people the right to happiness, all for the sake of so-called progress. There it is, the myth of progress, and 'Idle Hands' just blows it apart. The symptoms that come out of those conditions made up the other song titles, like 'Broken Home,' 'If,' and 'The Seed of Life.'"[14]

The *Harlem River Drive* album was not the commercial success that Palmieri had hoped for with this bold crossover experiment. Going with Roulette instead of Tico, and leaning so far in the direction of US soul and rock idioms, just what he had disdained in the boogaloo era, was explicitly an effort to "sell more units" and capitalize on the huge-selling recording success of Tommy James and the Shondells on Roulette. Perhaps the level of fusion and crossover was too much for the market, but the album has survived as a kind of "cult favorite" of leftist radicals and retro connoisseurs of early '70s funk. Most notably, "Idle Hands" became the anthem of the Weather Underground, the notorious urban guerilla group of those years, who made their adoption of the song widely known. While Palmieri was surprised at the attention it got from those quarters, he had no particular problem with it, though Morris Levy was of course infuriated when the FBI scrutinized him once again for the actions of his Latin

superstar. He called Palmieri in, as he had done a few years earlier because of the right-wing Cubans' protest against his use of
the Mozambique, and warned him not to bring him trouble for
something that was not even of his own doing.

During the time of that recording, Palmieri brought the
Harlem River Drive group to visit Sing Sing, the federal penitentiary in Ossining, New York, for a historic concert that led to the
Recorded Live at Sing Sing albums. There were two, but the first
one, volume one, is the best known. It was clearly a memorable
occasion in many ways, beginning with the number of quality
musicians present, as well as the reading by ex-Young Lord and
member of the Last Poets Felipe Luciano of his signature poem,
"Jíbara/My Pretty Nigger." Apparently the concert was intended
as a visit to Calvin Clash, who was doing time there, though it
turned out he had been transferred to another institution by the
date of the concert and wasn't even present. Though the event
was not specifically set up by the Young Lords Party, this was
one of many prison visits and concerts by Palmieri in those
years, most of them in fact arranged by members of the Lords.
The recording of the Sing Sing concert was done by Joe Cain
from Tico Records. The engineer was one Vicente Cartagena,
who assumed that it was an all-Latin band and was concerned
that the music wouldn't go over well with the mostly African
American prison population. "Eddie, the audience is 80 percent
black! They won't like our music!" To this Eddie responded con-
fidently, thinking of his unmatched popularity with the Black
dances and the Black Sunday nights at the Palladium: "'No kid-
ding! Just open the curtain, and don't worry about it, we got it
covered, you know.' And we played, and they went wild with it."[15]

The Sing Sing concert opened with a powerful Afro-Cuban
santería tune, "Pa La Ocha Tambó," and went on to offer new
r&b–inflected versions of his classic numbers from the La
Perfecta repertoire, "Muñeca" and "Azúcar." Felipe Luciano's

dramatic reading and the lively voice of the master of ceremonies reinforce the remarkable energy of the inmates audible on the recording. While the music has been described as the "most openly psychedelic" of all Palmieri recordings, in a remarkable feat of working with tradition and experimentation there can be no doubt as to the anchoring of the sound in the same Afro-Cuban structures that guided the composer and bandleader throughout his career. The *Live at Sing Sing* albums, the last that Palmieri did with Tico, attest to the boldly eclectic and socially conscious quality of his music during those exciting transition years between the fading of boogaloo and the coronation of the Fania All-Stars and baptism of "salsa." The coincidence of Palmieri playing his idiosyncratic Latin soul at Sing Sing prison while the Fania stable of all-stars, including Ray Barretto and Willie Colón, made history playing típico at the symbolic Cheetah Club, drives home the wide range of musical languages incorporated within the "salsa" frame, while at the same time dramatizing the divergent narratives that co-existed on the rise of "salsa" as the name for Latin world music.

Discussion of the late 1960s period in the history of salsa and its naming must include reference to the fascinating back-story of the scene in Venezuela during those years. Far from New York City and nearly a decade before salsa was called by that generic name in its place of origin, Afro-Cuban-based dance music enjoyed an enthusiastic reception in Caracas, especially in the city's populous working-class barrios. In 1966 the popular Caracas radio disk jockey Phidias Danilo Escalona founded a daily noon-time show which he called "La Hora de la Salsa, Sabor y Bembé," choosing the word salsa because the musical offerings were intended to delight the working people during their lunch break. In that same year, local bandleader Federico Betancourt and his band, Federico y Su Combo Latino, released an album entitled *Llegó La Salsa*, a selection of Cuban-style "tropical" songs, many of them achieving wide popularity among fans and the dancing public. In that context, "salsa" meant urban Caribbean music in general, especially as favored in the poor, marginalized barrios in opposition to the flood of American pop and rock cultivated by the middle classes across town. So there is thus some validity to the idea that the term "salsa" as a genre reference was first coined in Venezuela, at a distant remove from and well before it took hold in New York. Many New York–based Latin musicians—as I was informed by Andy González and Richie Ray among others—recall first hearing the word "salsa" when playing at the annual "carnivals" in Venezuela in the late 1960s, while Johnny Pacheco says he ran into the term when traveling in foreign countries, and not in New York. Caracas-born and raised pianist Luis Perdomo (now living in New York) remembers growing up with "salsa" by that name back in the late 1960s when he was still a teenager, while his music-loving father recounts what it was like to dance to the music of his foremost idols, Tito Puente, Tito Rodríguez, Eddie and Charlie Palmieri, La Lupe and Ray Barretto, and the many others who were often invited to play in clubs and stadiums in urban Latin American venues.[16]

However, though this pre-figuration is of some historical importance and needs to be better known to followers and students of the music, the first use of the umbrella generic term should not be confused with the music itself. After all, the repertoire played by Phidias on his lunch hour show and loved by his ecstatic listeners consisted mainly of recordings by the pioneers from New York: Eddie Palmieri, Ray Barretto, Richie Ray and Bobby Cruz, Willie Colón, Joe Cuba, and other mainstays of the New York scene. The style that caught the imagination of people from the Caracas barrios cannot be described simply as "urban Caribbean," or "tropical," but was actually created by second-generation Puerto

Ricans and Cubans in the New York diaspora, and it was music that reflected that reality; without the New York ingredients, salsa would not have been salsa. This is not to minimize the style's international roots and aesthetic appeal, qualities that would contribute significantly to its powerful global diffusion in subsequent decades. The Caribbean and Latin American grounding of the music is present throughout and is a crucial source of its contestatory power in the hegemonic context of US culture during the 1960s and '70s. It is that sense of Latino cultural difference and the refusal of rampant imperial assimilation that provide salient political content to the "revolt con swing" so prevalent in New York's Latin music of those heady years. While the term was only in widespread use far from the music's creative origins, it is in precisely that period that what would come to be called salsa came fully into its own. Without yet having an agreed-on name for it, in the dynamic compositions and performances of Ray Barretto, Richie Ray, Eddie Palmieri, and other Nuyorican pioneers, the listening and dancing public was indeed enjoying salsa avant la lettre. The music of the generation had arrived in full presence, "Llegó la salsa!"

5

Fania's Latin Thing

It was 1971. The prime time for "Latin music" had arrived. The masterminds of Fania Records, Jerry Masucci, Johnny Pacheco, and Larry Harlow, were planning the big hype. They needed the right venue. They thought of Fillmore East, Bill Graham's famed psychedelia space, but it had just closed. They thought of Central Park, but they couldn't get a permit. The historic Palladium Ballroom had closed down five years earlier. But there was the Cheetah Club, right around the corner, on 53rd Street and Broadway. It was huge, and run by Ralph Mercado, the premier promoter of those years, so it would be easy to reserve and publicize. It would be the event of the summer and a landmark in Latin music history. They could pull together the Fania All-Stars, the biggest names in music, do a huge promotion blitz, and pack the place. They could even have the whole thing filmed and recorded live for a boxed set of LPs. Sounded like a winning plan! The hour of Salsa had struck!

The Cheetah Club was indeed an ideal venue. Working with Bill Graham might have been exciting, especially as he loved mambo, was a regular at the Palladium, and had unique experience at putting together mega-events like this one: just two years prior, in 1969, he had been instrumental in booking Carlos Santana to play the Woodstock concert before the mob scene of over 400,000, and then viewed on the 1970 film by millions of others. But aside from its historic location in the shadow of the old, unforgettable Palladium, the Cheetah was also known to all Latin music fans by then, and when still called the Palm Gardens it had been the cradle of a lot of boogaloo and Latin soul concerts just five years earlier. Besides, it housed more than two thousand people and had a few other perks guaranteeing a wild time; as Harlow described it, "It had a balcony on top, and an upstairs room called the 'Love Room'—it was all black-light posters, the 'get high' room. And then there was a little room that hung from the ceiling with a few tables and chairs, and we used to go there to get blow-jobs."[1] Promotion could go into high gear, with empresario and long-term album cover artist Izzy Sanabria, who put the event in a larger cultural context: "It was the time of the sexual revolution, you know, and the Young Lords and all that shit. We were waking up. My mission was to improve the Latino image in a positive way. We recorded a commercial on a one-track, straight to vinyl, that then ran on Dick Sugar and Symphony Sid's show. The commercial for the Cheetah, I did a voiceover just using music from *2001: A Space Odyssey*, telling people to come and be part of the filming."[2]

To do the filming they recruited Leon Gast, a good friend of Larry Harlow and a known quantity to Fania as he had shot album covers for them and was gaining a reputation for his still photography work in *Vogue* and *Esquire*. Gast was to become best known years later for his Oscar-winning 1996 documentary *When We Were Kings* about the famed "Rumble in the Jungle," the 1974 heavyweight boxing championship match between Muhammed Ali and George Foreman in Zaire. As another part of its meteoric rise to world celebrity, the Fania All-Stars played that event, which was the reason for Gast's attendance; indeed, in the year of the fight he directed *Celia Cruz and the Fania All-Stars in Africa*, and during the same year came out with *The Grateful Dead Movie*, which he co-directed with Jerry Garcia. *Our*

FIGURE 28 Poster, Fania All-Stars, Historic dance at the Cheetah, Club, August 26, 1971. Courtesy of Izzy Sanabria.

Latin Thing — Nuestra Cosa Latina, the 1972 documentary about the Cheetah concert, was his very first film credit and the film met with impressive commercial success. It was a linchpin of Fania's stratospheric prominence and the promotion of "salsa" to world music stature. Its deft interspersal of concert and rehearsal footage with scenes from New York barrio life lent it a true-to-life quality and accounts for its fame as the "definitive salsa documentary."[3] It is one of the main sources of evidence for César Miguel Rondón, in *El libro de la salsa,* in his—perhaps overstated—description of salsa as music of the streets.

More than four thousand people flocked to the Cheetah that Thursday night of August 26, 1971, many of them sensing that history was in the making and all anxious to hear and dance to the Fania All-Stars. There was a superstar for everyone, be it Harlow or Pacheco, Willie Colón or Cheo Feliciano, Ray Barretto or Richie Ray, Hector Lavoe or Bobby Valentín, Barry Rogers or Pete "El Conde" Rodríguez. Singers, drummers, piano virtuosi, master trumpeters— the huge band was like a dream team, a Latin music glitterati collection, all part of the Fania "family." It was a night not to be missed, and from all who were present it was indeed memorable. No doubt the band felt the adrenaline as well, and they didn't disappoint; according to Gast, "it really is my firm belief that the band never sounded as good as it did that night, and I've listened to them and been to a lot of Fania shows."[4] Within months, the four live albums were released and the film premiered, and Fania was well on the way to establishing itself as the sole creative home of salsa. In what would emerge as the master narrative, Fania became salsa and the salsa story the Fania story. Fania Records became nearly synonymous with the Fania All-Stars, often referred to as the greatest salsa band ever. And in terms of sheer star power, could there be any doubt? That narrative has prevailed down to our own time, as evident in the 2009 four-part public television special *Latin Music USA;* the second episode, entitled "The Salsa Revolution," is faithfully close to the script of the Fania story, equating salsa with the record label.

Though there can be no denying the crucial historical importance of the Cheetah concert, the Fania All-Stars, and the film, getting behind this prevalent version of music history is key to uncovering a more nuanced account of events and the relations between innovation, social conditions, and the role of the music industry. Leon Gast's own comments are revealing in this regard, when he mentions his own outsider status in relation to the community as well as (to a lesser extent) that of his guide Larry Harlow. He recalls that the street scenes were done in a very casual, haphazard way, "just walking around the streets shooting." He mentions that the setting was not El Barrio in East Harlem, or the South Bronx, as is often assumed, but the rather less representative Lower East Side. Even the idea for the street footage was his own and not that of the musicians or Fania people, and "as much as style is concerned, it's all very formulaic, music and a little bit of the culture." And as for the scenes with the musicians interacting with the community, especially the depiction of flutist Pacheco as pied piper attracting the kids in the street, "Really corny."[5]

More important, the very idea that the music itself emanates directly from the barrio streets, as appealing as it may be, and as basic for Rondón in his stridently populist book-length account, can be very misleading and needs qualification. By the time the music reaches the lofty heights of Fania sensationalism, the mean ghetto streets are far removed, though of course many of the musicians and the fans in attendance do stem from those very streets. It's the distance rather than the proximity that is most characteristic of "salsa" in the Fania version, and this becomes increasingly so over the ensuing years of unabated Fania hype. As drummer Orestes Vilató said of the film's midtown premiere, comparing it with the times of the Alegre and Tico All-Stars, which prefigured and were the inspiration for the Fania grouping, "Jerry [Masucci] was very smart. They took all of us to the premiere . . . in limos and tuxes with our wives, all very classy, and a big, big deal. No one remembered Tico, no Alegre, no nothing."[6] Or as Pacheco had it, salsa was about class, or classiness: "What was beautiful about salsa was its glamor. We had class: openings with Rolls Royces, big stretch limousines, big parties and shit like that. And the people were proud to see Latinos on a par with Americans. When we showed the movie *Our Latin Thing* we had a big opening at one of the theaters on Broadway."[7]

Gast's point about the band being at its best ever on that particular night is also noteworthy, especially in view of the superlatives commonly attached to the Fania All-Stars in the annals of salsa history. Of course the group was not actually born, at least in name, on that occasion, since there had been the first engagement three years earlier at the Red Garter. But that earlier assortment of personnel was very different, including as it did, "special guests" from the Tico stable of the stratospheric stature of Tito Puente and Eddie Palmieri, as well as many of the musicians no longer present by the time of the Cheetah event. Though incarnations of the all-star band continue to vary, what has come to be known as the Fania All-Stars did in fact premiere for the Cheetah mega-concert and filming, and was reflective of the much more lucrative, commercially successful Fania enterprise. By 1971 Fania was well on its way to virtual monopoly status in the Latin music field, already eclipsing the waning Tico empire, whose catalogue it would purchase within a few years, and accruing handsome profits from its own swelling output of more than eighty albums and growing fast. It is thus fair to say that the special concert date is of foundational importance in the historical process, and that the Fania All-Stars may be considered the collective embodiment of what is known as "salsa."

But ultimately, the all-star band, increasingly the touchstone of Fania's output and identity, needs to be assessed in relation to other similar constellations and to regular work-a-day ensembles like the bands of Colón, Harlow, Barretto, Palmieri, and others. Does the superstar stature of the invited dream team members add to the quality and creativity of the music? Does it mean reaching new heights of experimentation and syncronicity, as seemed to be the case with the Alegre All-Stars ten years earlier, or with the seminal Cuban descarga sessions? Or does the emphasis on the sheer virtuosity of the individual stars occlude a limited musical concept and overly staged spontaneity? Is salsa according to Fania and its all-stars up to the challenging quality of the music in the hands of Palmieri, Colón, or Barretto when leading their own bands? Do the live Cheetah albums stack up to recordings like *Vamonos Pa'l Monte, Asalto Navideño, Que Viva la Música,* or Harlow's *Abran Paso* from those same years? Is it something other than mere sour grapes when Tito Puente and Eddie Palmieri goof about the "Funny All-Stars," or when even Fania's main arranger Louie Ramírez himself outgoofs those two giants by correcting them phonetically and calling it the "Funnier All-Stars?"

Insightful salsa historian César Miguel Rondón addresses just such issues in his extremely detailed discussion of the Fania All-Stars and the Cheetah moment. He argues knowledgably that despite their undisputed excellence, the musicians chosen were with few exceptions not the most accomplished or appropriate practitioners at their respective instruments, nor were the stellar vocalists the best fit with the musical styles represented in the repertoire. Of greater critical consequence, since the same might be said of any given selection of talent and achievement, the stylistic range of the group was markedly constricted in view of the rich eclectic nature of New York's Latin music repertoire at the time. For one thing, the lyrics were all in Spanish, without even an occasional expression in English. Along similar lines, the variety of African American musical styles, including both the jazz and soul continuums, is virtually absent. Indeed, even any Latin genres other than Cuban, such as the Puerto Rican, Dominican, Panamanian, or Brazilian admixtures, are also virtually excised from the repertoire. Beyond that, even among the Cuban styles, not only are any traces of charanga absent, aside from Pacheco's occasional flute riffs, but the only strongly represented genre is the son, and within that rich history, it is the legacy of the Sonora Matancera and to a lesser extent of Arsenio Rodríguez that predominates. Also noteworthy, there is not any reference to New York City or the diasporic reality lived by many of the musicians themselves and most of the public. Beyond that, the sharp political content evident in much of the music from the period immediately preceding was totally absent, with the lyrics generally restricted to the usual party and dance exhortations; love relations with strong sexual, and sexist, implications; and of course, mucho male bravado. Such thematic orientations are evident in the best-known numbers identified with the all-star group at the Cheetah concert and in the recordings and documentary, such as "Ponte Duro," "Macho Cimarrón," "Ahora Vengo Yo," and "Quítate Tú"—all classic tunes, beloved standards of the salsa repertoire, but all remarkably uniform stylistically and thematically.

The All-Stars' *Live at the Cheetah* quickly ranked among the bestselling releases in the Fania catalogue and set the standard for what came to be known, locally and internationally, as "salsa." As Rondón, puts it, "The golden age of salsa music began at this point when the record companies successfully combined what executives thought impossible: a spontaneous, freewheeling, and accessible music of high quality that was also highly profitable."[8] The impressive sales were achieved without losing "the two key elements of a jam session—its spontaneity and the freedom of the musicians to play and sing whatever they were enthused about." The problem is that musically that spontaneity is more illusory and staged than is true of the historic descargas or jam sessions that served as Fania's model, those of the Alegre All-Stars of Al Santiago and Charlie Palmieri, and the Cuban descargas led by Israel López "Cachao." Though the jazz-derived style of alternating solos gives the impression of freedom and extemporaneous inventiveness, the Fania All-Stars' delivery was based on well-scripted arrangements done by the inner circle of Fania musicians, including Louie Ramírez, Bobby Valentín, Larry Harlow, Ray Barretto, and of course Pacheco himself. A casual comparison between the structure and feel of the first Alegre All-Stars album, for example, with the *Live at the Cheetah* recordings illustrates this difference clearly. It is not so much the elite stature of the individual musicians in the respective groups as their live interaction, the collective chemistry among them, and their ability to co-create the musical text in action. Compared to the Alegre group, which actually rehearsed and practiced together frequently, the Fania band exhibits a relative formality and predictability foreign to the descarga modality, and they were as a group famously unrehearsed and reliant on prior scripting by Pacheco and his immediate planners. In fact, for the Cheetah concert the repertoire was actually devised in the wee hours of the morning the very day of the recorded performance. As arranger Bobby Valentín reports, "Pacheco had the music for the Cheetah concert a week before the show, but the music wasn't right. We needed more excitement, so we changed all the music in two days. Pacheco and I stayed up all night till four or five in the morning writing for the All-Stars."[9]

It is the idea and sound of the Fania All-Stars, more than any of the bands from the company's stable except perhaps Pacheco's own, that established the "Fania formula," a term used proudly by Pacheco himself, but less admiringly by some of the other, more experimental musicians and cognoscenti. For Pacheco it is a matter of his personal legacy as the founder of the "formula" for success; "I want to be remembered," he said, "because of the basic formula for salsa that I created with El Tumbao. I also want to be remembered because of what I did with the All-Stars which is still alive. It was a very prestigious thing. To be the organizer and have the top musicians follow my leadership. . . . One thing I believe is that once you have a formula, you don't change it."[10]

The formulaic quality of this brand of "salsa" is especially evident in the All-Stars' recordings, a sound that Rondón pointedly calls the "Matancerization" of New York Latin music because of the boilerplate model provided by Sonora Matancera. In the work of Pacheco's own band, El Nuevo Tumbao, the footprints of traditional Cuban dance music are everywhere, with many of the numbers sounding like attempts at direct imitation of the original; some commentators suggest that it is neither "nuevo" nor really "tumbao." In the All-Stars performance and recordings, the Sonora Matancera influence is to be noticed in the nasal vocals of the coros, sometimes called "fañoso coro," the trademarks of the high voice in Sonora's chorus, the legendary Caito. Another earmark of the Sonora model is the trumpet work, with its typical filigree-like flair at the ends of lines.

These are of course signatures of Pacheco's faithful adherence to the established practices, which is in itself not especially objectionable; rather, it is the predictability and imitativeness involved that give the music a mannered and stylized sound, the trace of a formula in the negative sense of the term.[11] The All-Stars provided the precedent in many ways for what would become the standard salsa band of the boom period, and as Rondón points out, "The salsa that developed during the boom had little in common with the music that initially had shaped it. The industry forced musicians to follow safe and easy formulas, and so the old Cuban guaracha increasingly dominated the repertoire." Speaking of Pacheco's collaboration with Celia Cruz on the retro 1977 album *Recordando el Ayer* ("Remembering Yesterday"), Rondón continues, "The old expression was reproduced and imitated to the letter without any type of innovation, without any new element that revealed the music's contemporary circumstances. . . . It is unacceptable—even false and disingenuous—. . . to mask this reproduction of the past as the legitimate and authentic expression of the present."[12] As the knowledgeable Mongo Santamaría once commented regarding Pacheco's adoption of the old Cuban standards, "He didn't even change the arrangement."[13] In an even more poignant remark, Mongo responded to the calls for strict típico orthodoxy by saying, "If I wanted to play típico, I never would have left Cuba!"

In the minds of Masucci and Pacheco, the business model for Fania Records was explicitly Motown; even the logo seems to be a take-off on the familiar Motown insignia. The idea of an assembly-line production, with its obvious time- and cost-saving advantages, increasingly underlies the Fania agenda as commercial interests came to supersede those of musical originality and collective creativity. But, just as explicitly, it was a Motown "for Latinos." Pacheco, and Larry Harlow, said it again and again; in Pacheco's words, "The Whites had their music, the Blacks had Motown, and here we come with Fania. But it was Latino."[14]

"Our Latin thing," "nuestra cosa"—the catchword of the project, as branded by the film and recordings—indicates the strong influence of Fania's bonus baby Willie Colón, one of whose early albums and whose whole musical persona was built around this allusion to organized crime and the mob mentality. That association, an effective pop culture allusion and marketing ploy for Colón, became increasingly germane when referring to the shady and at times extortionist financial tactics of Fania Records, as Masucci and associates gravitated ever more overtly to other hit men in the music field, most notably Morris Levy. But the "thing," "la cosa," in this case was emphatically "our" thing, the "our" just as unequivocally identified as "Latin" to the exclusion of other, closely interacting cultural realities. As Larry Harlow put it, evidently insensitive to the irony, "it was 'Our

Latin Thing,' it really was; the Hispanics were looking for something to identify."[15] But it was, again ironically, a market-driven and not so much a political or even cultural sense of "Latino," seemingly inclusive but in fact limiting because it had to do with marking off a niche in the musical marketplace. Trombonist and Latin music critic Chris Washburne explains the notion of a Fania "family" in these terms: "The notion of family extended beyond the musicians and was marketed to the communities to which they targeted their sales. This strategy capitalized on the newfound cultural pride being incited within Latino neighborhoods, as well as the calls for a unified Latino consciousness by new political movements. Fania deliberately constructed salsa as an exclusively Latino cultural expression, a discourse that reverberated through the barrios and swiftly transformed the fledgling company into an economic powerhouse."[16]

As much as the historic Cheetah concert did to establish the commanding role of Fania in defining the features of what was beginning to become known as "salsa," the company was to carry forward its ambitious agenda in the years following, reaching the apex of its towering hegemony by 1975. As if the massive attendance at that spectacle were not enough, in the fall of 1973 Fania staged an even more mammoth affair, in that venue of venues, Yankee Stadium. Even the Beatles didn't get to play there during their famed 1963 tour of the United States but opted for Shea Stadium. In fact, the old Yankee Stadium only became a choice site for mega-concerts in more recent times, so that Fania was breaking relatively new ground and entering the stratospheric levels of performers such as Elton John, Billy Joel, Bono, and Michael Jackson. Fania again engineered a massive publicity campaign and arranged for a recording and movie of the event; Masucci once more turned to Leon Gast to direct the filming. Indeed, the crowd was a record for a Latin music event, numbering close to forty thousand. The opening acts by El Gran Combo, the newly formed Típica 73, and legend Mongo Santamaría effectively warmed up the spacious home of the Bronx Bombers, and energy was high when the members of the All-Stars were introduced individually, culminating in the appearance of Johnny Pacheco.

A featured number of the concert was "Congo Bongo," a much-anticipated drum battle between Mongo Santamaría and Ray Barretto. The excitement level was running very high—so high, in fact, that before the celebrated drummers got into the heat of their performances the crowd went wild, breaking security regulations by massively storming onto the field, rushing to the stage, making off with amplifiers and instruments, and grabbing at the musicians and tearing their clothes. The band members had to run off in fright. As Roberto Roena recalls,

FIGURE 29 Fania All-Stars live at the Palladium. John Storm Roberts Collection, Photos and Prints Division, Schomburg Center, New York Public Library. Courtesy of Fania Records.

"about half-way through the song, the fans came out of the seats like a tsunami toward the stage. The music had gone into the people's blood. The number didn't even finish. Then we started running. I saw the audience running with our amplifiers, pieces of musicians' clothes. I didn't know who took my bongos. I yelled to Nicky [Marrero], 'Corre, corre!' Forget the timbales and run for your life!"[17]

So much for the new live recording, and the new film promotional. Not about to see their ambitious plans derailed, though, Fania soon thereafter set up a highly attended mega-concert at the Coliseo Roberto Clemente in Puerto Rico, which they proceeded to record and film. In 1975, the Fania All-Stars released *Live at Yankee Stadium, Vol. 1 & Vol. 2*, retaining the title even though most of the songs were actually recorded at the San Juan venue. The albums were characterized by more of the Fania All-Stars sound, and they had the added attraction of the participation of Celia Cruz, who joined them at the Roberto Clemente stadium and sang some of the most engaging selections. Fania thus played its business hand well, capitalizing twofold by retaining the Yankee Stadium reference on the album cover and at the same time drawing together a huge fan base in Puerto Rico.

The film version of the two-venue mega-event, which didn't appear until 1975, veered off much more significantly from the Cheetah idea as captured in *Our Latin Thing*, a change that indicates clearly the direction in which the Fania project and "salsa" concept were heading by that time. For while the primary intention of the 1971 documentary had been to ground the musical expression in barrio life and the sense of the community as creator of the new genre, by mid-decade, the time of the new film, the agenda was directly the opposite. The goal this time, as explained by Rondón, was to "make salsa—more than a modern musical expression from the barrio—the latest fad in the international pop music scene. They called their new film *Salsa*, and they intended for it to show the history of this musical expression."[18] In addition to the opportunism of using the recognizable, very Americanized, and poorly informed journalist Gerardo Rivera as narrator, the film does everything it can to divorce the music from all traces of its community origins and points of reference. In a totally mythified version of cultural history, the movie tracks the story of "salsa" from the wilds of Africa—depicted in pathetically clichéd imagery with drum-beating natives—directly to "America," meaning the contemporary United States. To avert any political repercussions, there is not even a stop-off in Cuba along the way, and no sense of the history of the Cuban and Puerto Rican communities in New York. By projecting images of Dolores del Río, Carmen Miranda, Desi Arnaz, and other reminiscences from the exoticized mass culture of the forties and fifties, this Fania product is intent on inserting salsa into the lineage of the "tropical" fads and dance crazes, with the implication that its main value is its contribution to American entertainment. The goal was, as Rondón rightly concludes, to divorce the music from its social roots and raison d'etre and establish "salsa" as a "fundamental part of [American] pop culture."[19] The very title given the film makes it clear that by that time the word salsa had arrived as the accepted designation for the music as a genre or stylistic modality.

Aside from its place within US mass culture, the commercial strategy was for it to gain a truly international identity, and a place within the repertoire of "world music." Fania was immensely successful along these lines as well, not only in the Spanish Caribbean and Latin American markets but also in Africa. A year after the Yankee Stadium mega-concert, the All-Stars were off to Zaire on the occasion of the Ali-Foreman "rumble in the jungle." There was a star-studded music festival to accompany the intensely publicized boxing summit, which included the likes of Bill Withers, B. B. King, Miriam Makeba, the Spinners, the Pointer Sisters, and the "Godfather of Soul" James Brown. And, of course, the Fania All-Stars. Remembering the moment when the entertainers landed in Zaire and were getting off the plane, Johnny Pacheco speaks proudly about how he outshone James Brown in the celebrities' reception by the host African fans. The thousands of Africans there to greet them "went past him [Brown]," according to the acknowledged leader of Fania, "and they started chanting 'Pa-che-co, Pa-che-co!' They went bananas, I swear to God. So he wanted to know who Pacheco was."[20] The story of the immense popularity of Afro-Cuban music, including salsa, in Africa is a long and inspiring one, to be sure, but one can't help sense a certain special glee on Pacheco's part to have received a warmer welcome in the ancestral homeland than that towering symbol of Black diaspora expression that is James Brown. Something other than racial and cultural solidarity seems to have been at play, something having to do perhaps with commercial supremacy. In any case, this historic trip, and the Academy Award–winning film by Leon Gast years later, were an integral part in the international reach of the booming Fania empire. As Masucci preened, "When we were really doing the great concerts with the Fania All-Stars, we would do more business in Latin America than the Rolling Stones. . . . We did Japan, Africa, England, we did all of South America, and wherever we went, we never had a loser. It was always big."[21]

Perhaps nothing is more indicative of the monopoly established by Fania over the Latin music market than its purchase, in 1975, of its main competitor of many years, Tico-Alegre. While they had worked on projects together for some time, Tico owner Morris Levy and Jerry Masucci reached a deal, and the notorious "hitman" Levy was able to unload his huge Latin catalogue in order to pay off some accumulated debts. Inheriting such headline acts as Tito Puente, La Lupe, and Joe Cuba, Fania thus stood virtually unchallenged in the Latin field, and "salsa" became synonymous with that brand name. Eddie Palmieri had shifted from Tico to Harvey Averne's fledgling (and short-lived) Coco label, and the upstart Mericana label took on some of the Latin market as of its founding in 1973. But while its commanding position was already present by the beginning of the decade, by 1975 Fania ruled the roost, nearly unchallenged in its supremacy at least until the formation of Ralph Mercado's RMM empire in 1987. Eventually even Palmieri, whose long career took off just as Fania was founded in 1964 and who steered clear of that affiliation through the years, put out one album, *Eddie Palmieri* (sometimes called the "White Album"), with Fania affiliate Barbaro records (echoing the nickname of Benny Moré, "El Bárbaro del Ritmo"). But that was 1982, when Fania's star was already waning.

While Fania's business plan was clear and remarkably successful, its musical project was more ambivalent and often had deleterious effects on artistic authenticity and quality. To some extent the ambiguity lies in the diverse intentions and emphases of its twin kingpins, Jerry Masucci and Johnny Pacheco. As we have seen, Pacheco's intent was largely to preserve the traditional Cuban musical styles, especially the son and guaracha, to the point of outright imitation, while Masuccci's was to look for the crossover splash, a way for Latin music to break into and conquer the American and world pop markets. Any kind of crossover or fusion would do, as long as it stood to capitalize on established commercial US or international acts. Once the euphoria of the Cheetah and Yankee Stadium mega-events began to fade, and no new inroads were visible in the well-worn típico field, Fania moved its All-Stars in this new direction by throwing together the 1974 album *Latin, Rock, Soul*. The title tells most of the story, the word of the day being "crossover." While the album included the first release of two important numbers from the Yankee Stadium/Roberto Clemente Stadium concerts, "El Ratón" and "Congo Bongo," most of the cuts were studio recordings based on collaborations between the All-Stars and invited guests from the worlds of rock and soul at the time, such as Carlos Santana's brother Jorge, percussionist Bill Cobham and pianist Jan Hammer from John McLaughlin's fusion group the Mahavishnu Orchestra, and soul fusion sensation of the moment Cameroonian sax and vibes player Manu Dibango. The result is a hodgepodge of mixes in different directions and combinations, with none of them congealing in a convincing or organic way. The jazz fusion pieces, like "There You Go" or "Smoke," allow little or no room for the "Latin" dimension, while the classic Latin compositions, "El Ratón" as immortalized by Cheo Feliciano when with the Joe Cuba Sextette, Cachao's standard "Chanchullo," and Tito Rodríguez's "Mama Güela," fall far short of their originals because of the unhappy attempt to weave in Jorge Santana's electric rock guitar (which is, by the way, not even a close match to that of his superstar brother). Though the conga duel between Barretto and Mongo on Harlow's "Conga Bongo" composition obviously aroused crowd excitement when performed live at Yankee Stadium, much was lost in the recorded version. Perhaps the most successful track is the least touted, the opening "Viva Tirado" based on a 1970 hit by the East Los Angeles group El Chicano.

The All-Stars' fusion album was clearly part of the company's business plan, but it showed few signs of success. Its sales didn't come close to that of the Cheetah concert albums and its release had little or no significance in any of the markets included in the three-way fusion: Latin, soul, or rock. Though the label was on a roll, reaching its commercial peak in just those years, its alternatives of a retro típico sound or a concocted crossover did not bode well for musical innovation. Between the imitative and repetitious Sonora Matancera re-run and the generic "Latin" admixture in what Rondón calls "rock con conga," Fania's glowing business achievements and prospects began to run afoul of its capacity for creative experimentation and stylistic breakthroughs of any historic note. Ironically, just as the monopoly tastemaker was entrenching its much-needed commercial term "salsa," the musical modality that it was banking on was quickly running out of fresh new paths to follow. Though some of the star vocalists on their roster succeeded in pursuing solo careers of some note, and their standby bands continued to release accomplished and sometimes memorable albums, no new acts were emerging or on the horizon. If visibility and occasionally impressive sales are the measure, the All-Stars continued their name brand publicity role for years to come, enjoying revival after rebirth in a campaign of everlasting hype. Despite its ongoing and often enthusiastic international following, the Fania All-Stars project was not a bellwether of where New York–based Afro-Cuban music was headed, nor an indication of what the new generation of urban Latinos was coming up with. That role was played by some of the label's bandleaders with their own ensembles, and increasingly by developments emerging outside of Fania's purview.

Its famed dream-team composite was obviously Fania's flagship band, where the company was putting its financial hopes and energy and realizing some of its most lucrative profits; more than any other group, the Fania All-Stars came to epitomize "salsa," and on a world scale probably does so down to the present. But the label's musical claims, its association with creative innovation, continued to rest on the prominent bandleaders in its stable, notably Willie Colón, Ray Barretto, Johnny Pacheco, and Larry Harlow, along with the perennial outlier Eddie Palmieri. Salsa historian Rondón offers a helpful typology of these paramount bands of the 1971–75 period by differentiating between "traditionalists" and "avant-gardists": the former category is represented by Pacheco and Harlow, the latter by Willie Colón and Palmieri, while Barretto hovers somewhere in the middle, oscillating between a hard-set típico format and his experimental work in jazz or soul. The countervailing gravitation toward an "authentic" Latin sound on the one hand, with lyrics in unmixed Spanish and repertoire comprised of re-workings of típico classics, and on the other hand, toward experiments with those traditions and fusions with other, mostly African American and Puerto Rican, styles, defines the spectrum of expressive possibilities included within the generic notion of salsa. A brief consideration of each of the major Fania artists within these parameters leads well to a discussion of the achievement of Eddie Palmieri during that same period, culminating in his being awarded the first-ever Grammy for a Latin album, *The Sun of Latin Music*, in 1975.

Johnny Pacheco was the first and by far the most voluminously recorded artist on the Fania roster. The debut album of his co-founded label and of his new post-charanga band, the 1964 *Cañonazo*, was an explosive seller and launched a string of dozens of LPs in the "tumbao" format, the typical trumpet-led conjunto playing true to the style of the popular Cuban groups of the 1940s like the Sonora Matancera, Cheo Marquetti, Félix Chappotín, and Arcaño y Sus Maravillas. The title of his 1967 release, *Sabor Típico*, probably best capsulizes the quality he was striving for. While his numerous albums contain some commercial hits and demonstrate an overall high level of artistic competence and swing, they are generally difficult to differentiate due to their repetitiveness and the uniformity of their stylistic characteristics. During the 1971–75 boom period, perhaps the outstanding albums are two of the many he made with his prime vocalist, Pete "El Conde" Rodríguez, namely, *Los Compadres* of

1972 and *Tres de Café y Dos de Azúcar* (1973), and his classic collaborations with Celia Cruz, *Celia y Johnny* (1974) and *Tremendo Caché* (1975). Though his mid-1960s switch from cha-ranga to the conjunto format, and from Alegre Records to his own company, were abrupt and significant, Pacheco generally is to be admired for his persistence in sticking to his tried-and-tested style and honing that established language to the utmost. His mastery of the típico sound allowed for a harvest of some of the all-time established versions from the salsa genre, most notably the classic songs identified indelibly with the towering Celia Cruz repertoire, like "Quimbara" and "Cúcula." His long-time "compadre" Pete "El Conde" allowed for a perfect match between vocal style and orchestra, a combination that also gen-erated many favorites in those years. All told, however, Pacheco's recordings were with few exceptions not among the bestselling releases on the label, and the bulk of his prolific output failed to leave any mark for innovative contributions to the music of that period. The strict orthodoxy and derivativeness tended to leave too many of the active stylistic options out of the picture, the result being a sizable body of work that left little lasting mark and remains largely forgotten by the salsa world except for a few followers and aficionados. In addition to his spectacular pio-neering pachanga of the early 1960s, Pacheco seems destined to be better remembered for his empire building than his specifi-cally musical accomplishments.

While Larry Harlow has been a Fania stalwart since his first recording in 1966 (just the third band, after those of Pacheco and Louie Ramírez, in the catalogue), he came into his own dur-ing the boom period, notably with *Tribute to Arsenio Rodríguez* and *Abran Paso* in 1971 and *Salsa* in 1974; mention is also made of his *Presenta a Ismael Miranda* (1968) and his salsa opera *Hommy* (1972), though in the latter case, most of the creative credit should probably go to the lesser known Heny Alvarez, who composed most of the songs, rather than to Harlow himself. He was also a kingpin of the Fania All-Stars project from its inception, their regular on piano, and their constant composer and arranger through the years. Stylistically, he was like Pacheco a devoté of the típico emphasis, sometimes combatively so, though he did have his own rock band and is often credited with bringing a rock aesthetic, with lights and smoke shows, into the Latin scene. Harlow was more inclined to side with his old running buddy from pre-revolutionary Cuba days, Jerry Masucci, in bringing salsa to a level of star-studded glory compatible with that of rock. He frequently boasts about being the first to use electric piano, "way before Eddie, way before Stevie Wonder,"[22] a step that brought some balks from the traditionalists but made sense given the condition of many of the pianos provided by the clubs in those years. He is also proud of being the first to work with a two-trumpet, two-trombone format, thus adding the trombone front line in the style of La Perfecta but combining it with the usual trumpet-led brass section. But his best-known tunes, like his adaptation of Arsenio's "La Cartera," "Abran Paso," and others, are decidedly in the traditional vein and hew closely though sometimes creatively to the established sound. Though a master pianist in his own right, and made famous by his longstanding hold on the piano chair with the Fania All-Stars, he was surpassed in power and originality by contemporaries like Eddie Palmieri and Richie Ray. No doubt by titling his album *Salsa*—Rondón considers it his "most successful and important" one—he contributed crucially to establishing that word as the catchall for music of the time, and Fania as its primary source and keeper. Again, and quite unfairly, more than for his specific musical contribution, Harlow goes into the history books for that baptismal act, and of course for his remarkable ethnic versatility in moving from orthodox Jewish roots into the heart of Latin culture. Such is the story of "El Judío Maravilloso" ("the

Marvelous Jew"), the nickname given him after that of his legendary blind idol, Arsenio Rodríguez, "El Ciego Maravilloso."

Ray Barretto was more restless and wide-ranging in his musical abilities and interests and underwent several abrupt changes in direction in his frequent oscillation between Latin traditions—be they charanga or son montuno—and the jazz drumming that had been so formative throughout his musical life. As we have seen, he was also drawn to variations on soul and funk and gave voice to his political persuasions in some of his strongest compositions. He started off the boom years strong, following up on his first albums with Fania with *The Message* (1971) and the solid compilation *Que Viva la Música* (1973). But immediately thereafter, his trajectory was derailed in a serious way by the departure of most of his band, after which he recouped his strength with the promising but subpar *Indestructible* that same year; the closing title track seems to draw a parallel between his own personal resilience after the loss of his band and an "indestructible" political determination on behalf of the cause of justice. His main achievement in the salsa field as of the time of the Cheetah concert was his role as musical director of the Fania All-Stars, a position he held through the decade. In this capacity it is clear that in spite of his idiosyncratic musical predilections, but perhaps because of his very eclecticism, Ray Barretto was located squarely in the inner circle of the Fania enterprise.

Though his own recording output was never to equal his finest work with Charanga Moderna or with his prolific conjunto on the Fania label as of 1968, his 1975 album entitled *Barretto* was a major contribution to the salsa repertoire. It was intended as a review compilation of some of his best previous work but with a new format and new vocalists, in this case the young Tito Gómez from Puerto Rico and Rubén Blades, who was making his first serious entrée into the higher echelons of salsa. The track

"Guararé," based on a Cuban standard written by Juan Formell, became one of the best-known hits of the salsa canon. In addition to that song and Blades's debut composing and singing appearances, the album features two memorable compositions by Tite Curet Alonso, "Testigo fuí" in tribute to the Puerto Rican people, and "Vale más un guaguancó," which Rondón considers "one of the most beautiful songs that this music has ever known."[23] Indeed, though it is actually one of Barretto's lesser known and difficult to acquire recordings, Rondón is all superlatives, referring to *Barretto* as "his high point in the salsa world and his most mature work, . . . one of the chief documents of salsa music."[24]

No doubt Barretto's own conga work contributes to that glowing judgment, but it is also clear that if this album represents a peak, it also marks the beginning of a decline from which the bandleader Barretto never fully comes back: by the following year, 1976, he dissolved his band and follows with two unsuccessful jazz albums with Atlantic Records. Barretto remained a consistent and celebrated presence in the Latin music scene for decades thereafter, but his days of greatest glory and original accomplishment were behind him. His in-between position regarding traditionalist versus avant-gardist tendencies in musical concept corresponded to his own dual attraction to both típico and varied shades of crossover into the jazz and soul fields.

Once he signed on with Fania in 1967 and formed his heralded partnership with vocalist Héctor Lavoe, Willie Colón was at the center of the whole enterprise and never veered from the salsa agenda, embracing the term once it came into currency. Indeed, he became the all-time bestselling member of the Fania stable and a regular member of the All-Stars. Unlike his fellow Fania standbys Barretto and Pacheco, though, his productive output continued unabated through the decade and beyond, with some of his most imaginative and commercially successful recordings dating from the boom years of the early to mid-1970s.

But he was not one to toe the line in terms of Cuban orthodoxy and the típico sound. Though Pacheco himself produced most of his early albums and had a lot to do with the end product, Colón ranged widely in defining the sources and related rhythms for his repertoire which, despite the unifying personae of the bad boy from the streets in league with his crafty jíbaro buddy from the Island, remained loose and experimental. As we have seen, more than any of the other major salsa bandleaders Colón emphasized the Puerto Rican roots of the New York Latin community and its music. In fact, some of his best and most popular material centers on the very relation between the Island and the New York setting, a relation captured in its complexity and intensity in his unparalleled Christmas album from 1971, *Asalto Navideño*. Here the cadences of Puerto Rican música jíbara resounded to the masterful and versatile cuatro of the peerless Yomo Toro and the unmistakable vocals of Héctor Lavoe, all in counterpoint with the familiar trombone and conga sounds of New York salsa. Small wonder that it has remained one of the most popular salsa albums both in New York and on the Island, and an all-time favorite Christmas album throughout Latin America.

During the boom years of 1971–75, Colón continued his prolific output unabated, producing a successful album or two every year, all remarkably consistent with his abiding, playfully enacted theme of street crime and the perennial "barrio bad boy." In rapid succession, and each including songs that became long-standing favorites of the salsa public, he and his band came out with *La Gran Fuga/The Big Break* (1971), *El Juicio* and *Asalto Navideño Volume 2* (1972), *Lo Mato* and *Crime Pays* (1973), and *Se Chavó el Vecindario/There Goes the Neighborhood* (1975). The last of these is of special interest because it was based on a collaboration with pioneering Puerto Rican plenero Mon Rivera and includes some of the classic bombas and plenas from the tradition, some of them composed by Rivera's father, one of the legends of those Afro-Puerto Rican genres. Songs like "Aló Quién Llama" and "Tingulikitín," which feature Mon Rivera's unique tongue-twisting ("trabalengua") skat singing, may by now be best known to modern audiences thanks to this album with Willie Colón. It is around this time, the mid-1970s, that the first signs of a revival of those forms in New York City became evident as part of a movement that was to continue growing and spreading throughout the country and even back to Puerto Rico over the subsequent decades.

Because of this and many other daring forays away from the usual salsa formats and traditions, Willie Colón, though faithfully in the Fania fold, stands out as an "avant-gardist" when his output is compared to the more predictable repertoire and stylistic range of bandleaders like Pacheco and Harlow, and even the eclectic chameleon Ray Barretto. Colón was very aware of the boldness and experimentalism of his compositions, and he attributed it directly to the diasporic origins of the new, mixed styles that were to engender such sharp rejection among the traditionalists. As he put it, "Our generation was mostly US born, so when I started a song with a Puerto Rican *Aguinaldo* that went into a Cuban *son montuno* and then into a Dominican *merengue*, with occasional English or Spanglish choruses, nobody flinched . . . except for some of the old timers who nearly had apoplexy. It was blasphemous! It was incorrect! It was . . . *salsa!*"[25]

Colón—as a Fania stalwart he was a major beneficiary of the boom—was also acutely aware of and outspoken about the pitfalls of that commercializing process and its impact on the music. He saw the "salsa explosion" of the 1971–75 years as a "double-edged sword." As Colón explains, "It gave us diffusion, but it also introduced the factor of commercial interests with a vengeance. When salsa began to take hold among the Latino public of the United States and in the Caribbean it also became a business, and right away the record companies began to look for formulas aimed at taking advantage of the success."[26] Colón mentions the practice of building the whole sound around the star vocalist, and the idea and common practice of dusting off the old Cuban hits of the 1950s, the songs of Benny Moré, Arsenio Rodríguez, Celia Cruz, and the Sonora Matancera, "salsa-ing" ("salsearla") them up a bit with new arrangements and instrumental formats, and being sure of a hit. "In that way," he goes on, "the boom became a brake on experimentation, and this has all affected me directly and significantly, since I have always tried to take it a step forward with each new record, and the only way I know of to do that is to let my creativity loose without having to think about whether you're going to have a commercial success with it."[27] To his credit, Colón was willing to take those risks, and he points to the bold new directions evident in his historic collaboration with singer-songwriter Rubén Blades, which with all its stylistic and thematic innovation also resulted in the bestselling salsa album of all time, their 1978 *Siembra*.

Eddie Palmieri wasn't invited to the Cheetah Club for the historic Fania All-Stars concert on August 26, 1971. And if he had been, chances are he would have declined. Things had changed since the prior All-Stars concert at the Red Garter in 1968, when the ranks of the Fania roster needed to be filled out with some "special guests" from Tico, like Tito Puente and Palmieri himself. But by 1971 Fania had full coffers of talent and could boast the overwhelming majority of the major Latin bandleaders, vocalists, and masters at the various instrumental roles. But Palmieri's absence at the Cheetah meant he made not even a cameo appearance in the film *Our Latin Thing*, nor a few years later in the sequel *Salsa*, nor for that matter in "The Salsa

Revolution," part 2 of the widely viewed 2009 public television documentary *Latin Music USA*. Just as "salsa" was experiencing its meteoric rise to international pop status, arguably the most important pioneer in forging that experience was being written out of the master narrative. That this outsider status was in large part self-imposed is clear, since it is known that Jerry Masucci's mouth was watering to incorporate Palmieri into his dynasty. But the lines were being drawn with little regard for historical accuracy or musical justice, such that this gross erasure in many accounts of "salsa" history only attests to the hegemonic power of Fania, the corporate empire of the Latin music industry in those years, to tell the story in its own image and attribute to itself and its inner circle creative rights over the generation.

This is not to say that Palmieri was left with his arms crossed while all the hoopla was going on. During the same year as the Cheetah concert, Palmieri performed at the massively attended concert at the University of Puerto Rico, resulting in the live recording three years later, in 1974. Fans in Puerto Rico remember that event to this day as a pathbreaking one for salsa on the Island. That same year also saw the release of the canonical album, *Vamonos Pa'l Monte*, and in 1972 the two volumes of *Live at Sing Sing* appeared, which together demonstrate the remarkable musical range of Palmieri's bands, whatever their personnel. And then, in 1973, the year of the Fania All-Stars mega-concert at Yankee Stadium and precisely when Latin music was being named "salsa," Palmieri released one of his most remarkable albums, *Sentido,* a veritable showcase of the bandleader's and composer's many modalities and voices.

Though the Fania releases of that year included such important contributions as Pacheco's *Tres de Café* and *Dos de Azúcar*, Ismael Miranda's *Así Se Compone un Son*, Bobby Valentín's *Soy Boricua*, Willie Colón's *Lo Mato*, and Ray Barretto's *Indestructible*, none demonstrate the degree of sophistication and sheer originality of *Sentido*. Every track of that often overlooked collection, which without being a thematic album and despite its vast range of different styles displays a surprising coherence and sequence, warrants admiration. From the gorgeous slow-tempo anthem to "Puerto Rico," surely one of the most memorable of that genre, to the wildly experimental funk-rock fusion number, "Condiciones Que Existen," which could well be an out-take from *Harlem River Drive*, to the nine minutes of carefully modulated descarga of "Adoración," there is vintage Palmieri here for every taste, all of the highest production quality and musicianship. This was Palmieri's first recording after leaving Tico for the fledgling Coco label owned by producer Harvey Averne, who bought his contract from Morris Levy for $35,000 at a time when Palmieri could well have chosen to move to Fania in its prime. "Sure," he recalls saying to himself, "a brand new company, I like challenges like that."[28]

Sentido was also Eddie's last album before his long-term vocalist Ismael Quintana was to leave him and go solo with Fania. The collaboration with such exciting experimental instrumentalists as Andy and Jerry Gonzalez, Nicky Marrero, Mario Rivera on flute and sax, veteran Vitín Paz on trumpet, and Harry Viggiano on tres and guitar allowed for a dynamic and varied sound, which was amplified further by the presence of the trusty trombone duo of Barry Rogers and Jose Rodrigues from La Perfecta days. Palmieri also luxuriated in collaborating once again with Rogers on the arrangements for most of the numbers. In all of Palmieri's extensive recording oeuvre, *Sentido* is no doubt one of the sadly overlooked jewels and offers a better sampling of Palmieri than any of the numerous "best of" compilations.

Perhaps the relative obscurity of *Sentido* in the Palmieri canon is due to its being almost immediately eclipsed by the two albums to follow, both of which were of towering importance and won the first two Grammies ever awarded Latin music recordings. *The Sun of Latin Music* and *Unfinished Masterpiece* from 1974 and 1975, respectively, were also on Coco, and both stand as peerless tours de force in the annals of New York Latin music. Importantly, they came out just as the music was being referred to as "salsa" in broad public (and commercial) discourse, the very years that also saw Harlow's album and the second Fania All-Stars film, both entitled *Salsa*. Though, as said, both were awarded Grammies, *The Sun of Latin Music* is the more remarkable of the two, in part because the bandleader had to identify and then train a new vocalist after having worked with Quintana in that capacity for over a decade, since the beginning of his career. The story of his "discovery" of the teenage Lalo Rodríguez while on tour in Puerto Rico, and then preparing him for the big stage and the pressure of studio recording, is a triumph in its own right, not to mention the inclusion of one of the initiate's own compositions, the unforgettable track "Deseo Salvaje," which became an all-time salsa favorite. The list of personnel was similar to that on *Sentido*, but this time it included Ronnie Cuber on baritone sax, Alfredo de la Fé on violin, and varied brass work including tuba and French horn, making for a truly fascinating sound on the consistently innovative series of tracks, most arranged by master pianist and arranger René Hernández of Machito and Tito Rodríguez fame. Though all of the selections carry their own distinctive quality, ranging in genre from bolero and guaguancó to danzón and cumbia, surely the tour de force is the extended, suite-like "Un Día Bonito," which meanders energetically through nearly sixteen minutes of shifting solos and counterpoints all centered around Palmieri's own inimitable piano work. Arranged by Barry Rogers, this remarkable, thickly atmospheric composition stands as one of Palmieri's foremost achievements, ranking with "Azúcar" of a decade earlier as a song of a musical generation. Along with the

Beatles-evocative danzón "Una Rosa Española," "Un Día Bonito" displays convincingly Palmieri's unique ability to range boundlessly in stylistic flavor while still keeping his firm grounding in both Afro-Cuban and jazz idioms and structural possibilities. As one of the rightfully glowing comments says, "Suitable for either the casual ear of the salsa fan, or the careful attention of the jazz aficionado, *The Sun of Latin Music* shines brightly, high above the horizon of its peers."[29]

FIGURE 30 Eddie Palmieri, *The Sun of Latin Music*. Courtesy Coco Records.

Eddie Palmieri remembers the eighteenth Grammy Awards ceremony when *The Sun of Latin Music* was selected to receive the first Grammy ever for a Latin Music Recording, a major historic event for all involved in Latin music everywhere. Of course, some of the key players from Fania Records were there—Jerry Masucci, Johnny Pacheco, Larry Harlow, Ray Barretto, Willie Colón (Eddie can't recall exactly)—since at least four of the seven nominees were Fania releases of that year, 1975: Mongo Santamaría's *Afro-Indio*, Barretto's *Barretto*, the Fania All-Stars *Live at Yankee Stadium, volume 1*, and Willie Colón's *The Good, the Bad and the Ugly*. Then there was the young Bobby Paunetto's exciting Latin jazz selection *Paunetto's Point* on Pathfinder Records, and Spanish pop singer Camilo Sesto's smash hit single "Quieres Ser Mi Amante." And then, the seventh, was Palmieri's *The Sun of Latin Music*. The excitement in the room was high, Chick Corea was doing the presentations, and then the announcement was made: Eddie Palmieri, *The Sun of Latin Music*. Like everyone else present, Palmieri was surprised, given that he was up against the powerhouse Fania dynasty at the height of its prestige and predominance in the field, and the nominated recordings were some of the most successful in their entire catalogue.

But Palmieri came out the winner against all odds. Corea told him "Here, Eddie, you deserve it" as he handed him the trophy. And however reluctantly and with whatever other resentments they might have felt, the Fania people had to come over and congratulate him for this supreme recognition. Here he was, recording on a tiny fledgling label, Coco Records, and he was able to conquer the Goliath on the sheer force and quality of his very idiosyncratic music. That moment, coming at a time when Latin music had definitively come to be called "salsa," carries strong symbolic significance in that it challenges the whole master narrative of salsa rising to prominence on the shoulders of the Fania corporation and its formula for success.

And just to prove that it was not a fluke, Palmieri received the second Latin Grammy the following year, for *Unfinished Masterpiece*, an album that he himself disavowed because it was released by Coco before he was able to finish his work on it (thus the title). This time he was running against more Fania powerhouses, including Mongo's *Sofrito*, Pacheco's *El Maestro*, the Fania All-Stars' *Salsa: The Original Soundtrack*, and Joe Cuba's *Cocinando la Salsa*, along with Eydie Gormé's collection of love songs recorded with the immortal Trio Los Panchos, the *La Gormé* album. And the winner against all of that salsa was none other than Eddie Palmieri, who has always despised the very term "salsa." Remember, whenever he encounters that word, the universally acknowledged prime creator of salsa has recourse to his favorite quote from that other pioneer of the genre, Tito Puente: "Salsa, salsa's not music, it's what I put on my spaghetti."

6

Salsoul Challenges

Joe Bataan was the first to break rank with Fania Records. One of the label's bestselling artists since his 1968 breakthrough hit "Gypsy Woman," Bataan had long felt unfairly compensated for his prolific output and popular success, and he brought increasing pressure on the company for a change. At the peak of Fania's success and predominance, the one-time street gang leader even tried to organize other musicians to form a union and stand up to the exploitative company and its obvious mob connections. The tension reached a high pitch in 1971 at the time of the historic Cheetah concert, when Fania declined to pay the musicians for appearances in the film. Bataan specifically remembers a meeting, held at the Castle Key Club in El Barrio in 1972, where a range of musicians—he recalls Tito Ramos, Ray Barretto, Joey Pastrana, and others—came together with the idea of uniting so as to secure better conditions from Fania. He recalls that he was blacklisted by Fania once Jerry Masucci got wind of the plan and learned that Bataan was the ringleader. Using a political style reminiscent of the boogaloo era, Masucci himself and other Fania powerholders reached promoters and radio DJs and urged them not to give any gigs or airtime to Joe Bataan and his band. In 1972, Bataan released his last album with Fania, *St. Latin's Day Massacre*, and then left the company, never to record with them again.

With no financial backing and only his name and popularity to bank on, Bataan struck out on his own, intent on dispensing with the middlemen standing between him and his fan base and skimming off an unfair share of the proceeds. Looking for an alternative to the monopolistic Fania empire, he landed on an obscure new label, Mericana Records, whose owners, the Cayre brothers (Joe, Ken, and Stanley), were relative novices in the New York market. Within a year of leaving Fania, in 1973, Bataan released his first recording with Mericana, the LP *Salsoul*. It was such a hit that the brothers changed the name of the label to Salsoul Records and gave Bataan a major share in the company. The popular DJ on WBLS Frankie Crocker played the whole album on his show, while promoter Héctor Maysonave defied Fania's dictate and continued setting up gigs for Bataan in venues around the city.[1] His career back on track, Bataan went on to build a wide international following, showing the world that it was possible to make New York–based Latin music outside the purview of Fania Records. Just as "salsa" was reaching the height of its boom years—virtually equated with Fania— this self-made bandleader from the streets of El Barrio was establishing Latin soul as an ongoing genre of Latin music in New York and worldwide, and giving it a new name of his choosing, "salsoul," salsa and soul.

Even though Bataan's main complaint with the music industry was economic—his not getting his share of the royalties and publicity—there were other important issues at stake that were not measurable in dollars and cents. In that same period, Bataan was being considered to host the first Latin soul TV program. It was to be aired on Channel 11, as an offshoot of *American Bandstand* and the "Latin" counterpart to *Soul Train*; well-established producers Alan Lorber and David Yarnell were on board, arrangements went out to the sponsors, and everything

FIGURE 31 Joe Bataan, *Salsoul*. Courtesy of Joe Bataan.

seemed to be set. But as Bataan recalls, "Fania and Izzy Sanabria caught wind of this plan, too, and quickly threw a wrench into the mix. Somehow they managed to contact the advertising agency and stated that Joe Bataan wasn't from a Puerto Rican background and shouldn't represent the Latin soul show on TV."[2] When they pressured the agency to replace Bataan with Izzy Sanabria, Channel 11 decided to drop the project altogether.

Despite Joe Bataan's strong roots and popularity in El Barrio and his extended success creating Latin music, Fania was able to throw doubt on his being a "real Latino," suggesting that because of this lack of authenticity he was not qualified to represent Latinos and their music. Thus, in addition to the sharp dissension over economic compensation and business ethics between Bataan and Fania, the record company was successful in questioning his ethnic representation and belonging, challenging his ethnicity so as to marginalize the troublemaker as an outsider to the culture. Somehow they didn't seem to have the same problem with Larry Harlow, for example, who actually had far less cultural credibility and social experience than Bataan but was squarely in Fania's inner circle and remained more loyal to its agenda, at least at that point. Perhaps in response to this questioning of his cultural background, Bataan titled his next album, released by Salsoul in 1975, *Afrofilipino*, thus describing his actual family heritage of Filipino and African American.

Beyond the struggle for adequate economic compensation, which was shared by most of the musicians of the Fania stable and even the hired arrangers and technicians, there were in Bataan's case also these charged issues of cultural identity. Perhaps most significant, however, though hardly addressed head-on, his break with Fania also had to do with musical style. Of course, the label voiced no explicit proscription against any given version of "Latin" musical genres, and as we saw had actually included many boogaloo and Latin soul recordings in its catalogue during the 1960s. But with time and increasing success the Fania "formula" tended to become more and more circumscribed, and its production and promotion more and more modeled after Motown's assembly-line technique. By the boom years of the early 1970s, the "Matancera" version of típico had become the privileged language of "salsa," with less room left for fusions and crossovers except with mainstream pop styles of the American repertoire. Willie Colón's ongoing inclusion of Puerto Rican genres and incursions into other international styles would seem an exception, though all of those innovations, including Colón's, were made compatible with the Cuban base of the music, with the tumbao. Most significantly, the strain of New York Latin music expressive of the interaction of Latinos and African Americans, including both Latin soul and Latin jazz, came to be relegated and marginalized in favor of a more unadulterated Afro-Cuban tradition and the Spanish-language, trumpet-led conjunto. We've seen how even Ray Barretto, who had been at the borderline between Latin and African American musical languages since early in his career, became more bound by the típico stylistic options in those early 1970s years.

Again, there were no stated exclusions or blatant suppressive measures, but Fania's "formula" for success, as Pacheco called it, and what came to be identified as "salsa," rested on a faithful, to-the-letter rendering of the Cuban original, with minor touches indicative of the New York location and sensibility. At the same time, the label, especially in the person of owner Jerry Masucci and others, was intent on moving into the big market with crossovers and fusions, in this case not so much with soul, funk or even jazz styles but rather more mainstream and more lucrative pop and rock idioms. The disastrous 1975 Fania All-Stars album *Latin Rock Soul* is the most prominent example of this "crossover dream" and its dismal musical consequences.

Despite his eclecticism, Bataan is squarely identified with the varieties of Latin soul sounds, from slow ballads to the most up-tempo dance styles of the time. His music, whether in Spanish with a strong Latin format or Latin-inflected, English-language interpretations of popular r&b compositions, was consistently expressive of that rich, creative juncture between Latino and African American social and cultural experience, especially among youth of the upcoming generation. As we have seen, the launching of Bataan's career, like that of Willie Colón, coincided with the boogaloo era, and while he never embraced the word, his subsequent musical output, unlike that of Colón,

remained strongly in that idiom. His performance and recording repertoire before and after leaving Fania was all Black-
Latin fusions of differing mixes and shadings, with some of his
somewhat less-known post-Fania output standing out as his
most impressive achievements. The *Salsoul* album itself is a rich
example, proceeding as it does from Bataan's Spanish-language
vocals in the first tracks, "Mi Nube" and "Muchacho Ordinario,"
to soul and funk compositions with only a tinge of Latin sound.
Notable differences between this 1973 recording and his early
work of the late '60s are the greater presence of electric guitar
and wa-wa reverberation reflective of a rock influence, and the
increasingly prominent hustle and disco tempos. Cuts like the
gorgeous ballad "Mujer Mía," the Bobby Rodriguez composition
"Fin," and Bataan's interpretation of the Deodato number "Latin
Strut" illustrate well the quality of his work at this stage, and
his engagement of caliber instrumentalists like Rodriguez on
bass and Barry Rogers on trombone assured a quality not often
attained in his earlier, better-known recordings. Also representative of this phase of Bataan's work is the disco-geared composition "Aftershower Funk," as is, in a different way, the live
recording of "Peace, Friendship, Solidarity," his contribution
to the international youth festival held in East Berlin in those
years. Through the years, Bataan retained his progressive politics and thematic concern for the common folk and poor people. Most famously in this regard, his subsequent album, the
1975 *Afrofilipino*, included Bataan's powerful disco version of
Gil Scott-Heron's canonical admonition on the trap of alcohol
abuse, the 1974 cult hit "The Bottle."

Attentive to the prominence and promotional hype surrounding the newly named "salsa" of those early 1970s years,
Bataan at the same time stayed in close tune with the dance and
musical styles of urban Latino and African American youth of
the post-boogaloo period. By the beginning of the decade, young

Nuyoricans were already extending and veering off from the more traditional mambo-based salsa style of their parents and creating a range of dance steps culminating in the Hustle, soon referred to as the Latin Hustle. Many of the fast moves, turns, and twirls associated with salsa dancing of subsequent years were actually developed as part of the Hustle, a chapter of New York Latin music as yet unanalyzed and in fact barely mentioned in the scant writing on the subject. While the origins of the Hustle and related dance fads of those years clearly stem from African American choreographic histories, young Latinos assured an unmistakably Latin stylistic affiliation to the most enduring of the variants of the Hustle, which is why like boogaloo before it and b-boying (breakdancing) thereafter, the "Latin" epithet becomes so indispensable and definitional of the style as a whole. Yes, it is firmly rooted in African American cultural traditions, but without the "Latin" component it wouldn't be what it is.

Pioneer Hustle dancer Willie Estrada recalls that of the early innovators in that dance style, all were New York Puerto Ricans except for one African American, Floyd Chisholm.[3] Estrada shows confident command in describing the intricate foot and body work and the many dance styles and substyles of the late 1960s and early '70s that led up to the Hustle in its full-blown expression. The emergence of the style is generally dated in the mid-1970s with the chart-topping recordings by Van McCoy, "The Hustle," which went viral in the summer of 1975, and the Fatback Band's "(Do the) Spanish Hustle" and Eddie Drennan's "Let's Do the Latin Hustle" of the following year. The Latin Hustle, increasingly identified as disco, then became an international sensation with the 1977 movie *Saturday Night Fever*. But Estrada and other early practitioners attest that a range of prior styles, like the 500, the Push and Pull, the Rope, Free Style, and others, were all evolving in the early years of the decade, just as salsa was attaining hegemonic status as *the* Latin style. By the time "salsa" came to be more broadly known by that name, many young Latinos in New York, and most specifically in that cradle of Nuyorican innovation the South Bronx, were already moving on to the "next big thing." Years before John Travolta and the Bee Gees established the disco fever of the late '70s and '80s, Nuyorican teenagers were creating new styles at house parties, disco clubs, and hookie jams (parties held during school hours by truant teens) in the area around 149th Street and Third Avenue at the hub of the South Bronx.

FIGURE 32 Willie Estrada and partner Millie dance the Latin hustle, ca. 1974. Courtesy of Willie Estrada.

The Hustle is best known to the world as "disco," its social origins virtually erased by the hype and multiple mutations of the stylistic forms as a result of commercial diffusion and re-appropriations. And while one of the upshots of those early '70s innovations was no doubt what became disco fever (as in the blockbuster John Travolta cult film *Saturday Night Fever*) and its varied social incarnations, another, more enduring consequence was the emergence of early hip-hop in the form of uprock and other prefigurations of b-boying. Again, the early emergence of hip-hop is generally regarded as a post-salsa phenomenon of the late '70s and early '80s, the release of the Sugarhill Gang's "Rapper's Delight" in 1979 marking a convenient starting point of the accepted narrative. But in its simultaneous creation with and surfacing out of the Hustle, the seeds of b-boying and the pre-recorded, street-level incubation of rap can clearly be traced to the early '70s as well, coinciding with the boom of Fania and its baptism of salsa. Interestingly, Estrada attests that the first b-boy went by the name of "Salsa."

Joe Bataan was the New York Latin bandleader most directly in tune with these developments of 1970s Latino and African American youth culture as they were unfolding, and he was intent on keeping his own performing and recording production firmly planted in this creative space. While many of the salsa musicians, including some of the most prominent of them, were fretting over the lack of gigs and opportunities, Bataan was recording for dance clubs, that is, for dancers moving to recorded music. He covered soul and funk hits by the major artists from Curtis Mayfield to the Philly sound to Deodato, all the while lending them a Latin rhythmic dimension or accenting further the Caribbean or Latin features already evident in the originals. He identified his compositions variously as soul, funk, strut, hustle, or continental, after the African American styles most expressive of that social experience of people of color. And, as might be expected but still little known by the general public, Bataan recorded one of the first hip-hop compositions, his own "Rap-o Clap-o," which appeared on his 1979 album *Mestizo* on the Salsoul label. Overshadowed among American audiences at the time of its release by "Rapper's Delight," Bataan's recording garnered great popularity in Europe, where it is viewed as one of the founding rap recordings. Thus, between Latin boogaloo and hip-hop, by way of Latin soul and the Latin hustle, Joe Bataan embodies the lineage of New York Latin music in its fusion and overlap with the African American sounds loved by young second- and third-generation Latinos in the inner city. It is precisely this evolving tradition—as of the early '60s an integral part of the musical expression of New York Latino youth that led up to salsa—that the Fania version of the music increasingly leaves out of the mix and loses touch with. Throughout the 1970s and beyond, it remains a crucial countercurrent to the master narrative and mainstream incarnation of the salsa story.

Grupo Folklórico was in the studio, in the midst of a recording session, when the goons showed up. They claimed to represent the union and asked for everyone's union card. But they had Mafia written all over them: the long trench coats, the fedora hats tilted to the side, the big cigar stuffed in the corner of the mouth. Jerry González, with his brother Andy the mastermind of the experimental band, was incensed: "What the fuck are you doing here? The union? You don't do shit for us, and here you come around interrupting a recording session. What are you, the Gestapo? Get the fuck out of here or we'll throw you out!" Jerry's threatening words and tone might have deterred the goons some, but it took the intervention of the record company that was paying for the studio time to get them to back off and leave. No further repercussions came of the event, but to all present it was clear that the unwanted visit at that particular moment was not fortuitous, and that someone wanted to derail the recording session by sending the union thugs to the scene. Many of them suspected it was Fania Records.

It was March 24, 1976, at the Bell Sound Studio on 54th Street, and the exciting new band with the long name, Grupo Folklórico y Experimental Nuevayorquino, was recording the song "Corte el Bonche" from its second album. Like its blockbuster first LP, *Concepts in Unity*, from the previous year (1975), *Lo Dice Todo* was contracted by none other than Salsoul Records, the modest record company owned and run by the Cayre brothers, as part of their business, Caytronics. Jerry and Andy and their band, then called Conjunto Anabacoa, had been introduced to Salsoul by their friends René López and Andy Kaufmann; the two record producers and collectors had been issuing compilations from López's extensive collection of historic recordings of Cuban music by performers such as Beny Moré, Arsenio Rodríguez, Arcaño y Sus Maravillas, Orquesta Aragón, and others.

As mentioned, the Salsoul label had been known as Mericana until Joe Bataan's 1973 album *Salsoul* hit it big, its neologistic title suggesting a convenient, catchy brand name for a new outlet of Latin music. Thanks to Bataan's example and intervention, the label had as its main focus the new dance style, the Latin Hustle, and eventually disco as it emerged in the mid-1970s. But the Cayre brothers were also keenly interested in breaking into the burgeoning Latin field and cashing in on the booming salsa market. Once they gained access to the abundant but unappreciated Latin catalogue owned by both RCA and CBS, the Cayres came to command a cornucopia of historic material from all genres of Latin American and Caribbean music. The prospects for attractive re-releases seemed boundless. López had already put out two important compilations, one of early Beny Moré recordings and the other a new release of Orquesta Aragón from their Cienfuegos years.

But Salsoul was also interested in bringing out new artists and made no bones about making inroads in the Fania behemoth, which had become more predominant than ever in the Latin market with their purchase of Tico-Alegre and by joining forces more closely with Morris Levy. As López and Kaufmann counseled the Cayre brothers, their eye on an exciting new recording: "You think the Fania All-Stars are big, and they are—no one can deny the musical prowess of that premier salsa band. But wait till you hear Anabacoa. It is much heavier, the real shit! It's sure to make it big!" It didn't take much convincing, and Joe Cayre promptly came up with a two-record deal for albums of new material by the upstart band. Conjunto Anabacoa at that time was basically an all-percussion grouping with the trumpet of Chocolate Armenteros and Nelson González on tres, who jammed on an irregular basis in the basement of Andy González's house in the Bronx and did their first gig at a jazz gathering at Wesleyan University. López and Kaufmann made plans with the González brothers and other musicians to expand the band by adding two trombones, flute, sax, and other instruments, and to change its name to the long descriptive one by which it has been known since, though the short version—Grupo, or Grupo Folklórico—has become its most familiar and accessible designation. The full name, with its dialectic of folklore and experimentation and its emphatic location in New York City, bore the stature of an entire program or aesthetic. Though fully in Spanish, in acknowledgment of their own bilingualism and that of their community, all of the words of the title are cognates and readily understandable to English-language audiences.

The programmatic title of the band was also indicative of the musicians, who were carefully selected as the most able to combine knowledge of and immersion in Afro-Caribbean musical folklore with an equally strong impulse to improvise and mingle those roots with new stylistic possibilities. While not the commercially successful superstars of Fania's dream team, Grupo prided itself on bringing together the acknowledged masters of each instrument. A core of them had played with Eddie Palmieri at different stages in his career, starting with Andy and Jerry González, and including Manny Oquendo, Chocolate Armenteros, José Rodríguez, and Julito Collazo, but none had yet been prominent bandleaders or superstar vocalists. With few exceptions, none had been part of Fania's extensive roster and were not part of "the family." But all excelled at their respective instruments, and all strongly endorsed the guiding principle of the project with its emphasis on grounding the music in the deep roots of Afro-Cuban music, most notably rumba guaguancó and the revolutionary breakthrough of Arsenio Rodríguez (Anabacoa is the title of a canonical Arsenio composition), along with a wide-ranging repertoire drawing from multiple traditions including jazz. Indeed, Andy and Jerry were both readily conversant in the jazz idiom, each having done stints playing with Dizzy Gillespie and other leaders in the field.

For the recording of *Concepts in Unity* Salsoul rented the top-of-the-line CBS Studios. Using sixteen-track equipment and the expert guidance of producer Fred Weinberg, Grupo took nine hours to record all nine songs, each in its own way a gem of folklore and experimentation. Soon after its release, the record was a towering success, receiving accolades from many critical quarters and outselling all other albums in the Latin field of the time. Not only was it praised to the skies by the local Latin magazines, *Latin New York* and *Latin Times*; it even was honored with a five-star review in *Downbeat*. According to Salsoul's accounts, *Concepts* enjoyed unexpectedly large sales in its first year, held its place for some time on the Billboard charts, and has remained a prized staple of international Latin music connoisseurs ever since. Because of its musical sophistication and its street credits—the band is comprised overwhelmingly of Nuyoricans born and raised in New York—that album (and its sequel, *Lo Dice Todo*) is sometimes referred to as the "filet mignon" or "champagne" of salsa.

It is no surprise, then, that Jerry Masucci and other Fania brass would feel piqued, and even threatened, by the meteoric rise of this makeshift assemblage of vintage New York Latin musicians and its hotly saleable productions. By that point, Fania ruled the roost in all senses and aspects and could not abide anyone deigning to diminish its stature. What to make of this upstart company run by outsiders, both to the music and to the New York scene? What was this "salsoul" gimmick, a name coined by its unruly renegade Joe Bataan and now appearing everywhere that salsa was being promoted and sold? In the historic June 12, 1976, issue of *Billboard* announcing the "salsa explosion" on the front cover, Salsoul Records ran a strategically placed full-page ad declaring themselves "Today's Revolutionary New Salsa Label for the People" and highlighting their prize product, Grupo's *Concepts in Unity*, "The Heaviest Brothers ever assembled on one album."

Of course, the Fania monopoly didn't really have much to worry about. Given its vast economic might, its engulfing in-house roster of artists and acts, and its foolproof promotional machinery, Fania's dominance was not actually threatened by a novice outfit like Salsoul, which held little promise of lasting long or holding its own in open combat. Indeed, Grupo's second album, while of equal musical fascination, did not fare as well commercially, and the band, always regarded as a work in progress, saw its members go separate ways, mostly to successful

CONCEPTS IN UNITY

FIGURE 33 Grupo Folklórico y Experimental Nuevayorkino, *Lo Dice Todo*. Courtesy of Andy Kaufmann.

careers. Salsoul was not going to outsell Fania or cut significantly into its market; eventually its stake in the explosive disco field took precedence over the Latin venture.

The real challenge of Salsoul, and of the success of Grupo Folklórico in particular, had to do not with profits but with musical quality and variety. As the Fania "sound" was becoming increasingly predictable and tired, Grupo came forth with a robust, deeply rooted, and boldly experimental repertoire that would also be called "salsa," though it was much more as well. Grupo's achievement made it clear that the Fania All-Stars, headlined as the summum bonum of salsa orchestras and boasting the marquis musicians in the business, were simply not producing the most interesting or innovative music at that time. And it wasn't the musicians themselves who were responsible, nor the arrangers and producers, all of whom were seasoned and accomplished. Rather, what made for the difference was the concept of an assembly-line, star-centered, formula-driven musical practice as against the genuinely improvisational descarga, the guiding principle of collective production, and original and complex musical structures and styles. To this day—and they have re-grouped in recent years—like the early Alegre All-stars before them, Grupo would go to work without any written arrangements. For good reason, then, Nelson González refers to Grupo as "el cuco de la Fania," the bogeyman, the thorn in the giant's side.

Fania's first move on sensing the power and depth of Grupo Folklórico might well have been co-optation, as it had been at various points with Eddie Palmieri: bring them into the fold. Failing that (and such offers and negotiations were made and fell flat), the next option is obvious: throw a wrench in the works, kill the competition. Again, there can be no outright claim or certainty, but there is at least reason to believe that it was Fania who tipped off the union goons to Grupo's recording session for the second album. All fingers seem to point in that direction, even though, according to knowledgeable arranger Marty Sheller, "none of Fania's sessions went through the union."[4] The episode, while ultimately inconsequential and unresolved, was no doubt a memorable one for the musicians and all present.[5] For it calls to mind the thuggery and chilling tactics at the heart of the music industry— where "salsa" is above all else a brand name and a bone of commercial contention. And the raid also attests to the treacherous conditions surrounding creative innovation, the risks inherent in striking off in new directions and against the current.

Grupo veers off from the Fania narrative by tracing a differ-ent lineage in the post-mambo stage of the history, more com-patible with the Tico-Alegre background, and especially with Eddie Palmieri and the Alegre All-Stars, than with Fania as a musical project. The Grupo version of salsa, if we stick to that name because of its universal currency, also differs because it suggests new and emerging forms of musical expression. Just as Joe Bataan's Latin soul going back to the doo-wop and boo-galoo eras anticipates Latin hustle, disco, and early hip-hop, so the inroads of Grupo lead to the re-emergence and flourishing revival of folkloric Afro-Cuban and Afro-Puerto Rican "roots music"—rumba, bomba, plena—that emerged in the 1980s and has grown as a movement for a full generation. While all the talk was of "típico," Grupo shows greater mastery of the rhythms and structures from the tradition and works a more eclectic range of Afro-diasporic traditions than other attempts in the popular music of the time; their seamless interweaving of these diverse sources within the musical text is unmatched within the field commonly called salsa.

At the same time, Grupo's language and sound also involve a constant dialogue with jazz. Examples abound in all of their work, and in fact there are very few cuts on the albums or in their repertoire that do not illustrate this ongoing, organically drawn fusion at some level. Though most of the band members share this cross-cutting of rumba and jazz to some degree, here again Jerry González plays a singular role, building as he does on his (and brother Andy's) intense experience at the seams and in earshot of both major components of the "experiment." This aspect of the Grupo project directly anticipated a goal of Jerry's in the Latin jazz field that he only came to realize a few years later, with the formation of the Fort Apache Band in 1980. As has become increasingly clear with the advantage of hindsight, if any musical expression of the 1980s generation (and beyond) illustrates the full creative potential of New York Latin music—what came to be called salsa—it has been in the broad rubric of Latin jazz. And as René López knowingly puts it, "If we're talking about Latin jazz, there's a before Fort Apache and an after Fort Apache."

The success of the *Concepts* album with Salsoul also had the unintended effect of opening doors for the González brothers in their other musical endeavor hatched during the boom period, their salsa band Libre. Originally called Conjunto Libre, and then renamed Manny Oquendo's Libre, the idea of this group was already congealing in the founders' minds while they were still playing in Eddie Palmieri's stellar band of the early 1970s, and with a view toward La Perfecta. Like Grupo, Libre has been called (again by their friend René López, and in admiring tones) an "Eddie Palmieri alumni band." Having left Palmieri in the summer of 1974, Andy, Jerry, and Manny were already inaugurating their new band, Conjunto Libre, on October 24, 1974. Andy remembers their debut concert well, a dance for Puerto Rican Discovery Day at John Jay College in Manhattan. The occasion evoked such patriotic fervor that the new band had to come up with its own "salsa" version of "La Borinqueña," the Puerto Rican national anthem. Before a year had gone by Libre had enough songs for their first album. Thanks to the success of Grupo's *Concepts in Unity*, Salsoul was more than willing to begin recording Libre as well. Between 1978 and 1980, Salsoul released three Libre albums, volumes 1 and 2 of *Conjunto Libre: Con Salsa . . . Con Ritmo* and *Los Líderes de la Salsa*.

Like Grupo, Libre was also a direct challenge to and defiance of mainstream commercial salsa and the hegemony of the Fania sound. As Fred Weinberg, the highly regarded engineer for the Libre recordings, wrote in the liner notes to the first album, "after so many cold, mechanical and lifeless albums, it is a pleasure to listen to music like this."[6] While the Grupo project resisted the commercial pigeonhole by producing Afro-Cuban based music that can hardly even be called "salsa" in the usual understanding of the term, Libre confronted the banalization of the category by getting back to the forceful, as yet unchristened Latin music of the 1960s, and especially that of La Perfecta and the pathbreaking sounds of Eddie Palmieri's bands. Both of the Gonzalez brothers' ensembles anticipated new and emerging stylistic innovations by reconnecting to earlier traditions that had been erased or blurred by the standardization and dilution involved in the mainstreaming process. But whereas Grupo emphasized the deep, age-old roots of Afro-Cuban and African diaspora musical heritages set in an experimental, jazz-oriented format, Libre was about connecting to and energizing the tradition of New York Latin styles of the previous decade, prior to their being watered down under the sway of the industry. As Rondón puts it, "After the salsa boom had made complacent rhythms, weak mambos, and repetitive montunos the norm and seemed incapable of getting beyond this malaise, Conjunto Libre represented not only a healthy change but also the return to the beginning of what would signal the end of a cycle. Without a doubt, this was one of the principal virtues of the group: they brought closure to this final period of the salsa boom by connecting salsa not so much to its long tradition but to its most immediate past."[7]

An important formative moment for Libre came in early 1976 when they played a benefit rent party for what was to become the Lower East Side cultural center, the New Rican Village. The band was such a hit with the crowd at that venue that they went on to play there regularly two nights a week. Their popularity grew over time as they attracted ever larger and more dedicated fans and followers. Since they had not recorded yet and were not in the Fania fold, Libre was still passed over by promoters and had few gigs at the larger clubs. Rather than a star status, they achieved a kind of underground, cult reputation among audiences seeking more solid, innovative, and socially rooted musical offerings. And who better than the remarkable assortment of mainly Nuyorican players associated with Libre, including Dave Valentín, Papo Vázquez, Oscar Hernández, Manny Oquendo, Alfredo de la Fé, Nelson González, Edgardo Miranda, Milton Cardona, Jimmy Bosch, Gene Golden, Chocolate Armenteros, and of course Andy and Jerry themselves?

Plenty of quality rumba- and son-based salsa and Latin jazz filled that humble space on Avenue A on many nights, but the New Rican Village was also a hub for creative young Latino poets, playwrights, actors, visual artists, political activists, and cultural workers of varied interests. The presence of Libre drew other musicians to the venue, notably the experienced and highly innovative Dominican sax player Mario Rivera. Best remembered for his two-decade association with Tito Puente among other greats, Rivera became a regular of the New Rican Village, first joining in with Libre and then forming his own group, significantly named the Salsa Refugees, which entertained and inspired audiences on alternating nights. Many of the participants in the center had been affiliated with or were admirers of the Young Lords Party of a few years earlier and maintained an active radical politics as part of the venue's cultural ambience. Libre and the González brothers thus became the central musical force of a vibrant, avant-garde setting that was outside the pervasive influence of the commercial network of record labels, DJs, promoters, and club owners.[8] As one New Rican Village regular states, "I figured out . . . why they're called Libre. Because they wanted to be free—free to express themselves, free from being confined to the controlled avenues of presenting themselves."[9] And among the many rave reviews that

Libre was receiving in those prime years of the later 1970s, one read, "At night the New Rican Village comes alive with sounds that can only be called 'improvisational Salsa,' a floating night-long jam session."[10]

Unwittingly perhaps, but in its incursion into Fania's virtual monopoly of the New York Latin music field, Salsoul Records helped to spawn alternative expressive movements and currents that were to emerge in the imminent "post-salsa" generation. These new alternatives also tended to reassert the centrality of aspects of salsa that had been sidelined or erased in its commercial mainstream version. On the one hand, Joe Bataan and his continuing of the Latin soul lineage after his break with Fania, found in Salsoul welcome support for staying at the pulse of Latino and African American youth as they forged new dance and musical styles in the Latin Hustle and early hip-hop.

FIGURE 34 Jamming at the New Rican Village, from left Jerry González, Chocolate Armenteros, Totico, René López, Papo Vázquez, ca. 1975. Courtesy of José Flores.

We might view this as the populist, barrio-based dimension of 1960s Latin cultural expression that attested to the strong bond with African American popular music; as we have seen, that organic Black-Latino linkage characterized the cultural setting during the pachanga and boogaloo eras and was also strongly evident in the projects of Eddie Palmieri, Ray Barretto, and Willie Colón in those mid- and late '60s years. On the other hand, Grupo Folklórico and Libre formed part of the creative, experimental avant-garde of the musical culture, with its attraction to the deeper roots of típico as manifested in rumba guaguancó and the breakthroughs of Arsenio Rodríguez, and as interwoven with sophisticated jazz innovations represented by such pioneers as Dizzy Gillespie, John Coltrane, Charlie Parker, Miles Davis, and Thelonious Monk.

Again, both of these important components of earlier, pre-boom salsa history tended to be elided by the Fania enterprise and musical "formula," and both harbored a strong political awareness that was also of minimal presence in the Fania products of the boom. Significantly, both also pointed in the direction of the deep Afro-Latin connection, one by way of the inextricable link to African American vernacular music and culture, the other by way of the strong Afro-Cuban and Afro-Puerto Rican anchor and the complex intersections with jazz.

Coda

Salsa played on while the South Bronx burned. In the mid-1970s, just as the catchy name for New York Latin music was gaining universal currency, the eyes of the world turned to its birthplace, the very streets that in earlier years had seen the creation and blossoming of mambo, pachanga, and other popular styles, as it went up in flames and became the symbol of urban blight. As the turning of the musical generation was marked by the standardization and commercial dilution of the stylistic language and the budding of new sounds and dance movements, the social landscape of Latin New York was also shifting, from the exciting self-discovery of Nuyorican and New York Latino identity to the devastation of the community's already fragile economic and political status. The consequences of massive working-class migration in the face of the city's drastic fiscal crisis of 1975 was epitomized by those nightmarish scenes of inner-city conflagrations, smoldering rubble, often violent street gangs, and the hulks of burned-out buildings. There was widespread torching of entire neighborhoods by landlords choosing to collect the insurance rather than deal with the upkeep of dilapidated housing stock, destitute tenants, and crime-ridden slums. The 1960s had seen a second generation of Puerto Rican migrants, their initial disillusionment, and cultural affirmation, and by the middle and later part of the 1970s, the vibrant energy of the Nuyorican movement and Young Lords Party had already

subsided; a different, more somber sensibility and social circumstance were setting in. It might not have been Howard Cosell
who—as legend would have it—was the first person to cry out
"The Bronx is burning!" while announcing a Yankee game, the
TV cameras fanning out to display the smoldering South Bronx
streets surrounding Yankee Stadium, but the human horror
story has remained familiar to many ever since. Indeed, the
image of that inner-city jungle, home to impoverished Puerto
Rican and African American families, has long been ingrained
in the public mind through dramatic representations like the
notorious 1981 film *Fort Apache, the Bronx* and Tom Wolfe's
1987 award-winning novel, *Bonfire of the Vanities.*

The new musical generation was marked by these conditions
and contexts. The exuberant dance party of salsa in its prime
peaked and was gradually eclipsed, especially among the youth
in those inner city settings. The new sensibility found its own
expression in the gritty, boisterous outburst of hip-hop issuing from those burned-out apartment buildings and the adja-
cent public housing complexes. Of course, New York–based
salsa still had vibrant life left after the boom of mid-decade, the
most striking case in point being the towering success of composer and vocalist Rubén Blades in partnership with the seasoned bandleader and producer Willie Colón; their 1978 album
Siembra is recognized as the bestselling salsa LP of all time, and
Metiendo Mano (1977), *Canción del Solar de los Aburridos* (1981),
and *Buscando América* (1984) also brought major sales and introduced the Blades compositions that have remained classics of
the salsa repertoire. Other New York–based salsa groups also
thrived into the later 1970s, the obvious and perennial example being Eddie Palmieri, whose ongoing album releases like
Lucumi, Macumba, Voodoo (1978), and *Palo Pa' Rumba* (1984) continued to garner awards and critical acclaim and added to that
pioneer's already voluminous repertoire. Típica 73, initially in

part a spinoff of Ray Barretto's popular band, gained avid attention in those years as well, in significant part because of their
bold experimentalism and creative renovation of charanga, as
in albums like *The Two Sides of Típica* (1977), *Típica 73 En Cuba
Intercambio Cultural* (1979), *and Charangueando con la Típica 73*
(1980).

But Rubén Blades is surely the richest instance of post-peak
salsa, and for some observers he represents the peak itself.
Yet despite the resounding and enduring success of his music,
Blades at the same time evidences a sense of the waning of the
New York salsa generation in those later seventies years. His
Panamanian upbringing, broad Latin American political per-
spective, and relatively privileged social background set him
apart from most of his musical role models and collaborators,
making for a sound which, with all the composer's adoration
of Cuban típico, is thoroughly infused with cadences and lyri-
cal usages more typical of Nueva Canción and Nueva Trova and
other international styles than those of guaguancó, son montuno, or charanga. Historical retrospective may come to view
Blades as an early sign of the transition between the classic
1960s salsa in which he was reared and the emergence of "salsa
romántica" which set in during the 1980s and has remained the
main manifestation of music called "salsa" in the past generation. Perhaps most indicative of Blades's nostalgic, tenuous relation to the heady years of salsa creativity is his 1985 feature film
Crossover Dreams. As represented by protagonist Rudy Veloz,
played by Blades himself, salsa appears here as adrift, rootless,
and desperately seeking its big crossover breakthrough in some
kind of incursion into the lucrative pop market. Perhaps reflecting the early years of Blades's own experience on the New York
music scene, the prospects are elusive, and an organic, fervent
dance and concertgoing community all but non-existent. The

heyday of the music and dance appear in retrospect, giving a sense of fading glory and the passing of an era of exuberance and novelty.

It was at that time, the later 1970s, when the story of music called salsa and the history of Latin music in and of New York City came to diverge. While new styles of expression began to emerge on the local level, "salsa" became the catchword for all "tropical," Latin music around the world, such that by the first decades of the new millennium there is hardly a major city anywhere without its salsa clubs, dance classes, concerts of touring icons, and homegrown practitioners. Salsa has become a key component of "world music," with strong anchors and native stylistic languages in key places like San Juan, Caracas, Havana, Cali (Colombia), Barcelona, and other European cities, as well as Tokyo and Accra. This global proliferation of salsa may be a source of pride for Latin New Yorkers as well as for Cubans and Puerto Ricans in their home countries, but the shift clearly involved the unmooring of the musical expression from its community base and social context. While the music itself remains guided by the examples set by Tito Puente, Celia Cruz, Eddie Palmieri, Willie Colón, Ray Barretto, and other New York pioneers, the meaning and reference point for the term "salsa" have mutated. Rather than convenient and commercially savvy shorthand for the varied Cuban and Nuyorican stylistic repertoire emanating from the New York setting, salsa has for several generations now served as a catchword for the "Latino" lingo of a global soundscape devoid of any particular geographic or cultural foundation. The international diffusion of all popular music forms tend to involve the same kind of de-contextualization, as evident, for example, in reggae, hip-hop, bachata, and many others, so that salsa is no exception on that score despite the particularly dramatic nature of the exposure and resultant transformations.

But when viewed in relation to the trajectory of Latin music in New York City, this change has clearly involved, and resulted from, the emergence of a new generational sensibility.

The post-salsa period in that history has witnessed two successive generations: one extending from the mid-1970s through the early 1990s, the other reaching through the first decade of the 2000s. If the first is signaled by the stylistic idioms of "salsa romántica," the merengue boom, emerging hip-hop and "roots" music, and the maturation of Latin jazz, the second witnesses the entrenchment (for better or worse) of hip-hop, including the acceptance of Spanish-language and bilingual "Latin" rap and the explosion of reggaetón, and the ethnic diversification of the repertoire as a reflection of the massive growth and variety of the city's new Latino immigrant populations. While the merengue fever of the 1980s, attesting to the city's burgeoning Dominican presence, made a non-Cuban, non-Puerto Rican Latin style preeminent for the first time, by the early years of the millennium, New York Latin included Mexican, Colombian, Brazilian, Peruvian, Haitian, Honduran, and a wealth of other Latin American and Caribbean musical idioms, all fusing in sundry ways with the jazz, salsa, hip-hop, and other styles at home in the New York setting. The large-scale settlement of Latinos from a broad range of countries—by the 1990s New York City was home to as many as five Latin American diasporas with populations exceeding 100,000 inhabitants—has engendered a cauldron of musical and cultural hybridizations unknown in previous generations.

Seen in the light of this extensive historical trajectory, the salsa era (what I have called the "sixties generation" and dated 1960–75) stands out and assumes a kind of internal cohesion as the apex of a pan-ethnic diaspora's long quest for its distinctive cultural voice and expressive modality, and as the opening of local styles to vast international audiences and to newly settling Latino communities. The salsa generation is, from that vantage point, the fulcrum of a century-old historical process, the axis on which turns the whole saga of Latino music-making in New York City, arguably the world capital and no doubt the cradle of music called salsa everywhere.

To understand the origins and consolidation of that ubiquitous stylistic category, it is necessary to track the finer grain of music history at the point of creation and learn where the ingredients of the sauce—pachanga, típico, boogaloo, Latin soul, political protest music, Latin jazz, and the Fania sound—came from, and what flavors they added to the mix over the course of a full generation of creativity and contention. Knowing the course of "salsa rising" as I have attempted to evoke that emergent process thus helps give historical substance and social context to the spectacular phenomenon of global salsa, that infectious Afro-Cuban-based dance music created by an immigrant working-class community that no contemporary student or fan of popular music can possibly ignore. At the same time, reconstructing that complex musical modality in its founding iteration also heightens our sense of what has been lost in the shuffle: it allows us to appreciate how wide transnational diffusion and a magnified market appeal may well be achieved at the dear cost of fresh creative originality and the special energy that comes from a grounding in grassroots community life and collective social struggle.

Notes

Preface

1. Among the wide-ranging tradition of thinking about generations, I have found most helpful the canonical treatise by Karl Mannheim, "The Sociological Problem of Generations," as well as the work of Spanish philosopher José Ortega y Gasset.

2. Morales, *The Latin Beat*, 55. In an early reflection on the meaning of "salsa," commentator Rudy García writing in the 1976 issue of *Billboard* noted, "some call it the political and social expression of young Puerto Rican New Yorkers, others the product of promotional genius by clever recording execs." (cited in Max Salazar, *Mambo Kingdom*, 248).

Introduction

1. José Luís González, "The 'Lamento Borincano': A Sociological Interpretation," in *Puerto Rico: The Four-Storeyed Country and Other Essays* (Princeton, NJ: Markus Weiner, 1993), 85–90.

2. See *Memoirs of Bernardo Vega: A Contribution to the History of the Puerto Rican Community in New York*, ed. César Andreu Iglesias (New York: Monthly Review Press, 1984).

3. John Storm Roberts, *The Latin Tinge* (New York: Oxford University Press, 1979, 1999), 50.

4. Ruth Glasser, *My Music Is My Flag: Puerto Rican Musicians in Their New York Communities* (Berkeley: University of California Press, 1997).

5. Roberts, *The Latin Tinge*, 87.

6. See Peter Manuel, "Representations of New York City in Latin Music," in *Island Sounds in the Global City: Caribbean Popular Music and Identity in New York*, ed. Ray Allen and Lois Wilcken (New York: New York Folklore Society, 1998), 23–43.

7. Roberts, *The Latin Tinge*, 88.

8. For a helpful account of the many musical innovations of Machito and His Afro-Cubans, see Bobby Sanabria, "Innovations by the Machito Afro-Cubans," Latinjazz.com, November 2, 2007. This information is also posted on the Wikipedia entry for "Machito."

9. Quoted in Donald L. Maggin, *Dizzy: The Life and Times of John Birks Gillespie* (New York: Harper, 2005), 223.

10. See interview of Santiago in Vernon W. Boggs, ed., *Salsiology: Afro-Cuban Music and the Evolution of Salsa in New York City* (New York: Excelsior Music, 1992), 220.

11. Ira Gitler, *Swing to Bop: An Oral History of the Transition in Jazz in the 1940s* (New York: Oxford University Press, 1987). This association was shared with me by David Carp, who elaborated on the concept of generational "cusps" in personal conversation, December 29, 2013.

12. Ibid., 123.

13. For numerous excellent examples of these fusions, see the multiple CD compilations by Rhythm and Blues Records variously titled *Rumba Jazz, Rumba Blues*, and *Rumba Doo Wop*.

14. Quoted in Paul Austerlitz, *Merengue: Dominican Music and Dominican Identity* (Philadelphia: Temple University Press, 1997), 74.

15. See David García, *Arsenio Rodríguez and the Transnational Flows of Cuban Popular Music* (Philadelphia: Temple University Press, 2006), 64–93.

16. Abe Santiago, "Hispanic Contribution to Doo Wop," Beaudaddy's Vocal Group Harmony Site. Abe.webarchive.

Chapter 1

1. Quote is from the film *Machito: A Latin Jazz Legacy* (1987), directed by Carlos Ortiz and Isabelle Leymarie.

2. See Max Salazar, *Mambo Kingdom* (New York: Schirmer, 2002), 246.

3. See Roberta L. Singer and Elena Martinez, "A South Bronx Latin Music Tale," Centro Journal, vol. xvi, no. 1, Spring 2004.

4. Ibid.

5. Ibid.

6. Conversation with Tony Ortiz. . .

7. Conversation with Herman "Pee Wee" López, December 20, 2012.

8. David Carp Interview: A Visit with Maestro Johnny Pacheco, May 12, 1997. Descarga.com. http://www.descarga.com/cgi-bin/db/archives/Interview2?G6saP2PX;;262

9. Mary Kent, *Salsa Talks: A Musical Heritage Uncovered* (Altamonte Springs, FL: Digital Domain, 2005), 330.

10. Ibid.

11. See for example WikiPedia entry for "pachanga."

12. Vernon W. Boggs, ed., *Salsiology: Afro-Cuban Music and the Evolution of Salsa in New York City* (New York: Excelsior Music, 1992), 223.

13. Salazar, *Mambo Kingdom*, 197.

14. See "Charlie Palmieri y Su Duboney," interview, by Néstor Emiro Gómez for herencialatina.com, August 6, 1981.

15. Ibid.

16. Santiago, cited in Boggs, *Salsiology*, 222.

17. Kent, *Salsa Talks*, 259.

18. See Santiago, "Louie Ramírez, 1938–1993," *Descarga Newsletter* 1, no. 10 (1993): 1.

19. Cited in Salazar, *Mambo Kingdom*, 198.

20. See David Carp interview of Charlie Palmieri, date?, p. 14.

21. See David Carp, "Profile: Alberto Santiago Alvarez," *Descarga.com*, December 1, 1996. http://www.descarga.com/cgi-bin/db/archives/Profile3?m8gsAM99;;792

22. Boggs, *Salsiology*, 212.

23. Roberts, *Latin Jazz*, 109–110.

24. Cited on backliner notes of 1996 re-release of *The Alegre All-Stars*.

25. Boggs, *Salsiology*, 224.

26. Cited on backliner notes of the 1996 re-release of *The Alegre All Stars*.

27. Ibid.

28. Al Santiago, "Column: The Other Side of the CD," *Descarga*, May 1, 1994.

29. David Carp, "35th Aniversary of the Alegre All-Stars," *Descarga Newsletter*, no. 25 (1996): 7.

30. Santiago, "Column: The Other Side of the CD," *Descarga.com*, May 1, 1994.

31. Carp, "35th Anniversary," 6.

32. See David Carp interview of Roy Ramirez, May 5, 1996. See also Carp, "35th Anniversary," 6–7.

33. See John Child, "Profile: Al Santiago," *Descarga.com*, February 23, 1999. http://www.descarga.com/cgi-bin/db/archives/Profile36

Chapter 2

1. Personal interview, February 24, 2011. Much of the information for this chapter is based on an extended series of taped one-on-one interviews done with Eddie Palmieri over the course of several weeks in February and March, 2011.

2. David Carp interview, "Profile: Eddie Palmieri: Substance and Form," in *Descarga*, October 10, 1998, 11.

3. See David Carp, "Salsa Symbiosis: Barry Rogers, Eddie Palmieri's Chief Collaborator in the Making of La Perfecta," *Centro Journal* 16:2 (Fall 2004): 42–61. See also Charlie Gerard, *Music from Cuba: Mongo Santamaría, Chocolate Armeneteros and Other Stateside Cuban Musicians in the United States* (Westport, CT: Praeger, 2001), 53.

4. Carp, "Salsa Symbiosis," 55.

5. Ibid.

6. Ibid., 49.

7. Mary Kent, *Salsa Talks: A Musical Heritage Uncovered* (Altamonte Springs, FL: Digital Domain, 2005), 330.

8. Robert Farris Thompson, "New York From the Barrios," *Saturday Review* (October 28, 1967), 53. Republished in Farris, Thompson, *Aesthetic of the Cool: Afro-Atlantic Arts and Music* (Pittsburgh: Persicope, 2011), 12–15.

9. See David Carp interview of Palmieri, May 12, 1997.

10. Kent, *Salsa Talks,* 260.

11. Ibid., 264.

12. Ibid.

13. Ibid., 260.

14. Ibid.

Chapter 3

1. Personal interview with Pete Rodríguez, February 24, 2013.

2. Miguel Gavilán, Mr. Pete Rodríguez, *Latin New York*, Vol. 1–3, February 1968.

3. See my "'Cha Cha with a Backbeat': Songs and Stories and Stories of Latin Boogaloo," *From Bomba to Hip-Hop: Puerto Rican Culture and Latino Identity* (New York: Columbia University Press, 2000), 79–112.

4. Max Salazar, *The Mambo Kingdom* (New York: Schirmer, 2002) , 223.

5. Ibid.

6. Flores, "'Cha Cha with a Backbeat,'" 96.

7. Ibid.

8. See my discussion of the song in ibid., 83–86.

9. Ibid, 100–104.

10. See Vernon W. Boggs, ed., *Salsiology: Afro-Cuban Music and the Evolution of Salsa in New York City* (New York: Excelsior Music, 1992), 272–73.

11. See Salazar, *Mambo Kingdom,* 230–31.

12. Flores, "'Cha Cha with a Backbeat,'" 79–82.

13. Mary Kent, *Salsa Talks: A Musical Heritage Uncovered* (Altamonte Springs, FL: Digital Domain, 2005) , 73.

14. Ibid., 74.

15. Ibid.

16. Ibid., 75.

17. Ibid.

18. Personal conversation with José Lebrón, March 16, 2013.

19. Ibid.

20. Ibid.

21. Izzy Sanabria, "The Lebron Brothers: Roots of Disco," *Latin New York*, January 1979, 78.

22. Salazar in Boggs, *Salsiology*, 247.

23. John Storm Roberts, *Latin Jazz: The First of the Fusions, 1880s to Today* (New York: Schirmer, 1999), 147 passim.

24. See David Carp, "Profile: Pucho and His Latin Soul Brothers," *Descarga.com*, December 1, 1996.

25. See, for example, the cover of the magazine *Waxpoetics*, October–November 2006.

Chapter 4

1. See Juan Flores, "Bring the Salsa: Diaspora Music as Source and Challenge," in *The Diaspora Strikes Back:* Caribeño *Tales of Learning and Turning* (New York: Routledge, 2009), 151–71.

2. See ibid.

3. Victor Hernández Cruz, *Snaps* (New York: Norton, 1967), 71–75.

4. Personal conversation with Victor Hernández Cruz, February 2013.

5. Personal conversation with Mickie Meléndez, April 1, 2013.

6. Pablo Guzmán, "Ray Barretto, 1929–2006," *Village Voice,* February 21, 2006.

7. Ibid.

8. Liner notes to *Que Viva la Música,* by Ernesto Lechner.

9. Personal conversation with Eddie Palmieri, March 14, 2011.

10. Conversations with Richie Bertrán, Pablo Guzmán, and Mickie Meléndez. Mention is often also made of the group La Protesta, formed by Tony Pabón and other former members of the Pete Rodríguez band; their song "Bandera" was a special favorite and figures prominently in the soundtrack to the 1973 documentary about the Young Lords, *El Pueblo Se Levanta.*

11. Cited in *Waxpoetics* 11 (2011): 71.

12. Ibid, 68.

13. Ibid, 63.

14. Personal conversation with Eddie Palmieri, March 15, 2011.

15. *Waxpoetics* 11 (2011): 68.

16. Based on conversations with many of the musicians mentioned and others during the course of 2013. Pablo Yglesias has kindly provided me with ample evidence of this Venezuela connection, including several compilations of early "salsa" recorded in Caracas in those years. René López has mentioned this early association many times over the years and more recently recalled a conversation he once had with Johnny Pacheco, who expressed surprise that his single titled "Salsa," of minor success in New York when released on his 1967 album (*El Gran Pacheco*) *Te Invita a Bailar*, had become a huge hit in Venezuela. He also pointed out that along with Pacheco, Jerry Massucci and Izzy Sanabria were also part of the entourage to visit Caracas in those years, which may suggest a causal tie between the term salsa's use in the Latin American context and its spectacular commercial adoption by Fania and *Latin New York* magazine a few years later. Venezuelan music journalist César Miguel Rondón makes passing reference to this Venezuela connection in his important book *El libro de la salsa*; see page 24 of the English translation, *The Book of Salsa*.

Chapter 5

1. Cited in Matt Rogers, "Grand Slam," *Waxpoetics* 49 (2011): 39.

2. Ibid.

3. See Russ Slater, "It Was Our Thing, Our Latin Thing: An Interview with Leon Gast," (http://www.soundsandcolours.com/author/admin/), November 29, 2011.

4. Ibid., 3.

5. Ibid.

6. Rogers, "Grand Slam," 39.

7. Mary Kent, *Salsa Talks: A Musical Heritage Uncovered* (Altamonte Springs, FL: Digital Domain, 2005), 260.

8. César Miguel Rondón, *The Book of Salsa: A Chronicle of Urban Music from the Caribbean to New York City* (Chapel Hill: University of North Carolina Press, 2008), 43.

9. Rogers, "Grand Slam," 39.

10. Kent, *Salsa Talks*, 264.

11. I thank several musicians, notably Andy González and Nelson González, for these critical comments.

12. Rondón, *The Book of Salsa*, 132–33.

13. Private conversation with Marty Sheller, May 7, 2013.

14. Rogers, "Grand Slam," 40.

15. Rogers, "Grand Slam," 38.

16. Washburne, 18.

17. Rogers, "Grand Slam," 40.

18. Rondón, *The Book of Salsa*, 93.

19. Ibid., 95

20. Rogers, "Grand Slam," 42.

21. Ibid.

22. Cited in David Carp, "Profile: Larry Harlow: Salsero Maravilloso," *Descarga*, August 15, 1998.

23. Rondón, *The Book of Salsa*, 80.

24. Ibid.

25. Willie Colón, "The Rhythms," *The Portable Lower East Side* 5: 1–2 (1998): 11.

26. Colón, "Los reyes de la salsa no solo tocan canciones de amor," in Leonardo Padura Fuentes, *Los rostros de la salsa* (Havana: Ediciones Unión, 1997), 51–52.

27. Colón, "The Rhythms," 9–12.

28. Personal conversation with Eddie Palmieri, March 21, 2011.

29. Evan C. Gutierrez, *Review of The Sun of Latin Music, AllMusic.com*, *http://www.allmusic.com/album/the-sun-of-latin-music-mw0000095522*

Chapter 6

1. Conversation with Héctor Maysonave, March 27, 2013.

2. Personal conversation with Bataan, June 18, 2013.

3. Interview with Willie Estrada, April 13, 2013.

4. Conversation with Sheller, ca. August 5, 2013.

5. Recounted to me in individual conversations with Andy and Jerry González, René López, and Andy Kaufmann, June 2013.

6. Cited in César Miguel Rondón, *The Book of Salsa: A Chronicle of Urban Music from the Caribbean to New York City* (Chapel Hill: University of North Carolina Press, 2008), 250.

7. Ibid., 249.

8. See Wilson Valentín, *Bodega Surrealism: The Emergence of Latin@ Artivists in New York City, 1976–Present* (Ph.D. dissertation, University of Michigan, 2011).

9. Cited in Marina Roseman, "The New Rican Village: Artists in Control of the Image-Making Machinery," *Latin American Music Review*, vol. 4, no. 1 (1983): 150.

10. Ibid., 145.

Selected Bibliography

Boggs, Vernon W., ed. *Salsiology: Afro-Cuban Music and the Evolution of Salsa in New York City*. New York: Excelsior Music, 1992.

Diouf, Mamadou and Ifeoma Kiddoe Nwankwo, eds. *Rhythms of the Afro-Atlantic World*. Ann Arbor: University of Michigan, 2010.

Fletcher, Bill. *All Hopped Up and Ready to Go*. New York: W. W. Norton, 2009.

Flores, Juan. *From Bomba to Hip-Hop: Puerto Rican Culture and Latino Identity*. New York: Columbia University Press, 2000.

Flores, Juan. *The Diaspora Strikes Back: Caribeño Tales of Learning and Turning*. New York: Routledge, 2009.

García, David. *Arsenio Rodriguez and the Transnational Flows of Cuban Music*. Philadelphia: Temple University Press, 2006.

Gerard, Charley, with Marty Sheller. *Salsa! The Rhythm of Latin Music*. Tempe, AZ: White Cliffs Media, 1998.

González, José Luis. "The 'Lamento Borincano': A Sociological Interpretation," in *Puerto Rico: The Four-Storeyed Country* (Princeton, NJ: Markus Wiener, 1993), 85–90.

Glasser, Ruth. *My Music Is My Flag: Puerto Rican Musicians and Their New York Communities*. Berkeley: University of California Press, 1995.

Kent, Mary. *Salsa Talks: A Musical Heritage Uncovered*. Altamonte Springs, FL: Digital Domain, 2005.

Leymarie, Isabelle. *La Salsa et le Latin Jazz*. Paris: Presses Universitaires, 1993.

Loza, Steven. *Tito Puente and the Making of Latin Music*. Urbana: University of Illinois, 1999.

Maggin, Donald L. *Dizzy: The Life and Times of John Birks Gillespie.* New York: Harper Collins, 2005.

Manuel, Peter. "Representations of New York City in Latin Music," in *Island Sounds in the Global City: Caribbean Popular Music and Identity in New York,* ed. Ray Allen and Lois Wilcken. New York: New York Folklore Society, 1998, 23–43.

Morales, Ed. *The Latin Beat: The Rhythms and Roots of Latin Music from Bossa Nova to Salsa and Beyond.* Cambridge, MA: Da Capo Press, 2003.

Pérez, Hiram Guadalupe. *Historia de la salsa.* San Juan: Editorial Primera Hora, 2005.

Roberts, John Storm. *The Latin Tinge: The Impact of Latin American Music on the United States.* New York: Oxford University Press, 1979, 1999.

Roberts, John Storm. *Latin Jazz: The First of the Fusions, 1880s to Today.* New York: Schirmer, 1999.

Rondón, César Miguel. *The Book of Salsa: A Chronicle of Urban Music from the Caribbean to New York City.* Chapel Hill: University of North Carolina Press, 2008.

Salazar, Max. *The Mambo Kingdom.* New York: Schirmer, 2002.

Sanabria, Bobby. "10 Innovations by the Machito Afro-Cubans," posting to the *Latinjazz discussion list* http://launch.groups.yahoo.com/group/latinjazz/

Steward, Sue. *¡Musica! Salsa, Rumba, Merengue, and More.* San Francisco: Chronicle, 1999.

Sublette, Ned. *Cuba and Its Music: From the First Drums to the Mambo.* Chicago: Chicago Review Press, 2007.

Vega, Bernardo. *Memoirs of Bernardo Vega.* New York: Monthly Review Press, 1984.

Yglesias, Pablo. *¡Cocinando! Fifty Years of Latin Album Cover Art.* New York: Princeton Architectural Press, 2005.

Index

CPSIA information can be obtained
at www.ICGtesting.com
Printed in the USA
FSHW011116190121
77642FS